Beautiful Ghosts

Beautiful Ghosts

A Queer Memoir
of San Francisco

SHERILYN CONNELLY

Exposit

Jefferson, North Carolina

ISBN (print) 978-1-4766-8633-2 ∞
ISBN (ebook) 978-1-4766-4543-8

LIBRARY OF CONGRESS AND BRITISH LIBRARY
CATALOGUING DATA ARE AVAILABLE

On the cover: Photograph of the author in July 2006 (author collection)

Printed in the United States of America

Exposit is an imprint of McFarland & Company, Inc., Publishers

Exposit

*Box 611, Jefferson, North Carolina 28640
www.expositbooks.com*

For Matthue Roth and Mikl-Em,
who taught me what it means to be kind.

Hymnal

Be ye wicked, know ye woe
Be ye righteous and Satan's foe
Remember ye the tale of Job

For life is struggle, and not reward
The truth will too often be ignored
Until triumphantly speaks the Lord

Then the Lord answered Job out of the storm:

> *"Who judges creation?*
> *Who dares question why?*
> *Providence is not earthen,*
> *Not for thou to decry*

> *"Yours is not understanding*
> *Yours is utterly this:*
> *You must worship in sadness*
> *As you worship in bliss."*

All ye in witness must have a care
And give yourself not into despair
For sin and sorrow lie waiting there

Remember always, and always know
The Lord stands next to you 'ere you go
Lest ye forget the tale of Job.

—Jim Fourniadis, "The Tale of Job," *The Wicker Man*

Table of Contents

Introduction

Out of the Bag and into the Abattoir

When Tom Hooper's film *Cats* was released in December 2019, I had never seen or listened to any version of Andrew Lloyd Webber's Broadway musical, though I've known Webber and Tim Rice's rock opera *Jesus Christ Superstar* by heart all my life. *Superstar*'s Judas was the first literary character whose arc made emotional sense to me, and I appreciated that the Apostles were following Jesus so they could become famous by writing about Him. I had no strong feelings about Webber otherwise, but as my niece Shandon put it at the time, ***someone was describing this movie to me and i kept saying, this sounds like something my aunt sherilyn would love!*** Shandon was not wrong, and I would be seeing *Cats* as a civilian, for I was no longer a professional film critic.

Once upon a time, the print newspaper *SF Weekly*'s Assistant Calendar Editor Hiya Swanhuyser was a fan of Bad Movie Night, a movie-heckling show I produced at a community theater called the Dark Room. She also enjoyed my silly-yet-thoughtful write-ups for each film on the Dark Room's website, and in August 2011 she invited me to write for *SF Weekly*'s blog. Hiya gave me free rein, so I wrote dozens of pieces about subjects close to my heart such as the public access television station Access SF, the Jerry Lewis Cinema franchise, and monologist Spalding Gray's porn career. (I worked at a video store called the Video Zone as a teenager, and I knew liberating our VHS copy of Zebedy Colt's 1976 *The Farmer's Daughters* starring Spalding would pay off someday!) *SF Weekly*'s Managing Editor Alan Scherstuhl was impressed enough with my nonsense to ask if I'd like to start reviewing new movies. Sure! After some corporate changeovers cleared the neighborhood around my orbit, I became *SF Weekly*'s main film critic in January 2013, and I stopped writing in the online diary which I had launched in 1999.

I got the cold shoulder from other Bay Area film critics at press screenings, and in January 2015 they declined my application for membership in their professional guild. To make sure I understood that I lost a popularity contest, they wrote that *we trust you realize that this decision was based solely upon the results of our secret ballot, and implies no criticism or judgment of your professional qualifications.* Cool! Cool. Cool cool cool. That cut through many layers of emotional skin, but a few days after the guild's rejection, the North Carolina–based academic publisher McFarland greenlit my proposal for a scholarly nonfiction book called *Ponyville Confidential*, and I discovered that strangers in the Eastern Time Zone liking my brain salved the laceration of acquaintances in my own area code disliking everything else about me. Though I maintained the grind of reviewing two to six new movies per week for *SF Weekly*, as of Bad Movie Night's ninth anniversary I had decided to end the show on our 10th anniversary in March 2015. A decade of making us all that much more stupid every Sunday night was plenty, and we always did John Milius' 1985 *Red Dawn* on our anniversary, meaning I had to watch that miserable movie 11 times over the course of 10 years. After the final heckling of *Red Dawn* at the final Bad Movie Night, I started writing *Ponyville Confidential* in earnest.

I did not re-apply to the critics guild because I am not in the habit of clawing at doors I've been locked out of, and being a stray meant I did not have early access to the year's prestige pictures the way members did. The practical upshot was that when I wrote my paper's Year in Film feature, I was free to champion movies which spoke to me emotionally and not the ones critics were expected to rally behind. *SF Weekly*'s Best Film of 2014 was Stuart Murdoch's *God Help the Girl* and not the guild's choice of Richard Linklater's *Boyhood*, and in 2015 I chose David Zellner's *Kumiko, the Treasure Hunter* and not Tom McCarthy's *Spotlight*, and neither *Boyhood* nor *Spotlight* made it onto my lists.

When *SF Weekly*'s more respectable sister publication the *San Francisco Bay Guardian* ended its run in 2014, I found it hilarious that many people went the full *Walk Hard* with their disdain for my outlet: *the wrong paper folded!* In early 2015, the paper which should have folded got a new Arts Editor in the form of the nonbinary queer Peter-Astrid Kane, writing at the time as Peter Lawrence Kane. In addition to reviewing new movies for the print edition I was covering Criterion Collection and Shout! Factory video releases for the blog, and after reading my article about Shout!'s *Sgt. Bilko: Season Two* DVD, Kane emailed me to say *i really enjoy your digressive writing style and the fairly dazzling breadth of your knowledge, but mostly i love that you know how to use an em dash.* So, we got off to a good start, and under Kane's editorship I was able to boost the signal for events like Sheila Malkind's local Legacy Film Festival on Aging, Nick Prueher and Joe Pickett's touring Found Footage Festival, and rare screenings of Joe Dante's *The Movie Orgy* and Neil Young's *Human Highway*.

My name appeared on the cover of the print edition several times for film-related features, but also for non-film things like the pirate radio landscape, the transgender bar Divas, and the sex club known as the Power Exchange. I also never missed an opportunity to point out that Orson Welles' *Citizen Kane* is a better movie than Alfred Hitchcock's *Vertigo*, despite the British Film Institute's every-decade critics poll of the greatest films ever putting *Vertigo* in the #1 spot in 2012. I was underpaid even by the low standards of print journalism in the 2010s, and since I was an independent contractor the lack of withholding on those meager paychecks kicked my ass during tax season, but the freedom to express myself made up for it. For as much as I reveled in the wonderful feeling of *getting away with it*, I was professional in the ways that mattered: I met my deadlines every week, and I turned in words which were ready to be printed in the 65,000 news papers which would be available for free all over San Francisco in kiosks bearing the paper's slogan *raising hell and hella fun*.

One of the last, best things I wrote for *SF Weekly* was a longer-than-usual piece about the July 2019 re-release of Jenny Livingston's 1991 documentary *Paris Is Burning* and the impact that seeing the transgender woman Venus Xtravaganza in that film had on me when I was in the closet at 18. The article was one of about a half-dozen times I wrote about being transgender in *SF Weekly*, since it was never relevant otherwise. Arts Editor Kane had become Editor-in-Chief Kane by then, and they never made me tone down the opinions they disagreed with, such as my belief that mainstream drag culture in the 2010s was a form of outdated, misogynistic minstrelsy. The few complaints I received about my *SF Weekly* words were usually because I didn't like a movie everyone else had agreed to like, and yikes, some randos got very cross at me because I did not enjoy the sun-dappled depiction of statutory rape in Luca Guadagnino's *Call Me by Your Name*! When it did happen, Kane and I always shared a chuckle over the complaints.

The nonbinary queer Kane stepped down in August 2019, and their replacement was a well-meaning straight cis man. This New Editor and I immediately clashed over issues including but not limited to my criticisms of mainstream drag culture, which he removed from my writing because my words *could potentially be misinterpreted by readers as homophobic*, and, far scarier, might *inflame some readers*. I pointed out that I had been writing such things for several years without inflaming any readers, the New Editor's predecessor Kane was a super-queer person who supported my right to express those criticisms, and since I was a queer transgender woman it wouldn't make sense to accuse me of homophobia. The

New Editor was unimpressed by both my *curriculum vitae* and my queerness, and he defanged my work accordingly. It was not the first time I faced negative consequences for my writing, I knew it would not be the last, and I also knew that if Phil Ochs were alive, he could have written a new verse of "Love Me, I'm a Liberal" about the absurdity of a straight cis man scolding a queer trans woman for criticizing the misogyny of gay cis men. In November, the New Editor diminished me in favor of a straight cis person fresh out of Harvard who lacked my experience, my familiarity with San Francisco, and my *je ne sais quoi*, but who would write what the New Editor told them to write without sassing back or trying to sneak in incendiary opinions.

All I had left was the Susan Alexander Kane power move, and I used it: I walked the hell away and did not look back.

I was writing the Year in Film feature when I walked away, and Ari Aster's *Midsommar* would have been *SF Weekly*'s Best Film of 2019. One thing I appreciated about Bay Area critics was that they kept their yaps shut during movies, so when I first saw *Midsommar* in the quiet context of the June press screening I found it to be a breathtaking meditation on loss, with Florence Pugh's performance tapping into something real about grief. (The spot-on depiction of a psilocybin trip didn't hurt, either.) *Midsommar*'s themes resonated in the months that followed because getting marginalized out of my newspaper was the latest wrinkle in a year of loss, including the impending loss of my two closest friends. One was battling cancer and would pass away in early 2020, and the other stopped talking to me around the time I walked away from *SF Weekly*. The three of us had been close throughout the decade, and our friendship magic was strong, but it was not fated to carry on through the ages.

The foundations of my life first started to wobble in March 2019 with the closure of Divas. It was sad but not unexpected, for it was hard to miss the symbolism when the decades-old purple neon sign reading **The Motherlode** behind the bar died, and the owner told me he couldn't get it fixed because the neon repair shop had been replaced by a Verizon store. When I attended the final Sunday night karaoke, I only went to pay my respects by singing a few songs, not to cruise. I had been single since I was 40, and by the time I was 43 I had to admit that I was no longer 33, plus being 33 had been best when I was able to act like I was 27, and *that* wasn't going to happen again. The point is that math is hard, and after several one-and-done-dates with a series of cis and trans women who could have put on a new Bad Date Show with their stories about me, I solved the equation by deactivating my OkCupid account and spending Friday nights in my pajamas with my cat Hineni on my lap. My fuckable years may have been over, but I emerged from my journey through dark heat with many fascinating scars yet free of both venereal disease and chemical addiction, so I had no complaints.

It helped that I enjoyed my day job as a Youth Services Librarian at the San Francisco Public Library's Potrero Branch. I graduated from San José State University in 2014 with the Master of Library and Information Science degree required to become a capital-L Librarian, but the muscles I used most were from my years at the Dark Room. During the job's most unglamorous moments, like cleaning up Potrero's program room after a messier-than-usual Saturday Morning Snacktivity, I would think to myself, *what, and quit showbiz?* It also helped that librarians welcomed me as warmly into their fold as film critics had coldly shut me out of theirs, and my contentment with my imminent spinsterhood was why I paid the black-haired Mifkit no mind when they entered the fourth-floor lounge at Divas that Sunday night in March 2019. They were one more piece of non-binary Millennial eye candy in a room brimming with it, and I didn't notice the Mifkit was on the barstool next to me until I felt their leg against mine. Leg-to-leg contact in a crowded bar is not the same as wanting attention, but the Mifkit got up in my grill like Lux Interior about what I was drinking and had I been here before and what I was going to sing (they joined me for my third-favorite Rolling Stones song, "Paint It Black") and verbally confirmed that they were looking to buy whatever I was selling. And what the heck. Gregg Araki's new Starz series *Now Apocalypse* had been making me nostalgic for my days of colorful adventures on nighttime streets, so I decided to take my 45-year-old carcass out of retirement and see where the Mifkit would lead me.

The day after I met the Mifkit, I was in an automobile accident on the way home from Potrero. No humans were injured, but my car was totaled. She was the second used Saturn I'd owned, and I named her Spectra both for her chromium pallor and the recurring protest chant ***a specter is haunting the world!*** from my favorite film of 2012, David Cronenberg's *Cosmopolis*. She didn't have long to live by any metric when the accident happened: her organs had been failing, her dashboard lights were dimming, and that's without factoring in the existential terror of being abandoned by her once-beneficent creator Saturn. Spectra deserved better than to die on Lake Merced Boulevard between Winston and Font as her antifreeze bled out on the rainy pavement, but we don't get to choose our deaths.

I was driving a rented Hyundai Elantra when the Mifkit and I had coffee a few days later at the kink café Wicked Grounds, where we talked for an hour about our histories and our wants and desires. My ears perked up when the Mifkit said they wanted to get their fangs sharpened, and I soon felt their unsharpened fangs when we relocated to the SF Eagle and made out against the Harrison-facing wall. Evidence seemed to suggest I was aging further into Mehitabel, and *toujours gai toujours gai*, there was a dance in the old dame yet. We scheduled three more dates, including for the Mifkit to visit the apartment which I called the Black Light District to meet Hineni and watch Nicolas Winding Refn's *The Neon Demon*, which was *SF Weekly*'s Second Best Film of 2016 (after Beyoncé's *Lemonade*, obviously). They canceled each date at the last minute before lying to me on an emotionally brutal April night, and I never saw the Mifkit again.

It took my self-esteem the rest of 2019 to recover, and when I wasn't singing along with Sia's "Waving Goodbye" on repeat, I hit the clubs and danced the pain away. There was a well-timed influx of black dresses with white collars at Hot Topic, and I was wearing one of those dresses when two different people at Club Frolic in early May told me I reminded them of Courtney Love in the videos from the Hole album *Live Through This*. They both specified the *Live Through This* era, and both hastened to add that the Courtney comparison was a compliment, though I would have counted it as a win even if it had been meant as a sick burn. But lightning did not strike on that night or any other night.

*   *   *

I had to step away from Gregg Araki's 2019 series *Now Apocalypse* after the Mifkit incident because Kelli Berglund's character made me think of a puppy I had once known, and that was one too many painful feelings, so I instead practiced self-care by digging into the Blu-ray box set of Francis Ford Coppola's 1979 film *Apocalypse Now*. After watching all three versions in a row and remaining convinced that *Redux* was a bad idea poorly executed—and don't get me started on how *Final Cut*'s new color timing ruins Vittorio Storaro's cinematography—I was struck by Marlon Brando's Colonel Kurtz ruminating about ***real freedoms***, including freedom ***from the opinion of others***. More than ever I found myself identifying with Sam Bottoms' character of Lance, since taking drugs and embracing one's inner animal strikes me as the only sane reaction to war, but the bald whackjob Kurtz was on to something about freeing yourself from others' opinions. It felt more relevant since I was finishing up my second McFarland book, *The First Star Trek Movie*, and was about to start working on my third, *Presenting Persis Khambatta*.

The First Star Trek Movie was published in October, just in time for the 2019 San Francisco LitQuake Festival's Book Fair. I was honored that my old friend Tira traveled from the East Bay to buy a signed copy, and Carol Queen was kind enough to give me some space at the Center for Sex and Culture's table even though my books were not about sex. I also hung out briefly at the table of the publisher Last Gasp, where I was happy to see that Michelle Tea's 2004 *Rent Girl* was still in print and doing well. I was otherwise busy writing *Presenting Persis Khambatta* that October, and like *Ponyville Confidential* and *The First Star Trek Movie* before it, much of the research required reading strangers' vile words about people and things I felt connected to. Strangers had been writing vile words about people and things I felt connected to all my life, so that was nothing new, but I was also over it. I wanted to enjoy the people and things I felt connected to and not know if or why strangers hated those people and things. To be clear, those strangers were free to hate anything they wanted to hate! They had the freedom to write vile words about whatever they wanted, and I had the freedom to not read their words, so I began weaning myself off social media and stopped reading pop-culture news sites. But the opinion of others still snuck through like an eclipse through a pinhole viewer, and I became aware that the as-yet-unreleased *Cats* movie was being called the worst thing in the history of ever and attacked with an even greater ire than John M. Chu's 2015 *Jem and the Holograms* and Paul Feig's 2016 *Ghostbusters*. I had examined the backlashes against those movies at length in *SF Weekly*, and the relentless negativity toward *Cats* raised a familiar sense of empathy.

I saw *Cats* at 10:50 a.m. on Sunday, December 22, 2019, at the Regal Manchester in Fresno while I was visiting my mother for Christmas. The auditorium was empty except for three women around my age wearing shirts from the Broadway production and a pair of elderly theater-hopping men. One of the men went right to sleep and snored through the film, and the other tried to drown out his companion's snoring by eating as loudly as humanly possible. Those distractions aside, I spent most of that screening marveling at how few fucks *Cats* gave, at how the film dared to be itself and didn't care whether the viewer sank or swam. I was also grateful that the closed captioning allowed me to parse the obtuse T.S. Eliot verses sung in thick British accents as well as the new song written for Francesca Hayward's character Victoria. But I sensed there was something I was missing, something which would require seeing the movie again in a theater.

The tricky part was that people were starting to hate-watch *Cats*, and some San Francisco theaters were scheduling **hoot and holler at this kuh-razy new cult classic** screenings. It had happened with jet-age speed to *Midsommar,* whose distributor A24 leaned on the same **come laugh at all the wacky faces the chick makes** approach they used for Aster's previous film *Hereditary*. When I saw *Midsommar* a second time in July 2019 after the initial press screening, I decided to take a chance on the Alamo Drafthouse New Mission. I tended to avoid the New Mission because the two-story lobby was decorated with posters of 1970s martial arts movies, floor-to-ceiling violent images of angry men punching and kicking each other. The whole place was one St. Pauli Girl sign away from being a man cave, but I appreciated the Drafthouse's zero-tolerance policy regarding disruptive audiences. That policy was ignored for *Midsommar,* and the audience's ironic laughter was non-stop. It's so funny when women experience emotions!

* * *

I attended a double feature of Dario Argento's 1977 *Suspiria* and Refn's *The Neon Demon* at the Castro Theatre in September 2018, and I had seen enough old movies there over the decades to know I was in trouble when a group of bears sat in front of me. Dario Argento is a master of style over substance, and *Suspiria* is considered his masterpiece, but since it's mostly Italian women in 1970s clothes, the bears laughed whenever anyone said or did anything. Adding to the *Earthquake*-in-Sensurround of it all was the man behind me who exploded with a mirthless *ha ha ha!* at regular intervals like Max Cady in Martin Scorsese's 1991 *Cape Fear* (which I've always thought was a better film than Scorsese's 1990 *Goodfellas,* though his 1993 *The Age of Innocence* is my favorite of the three). The bears were also heckling *Suspiria,* and I could tell many of the quips they were shouting had been well-practiced in living rooms over the years.

I had produced a movie-heckling show for the better part of a decade, but context is everything: Bad Movie Night was a weekly $5–7 event in a 49-seat black-box community theater in which the movies were DVDs played through a standard-definition video projector, and we encouraged the audience to yell at the screen. In the spirit of *Mad Magazine,* we were open about and proud of the fact that our show was a noisy and stupid experience utterly without redeeming social importance. We even had a *Hee-Haw*-inspired sing-along theme song which my friend Jim Fourniadis played on his banjo most weeks, and I led *a cappella* renditions in Jim's absence.

> I went out last Sunday evening
> Wanted to see a film that was good
> Instead, I ended up at the Dark Room
>   (*2263 Mission, in the heart of the Mission!*)
> The people there were noisy and rude (*fuuuck you!*)
> Why oh why, Bad Movie Night?
> I'm sitting here, dejected and sad
> I searched the world over for a genuine good film
>   (*like [whatever lousy film just opened]!*)
> But I'm here at the Dark Room, and <*pfft*> it was bad!

By contrast, the attendees of a one-time, $13-per-ticket screening of the new 4K restoration of a classic film in a 1,400-seat movie palace which featured preshow musical performances on the Mighty Wurlitzer had a reasonable expectation that the audience would be respectful. Those attendees would often be disappointed, as I was for *Suspiria*, but that didn't make the expectation of being able to enjoy the film in peace any less reasonable.

When one of *Suspiria*'s few male characters is being chased through a vast plaza by an unseen witch, there is a hard cut from a spooky moon to a tight medium shot of burly men in lederhosen doing what at first glance appears to be Monty Python's Fish-Slapping Dance. The juxtaposition was intended to be humorous—you made a funny, Dario!—but there was nary a chortle from the bears nor Max Cady nor anyone else in the Castro Theatre. The picture then pulls back to reveal that the men are dancing on a table in a crowded pub with a Tyrolean-hat-clad band playing behind them, and though that is an empirically hilarious image, the audience remained silent. Once the story returned to the women, the laughter and heckling resumed like a switch had been flipped: **look at what she's wearing and how she's made up! she's trapped in a witches' coven and it's so funny how she's freaking out about her impending death by razor wire!**

Argento's *Suspiria* was an acknowledged laugh-a-minute camp classic, but the jury was still out on Refn's cool, rigorous *The Neon Demon*. As I had written when praising it in *SF Weekly*, *Demon* is not the schlocky T&A-fest one might expect from a horror movie set in the fashion world and thus is not a successor to Paul Verhoeven's *Showgirls* for ironic screenings hosted by drag queens. The Castro audience members who remained tried their best to laugh at all the by-definition-hilarious femininity on display in *Demon*, but since it was a recent American movie shot in English with live sound, they weren't able to Other it as easily as they had the older, foreign, and sloppily-dubbed *Suspiria*. There's no sex or nudity in the Refn film until a third-act scene which pushed the audience so far out of their comfort zone they couldn't generate nervous laughter, and by the time Sia's "Waving Goodbye" began playing over the end credits, I had fallen in love with *The Neon Demon* all over again.

Though it did not push the R-rated *Demon* into NC-17 territory, the mysterious cabal at the MPAA called it *a scene of aberrant sexuality*, which always made me think, *challenge accepted!* The finger-wagging tone of the phrase cracks me up, and when you've been told all your life that you are sexually aberrant, you can't help but have a different concept of what aberration is.

*   *   *

I continued to keep myself isolated from the *Cats* backlash as 2019 gave way to 2020. I mean, I could guess why it was hated, but I preferred not to know. I didn't see it again until I was back in Fresno during one of my research trips to Los Angeles, this time for a long-gestating book about the history of screen credits with the working title of *The Names Below the*

Title. (Ya burnt, Frank Capra!) Though I stayed with my brother Jim while in Southern California, my first stop on these trips was always Fresno to drop off Hineni so my mother could cat-sit her. As a result, my second *Cats* viewing was on February 6 at the Regal UA Clovis Movies, a dilapidated, second-run multiplex which was one of the last remaining theaters from my childhood. Speaking of childhood, the only other attendees were a woman accompanied by two boys and a girl, all three of whom were under the age of 10. It would be another six weeks before both schools and movie theaters were shuttered due to the COVID-19 pandemic, and the screening was at 12:40 p.m. on a Thursday, so I had no idea why they weren't in school. But there's a reason I became a librarian and not a truancy officer, and the way the kids were digging *Cats* gave me hope for the future: those three were going to grow up to become interesting adults who made the world a more interesting place.

I sang along with Victoria's new song during the film and then with Taylor Swift's version over the credits, and when I sent it to my friend Helena later that day, she diplomatically described it as **a very sherilyn song**. But it was during this second theatrical viewing of *Cats* that I realized why this reviled film was resonating with me so much, and it wasn't only because I had been reviled many times myself. *Cats* made me realize that the sense of loss I felt in 2019, the way so much of my life's slate had been wiped clean, was an echo of the similar but far more fundamental breakdown and reconstruction I endured twenty years earlier. I could not think of a shinier, more flattering metaphor for how I felt at the turn of the century than the story of a cat who gets put into a bag and tossed into the street, only to find a new community among the phantoms of night. That I was seeing myself in art which everyone else found distasteful was also a familiar sensation.

*   *   *

Everything in *Beautiful Ghosts* is true, based on my own writing at the time as well as hundreds of saved chats and emails and other bits of ephemera. I am not and never will be Pamela Holm, so names and other identifying details about many (but not all) people, homes, and drugs have been changed. Being a fan of the Copenhagen Interpretation of quantum mechanics, I tend to think of the past as existing in a superposition until measured as a narrative, and *Beautiful Ghosts* is how the wave function collapsed for me. Put in a more macroscopic way, while I have all the receipts needed for an epic Robert Caro–style every-belch-and-fart-has-a-citation multivolume biography, what follows is closer in spirit to a streamlined, all-killer-no-filler Scott Alexander and Larry Karaszewski biopic. This means everything is true and causality is never violated, but sometimes after *Glen or Glenda?* you have to skip *Jail Bait* and go straight to *Bride of the Monster,* and since *Plan 9 from Outer Space* has to be the climax, the story ends before *Night of the Ghouls* and *The Sinister Urge* and even *Orgy of the Dead.*

While *Beautiful Ghosts* is about being a transgender woman, it is only my story. This book does not reflect the thoughts, feelings, politics, desires, tastes, experiences, aesthetics, or proclivities of any other trans woman, and I can think of a few who will facepalm because I mentioned *Cats* in the first sentence. Goddamn *Cats,* of all things! Was I living under a rock that didn't have Wi-Fi in 2019? (They'll also acknowledge that *Cats* is on-brand for me, which only proves that I am not helping.) The way trans women were regarded and more often disregarded in the late 20th and early 21st century is a major theme, but the granular evolution of the terminology is beyond the scope of this book, such as *transsexual* being succeeded by *transgender* or *tranny* becoming a slur. Proper names like Trannyshack or the touring Tranny Roadshow will remain the same, but to avoid getting stuck in the linguistic weeds I'll be using some anachronistic terminology, in particular the words *cisgender* and *transgender,* most often shortened to *cis* and *trans.*

The Power Exchange on Otis was shuttered in November 2008, the Dark Room and the Lexington Club closed in 2015, Divas closed in 2019, the Mitchell Brothers O'Farrell Theatre and the Stud closed in 2020, and *SF*

Billboard in the Teen section of the Potrero Branch library announcing soon-to-be-canceled screenings of *Cats* and *Charlie's Angels,* San Francisco, March 2020. Read? READ (author photograph).

Weekly folded in 2021. I can also say without fear of contradiction that the greatest missed opportunity of the COVID-19 pandemic *vis-à-vis* library programming is that a few weeks before the system shut down in March 2020, I had scheduled *Cats* to be June's feature in my monthly Teen Movie Night series at Potrero. I was promoting it as the Final Unironic Screening in San Francisco, which I'm sure would have totally rehabilitated the film's reputation.

I've done all I can for *Cats*, but if *Beautiful Ghosts* inspires you to watch David Cronenberg's *Crash*, please do not judge that good movie by the bad cover of the Criterion Collection's 2020 Blu-ray. I could write a book about how Criterion bungled the key art and how it misrepresents the film. In a way, you're about to read that book.

So let the revels begin and let the fires be started, and though what follows is a work of nonfiction, it should nevertheless be read aloud at maximum volume. Don't be afraid.

Prologue

Infernal Cartography

    The parking was ample if you arrived early. The building was located on a street called Otis which was only two blocks long, making it obscure on paper maps and all but impossible for out-of-towners to find, and yet both out-of-towners and townies managed to find the Power Exchange. It was discreet while the sun was up, sharing its block of Otis with a car rental lot, a rug store, a machine shop, and other offices and storefronts which had long since closed for the day before the Power Exchange opened. It remained discreet after night fell, since the windows were covered with black-painted boards and the music coming from the lone door was never too loud, though the pinkish light surrounding the door caught the eye, as did the neon sign reading ***Power Exchange***. Business hours were Thursday through Sunday from 9:00 p.m. to 5:00 a.m., during which time there were always a few employees out front, large men wearing black shirts which read *Sex Squad* on the front and *America's Naughtiest* on the back. Parked close by were the Sex Squad cars, glistening police cruisers featuring those slogans as well as the logo of the club: the initials "PE" and an illustration of Bettie Page holding a riding crop.

    The crowd outside grew throughout the evening: smokers, newbies trying to find the courage to go inside, sex workers making negotiations, gawkers, the curious, the unhoused, the tweakers. Before you went inside, the nice man at the door checked your ID and determined that you weren't drunk or out to cause trouble and that you had a basic understanding of what the club was about. This took a while for some people, especially as the pricing was exposited: on Thursdays and Sundays, men got in for $15, hetero couples were $10 total, and women got in free, whether cisgender or transgender. The Power Exchange's definition of the latter word was broad, running the gamut from weekend crossdressers to full-time trans women such as myself, and we were all referred to in the local argot as T-girls. (I was fine with the term in the context of the Power Exchange, and it helped that it never leaked into the mainstream to become a slur like *tranny*.) Couples were a mere $20 on Friday and Saturday nights, and cis and trans women still got in free. Male-presenting men paid $75 wearing their street clothes or $35 if they took off their pants and wore a towel around their waist—or, if they were so inclined, went naked. (Single men were Tourists, and those wearing towels were Towelboys. All Towelboys were Tourists, but not all Tourists were Towelboys.) The third Saturday was the monthly Fetish Ball, and everybody paid $20.

Inside the front door were steps leading to a line of reflective tape which glowed neon yellow under the black lights. As you waited to be called to the counter to pay, it was expected that you would read the hard-to-miss sign to the left listing the Rules:

SAFE SEX MUST BE PRACTICED AT ALL TIMES. NO EXCEPTIONS.
ILLEGAL SUBSTANCES OF ANY KIND ARE NOT ALLOWED.
RUDE, OBNOXIOUS BEHAVIOR WILL NOT BE TOLERATED.
"NO" MEANS "NO." DO NOT TOUCH ANYONE WITHOUT THEIR
PERMISSION.
KEEP LOUD TALKING, GIGGLING, AND LAUGHING, ETC. TO A
MINIMUM.
RECORDING DEVICES ARE NOT ALLOWED AND WILL BE
CONFISCATED.
NO SOLICITATION OF ANY TYPE, INSIDE OR OUTSIDE THE
BUILDING.

The person behind the counter called you over and asked if you had read the Rules. If the answer was *yes* you paid whatever you had to pay, then got your hand stamped. Across from the counter was a red-walled lobby with couches and a pay phone, and just inside the door was a table with a rotating fiber optic tree and flyers for upcoming events. The room was partially illuminated with black light, as was most of the club, and the art on the wall included black-and-white cityscapes and porn holograms. There were usually a few men on the couches, watching people go by. A door to the right lead to the Comic Hallway, which contained the coat check and the Impulse Boutique, the latter being perfect for that pick-me-up Red Bull or reasonably priced fetish gear. The Hallway itself was decorated from top to bottom in a superhero theme, with a hand-painted Superman logo on the door and ginormous Powerpuff Girls near the ceiling. A display case on the far wall was home to an impressive array of action figures, and below that was a pair of old washing machines containing televisions showing animated porn from the 1970s. Capping off the superhero theme was a statue of Elvis Presley, the greatest superhero of them all.

Back in the lobby, the door to the left led to the Juice Bar. Elvis was also represented in the Juice Bar by a neon sign simply reading **Elvis**, but it was easy to miss with so much else vying for your attention, including but not limited to a stage with two stripper poles, air hockey, ping pong, and billiards tables, two classic video arcade machines, and a vintage gas pump. Most poignant was the sign from the late, lamented Jezebel's Joint, a bar at Turk and Larkin which had been owned by the man who owned the Power Exchange, and which he named after his daughter. (The Joint went out of business before Jezebel was old enough to legally enter.) Past the lobby and parallel to the Juice Bar was a red hallway with hip sixties-style cartoon concert posters on one side and BDSM drawings on the other. The hallway led to the Electric Zebra, a corridor painted in black-and-white stripes and lit with a strobe.

A doorway at the beginning of the red hallway led to the first play space on the main floor: the King Arthur Room, so named for its Camelotian decor. Across from the doorway to the King Arthur Room was Check point Charlie, the stool from which an employee named Artwhore checked hand stamps to make sure everyone was properly attired. He mostly paid attention to men's wrists, making sure they weren't trying to avoid taking their pants off if they only paid the $35 admission, and he didn't have to check anything with women unless they came as a part of a couple. The Egyptian Room was easy to miss unless you thought to turn right at the otherwise nondescript doorway at the end of the Electric Zebra, and its best design element wasn't visible unless you walked all the way inside: neon-green pyramids near the ceiling, set against a backdrop of stars which glowed green under the black light. Both the Electric Zebra and the Juice Bar led to the Pirate Room, a series of jail cells gussied up with pirate accoutrement—and thanks to the pirate store which had recently opened at 826 Valencia, such accoutrement was plentiful in San Francisco. The Pirate Room had once been decorated in the prison theme implied by the cells, but that mostly appealed to gay men, while everybody loved pirates. Within the cells there were slings, spanking horses, and a television which was forever showing the big-budget porn movie *Pirates*.

Across from the Pirate Room were the stairs to the basement Dungeon. The black walls of the stairwell were like the Egyptian Room, with neon stars and planets shining in the black light. There were two different Exit signs on your way down and often a few hopeful and/or disappointed men passing by in either direction. At the foot of the stairs in the Dungeon was a small lobby-type area with a few couches, and after that was the Red Room—a room in name only, being more of a sectioned-off area with a low wall and appropriately featuring red lights on red boudoir-style furnishings. Beyond the Red Room was the Blue Room, with low white walls and a large circular bed and other sparse furnishings bathed in blue light. When the regular house lights were on it was all white, but when lit for business, the Blue Room wouldn't have looked out of place in a 1960s Michelangelo Antonioni film. After the Blue Room was the Frankenstein room, done in a wood-and-fake stone theme, with a statue of the eponymous monster, a medical table, and the all-important Mad Scientist's Lightning Disc. Beyond that was the doorway to the Porn Room, an actual room which was decorated like the Connelly family room in the 1970s, with brown walls, horrid paintings my parents would have thought looked classy, and multiple televisions showing porn. Our family room only had one television, and it never showed porn while I was awake.

The centerpiece of the Dungeon was a spacious, fenced-off area known as the Cage. Within the Cage were plenty of furnishings such as a double-sided St. Andrew's Cross, a few different spanking horses, a rack and a sling, a long table for storing one's own weapons, and a red couch. If you were a Tourist or a spectator you had to stay outside the Cage, but if you were invited to participate or were accompanying someone who was going to play, then you were welcome. When I became a regular in late 2006, I always went straight into the Cage. It was a place where I felt loved and accepted, and I did not take that for granted.

1

Six Feet Down
at Age Twenty-Five

How the End Always Is

My girlfriend Tira was unhappy but not surprised when I came out to her as transgender in 1997. She was supportive of my nonzero level of interest in crossdressing, which I revealed to her about six months after we became a couple, but she always feared it was more than that. We ended our long-standing engagement after I came out to her, and in early 1998 I started having my natural brown hair colored and cut at a salon in the black-with-bangs Bettie Page style. I hadn't yet come out to my mother as trans when we visited Fresno over Mother's Day weekend in 1998, nor had I told her I was no longer engaged to Tira, whom my mother considered to be the Daughter She Never Had. Tira and I almost broke up on the Friday morning of Mother's Day weekend before we left San Francisco, making it one of many things which should have happened that weekend but did not, and we arrived in Fresno late on Friday night after a tense drive which was not made any less tense by me playing the Cure's *Disintegration* on repeat.

The first thing my mother said when she saw me on Saturday morning was, **is this the egyptian look?** It was a solid zinger which the Russian judges would have given a 7.5, but a look of horror crossed my mother's face when I said my hair was wavier than I'd like because I'd forgotten my flat iron. The horrorshow continued when we went for our traditional Saturday morning walk, and as El Niño spat on us, *mi madre* tried to shame and humiliate *su hija pródiga* into proper masculinity, saying **you're ugly** and **you're so skewed** and **you're flouting society's conventions** and **people are staring at you** and **your appearance is insulting to other people** and **i'm embarrassed to be seen in public with you**. When insulting me to my ugly face didn't get me to renounce my hairstyle, my mother lied to my ugly face, telling me the black dye and the flat iron were making my hair fall out, and she could see a bald spot developing. I told her my hair made me happy, and her reply summed up the impasse between us: *we're not here to be happy*. I asked why we're here if not to be happy, and she thought for a moment before saying *obligation. loving god and helping other people.*

When I asked how my hair being black with bangs prevented me from doing any of those things, she did not have an answer, instead lamenting that *you never gave me any real trouble before*. Because I was a proponent of what my brother Jim called the Eleventh Commandment, *thou shalt not get caught*, the best my mother could come up with was the day I cut class when I was 16 because I was lovesick over Tira. Now I was almost old enough to rent a car, but I had black hair with bangs, which qualified as me giving my mother *real trouble* because it was *her* that this was being done to. It wasn't me at all, not what it meant to me. I knew much of what scared her was how I was overcoming my once-stifling self-consciousness, which was why she was now asking me *why do you have to change? why can't you just be the way you were before?* Since I was the youngest of her four children, she had always referred to me as *the baby of the family*, a semantic infantilization which never sat well with me and which I knew was making it that much more difficult for her to view me as a free, self-reliant grownup. The best I could do in the moment was to talk about *free will* and how *it's more important to be myself than to be what everyone else thinks i should be*, to which my mother retaliated with the Tsar Bomba of white middle-class 1990s Fresno: *you need to see a shrink!*

Coincidental to my mother's attempt to shame and humiliate me into proper masculinity by telling me I needed to get my head shrunk, I had already scheduled the first of twelve hour-long weekly appointments with a Licensed Psychologist for my 25th birthday on June 16, 1998. We were going by the already-outdated book known as Harry S. Benjamin's *Standards of Care for Gender Identity Disorder*, and the Psychologist told me at the end of that birthday session that she had read me as female as soon as I walked through the door. We were still going to do the whole twelve weeks before she signed the paperwork which would allow me to start transitioning hormonally, which I was fine with both because I was relieved to have someone to speak to about this most unspeakable of subjects and because I hoped going *by the book* would set my mother at ease when I finally came out to her. (I was naïve.) I began electrolysis to remove my facial hair, and I started taking endocrinologist-prescribed estrogen as well as the testosterone blocker spironolactone on September 18, 1998. The day before I took my first pills, my mother wrote to say she'd had a dream in which *a younger version of you was kidnapped*. She ruminated that *it could mean that you've been taken from me in the sense that i don't know you anymore—the atheism and the hair and the attitudes i don't understand.*

I came out to my brothers John and Jim before we all gathered in Fresno for Christmas, and Jim joked that he was relieved someone else was going to be the lightning rod for our mother's disapproval. It was funny because it was true: when my mother saw on Christmas Day that I still had black hair with bangs, she started dropping references to my engagement to Tira, about how great it was that Tira and I would be getting married, how Tira was the best thing to ever happen to me and marrying her would be the best thing I could ever do, and how happy my mother was that the Daughter She Never Had would always be a part of her life. Awkward!

so, yeah, about our engagement … we've ended it. tira and i are not getting married.

My mother said nothing at first. She just looked at me, her chin resting on her hand, an unreadable expression on her face. It was like a loaded blankness, a sense of shock and despair so profound that her facial muscles had no idea how to represent it. When she finally spoke, my mother told me how disappointed she was in me and how terrible a mistake I was making by not marrying Tira. Not how terrible a mistake Tira and I were making, because Tira was blameless. My mother made it clear that this was my mistake alone, and I was doing a very bad thing by not marrying Tira, making the worst mistake I could possibly make. Tira herself was in the room but remained silent. I glanced over at her occasionally, and she would smile and nod sadly, as if to say **good luck, baby. i wish i could help, but you're on your own for this one.**

I almost came out as trans to my mother right then because I'd already ruined her mood with the engagement news, so maybe the best thing to do would be to bring my secret into the light and make this a Christmas worthy of a Lifetime Channel movie. But I did not, because my mother's lack of compassion hurt too much. Her disgust with me, her *revulsion* was growing more intense by the second, and I could only handle so much concentrated negativity. I also figured that was why even though she had struggled with her own weight for most of my life, my mother did not comment on the fact that I had dropped about 100 pounds over the past year: any positive feedback about my appearance might be misconstrued as condoning my behavior. A few days after Christmas, she wrote that she was worried that **if you are choosing an alternative lifestyle, life will never be easy for you, and you will never be happy.**

I was a temp at the software company Autodesk up in Marin for most of 1998, and after a series of nail-biting interviews in December, I was hired at the San Francisco dot-com company CNET Networks with a start date of January 4, 1999. Over New Year's Eve dinner at the Old Spaghetti

Factory, Tira told me she was reluctant to go on my new health insurance as a domestic partner, pointing out that she herself had nearly broken up with me several times over the past year. We should have broken up right then, as the complimentary spumoni spheres were arriving at our table and the big electric sphere was dropping in New York. Instead, the final impetus came when I misinterpreted my new CNET coworker Ligeia's meaningless flirting as meaningful flirting. Ligeia may have found me shiny at first, but my luster had worn off by the time I broke up with Tira sometime after midnight on Friday, January 14. Tira and I were in the bedroom of our small in-law apartment Lascaux West, and there was no yelling and no violence; we had agreed from the start that we would never nonconsensually hit or otherwise physically mistreat each other, and breaking up did not change that agreement. It was instead a long, somber, painful talk with no small amount of anguish and crying from both parties, though Tira would tell me many times in the months to follow that I had broken up with her *in the worst way possible.*

When I emailed my family about the breakup, my mother replied that she was very sad but not surprised and that *i have the uneasy deep-in-the-gut-feeling that you are almost as self-destructive as your brother tom, only in a different way. i pray to god that i am wrong.* Tom had wrestled with addiction since he was a teenager; he started smoking crack in his twenties and broke into our homes and stole our electronics to sell for drug money. (Because he was a straight white cis man, he only spent a few weeks in jail.) I graduated from high school in 1991 during the worst of Tom's self-destructiveness, then plowed straight through to Fresno City College and then San Francisco State University, where I graduated with a Bachelor in Cinema in 1997. I did not have a criminal record, I was only the second of my mother's four children to earn an undergraduate degree, and I had landed a full-time job with benefits in a booming industry. Throughout the 1990s I had harbored a fantasy that my academic and professional accomplishments would earn me the leverage to reveal my true self to my mother, that if I graduated from college and got good, steady work it would prove I was a mature grownup capable of making a mature grownup decision. Maybe she would say she was proud of me for taking such a difficult step! Instead, even before I came out to her, my *curriculum vitae* was not impressive enough to absolve me of my sins of breaking up with my high school girlfriend and looking faggy.

So, the timing was not great when I came out publicly as transgender in February 1999. There was no cultural imperative in those days to show kindness to emerging trans people, and my queerness removed any shades of gray from the breakup (which still would have happened if I was cis because Tira and I had grown apart from each other). Blame fell on me from all directions, as did the message that I had done two very bad and wrong things by breaking up with Tira and coming out as trans, that I had broken everybody's hearts and I was damned for all time and all the bad things which were going happen to me going forward were my fault and my fault alone. Tira's family cut me off after the breakup but before I came out as trans, while my family made it clear they were always going to consider Tira to be a Connelly despite the very bad and wrong thing I'd done by breaking up with her. The outlier was my niece Shandon, who was not angry or disappointed in me—but Shandon was a 14-year-old cis girl, and thus the only creature on the planet whose feelings were less important than a 25-year-old trans woman.

I was doing all right by the minimum standards of Maslow's Hierarchy of Needs: I had a steady job, and Lascaux West was close to the Pacific Ocean in a safe, quiet neighborhood in San Francisco's Outer Sunset district. But everything above the first tier disintegrated, and the early months of 1999 were the bleakest time of my life. I was feeling fear and guilt and shame in equally overloaded measures, painful emotions made more painful because of my heightened and ever-shifting hormone levels. The early stages of hormonal transitioning were often described as a second adolescence, and that's putting it mildly, because I was a godforsaken mess. It took Tira a few months to find a new place to live, and she seldom missed an opportunity to remind me that I had dashed all her dreams and fucked everything up.

When my supervisors at CNET invited me to lunch one day in February, I expected the worst: they were going take me to a neutral location and tell me that I'm not meeting minimum expectations and they're letting me go, the dot-com equivalent of the execution at Miller's Crossing. Instead, after we settled into one of the many eateries between our office and Pier 39, they looked into their hearts and told me they were pleased with my job performance. I was surpassing their expectations, but never mind all that because it wasn't a business lunch—they wanted to get to know me better. I had been at CNET for over a month, after all! When I made a passing reference to breaking up with my longtime girlfriend, they were flabbergasted. They said there was no way I could be a few weeks out from a nine-year relationship and be so … well, so **undramatic**, and they never would have guessed anything was wrong at home if I hadn't told them. I appreciated that they didn't ask if the breakup had anything to do with my eyeliner and pigtails, considering I wasn't out as trans to anybody in the office other than Ligeia. Everybody knew me as the tall, vaguely femmey weirdo who wore long Marilyn Manson shirts over stripey tights and stark black-and-white makeup in a way that made sense in early 1999 San Francisco. I was male-presenting during the interview process, and I didn't start feminizing my appearance until my second week, but I was later informed that in addition to having the qualifications and experience, one of the reasons I got the job was my department's philosophy of hiring *interesting-looking people*.

In March, the department head called me in and said they were going to cut my probation period from six months to three, give me a raise, and let me in on the stock options sooner rather than later. Ah, the glory days of the dot-com boom. Over the next decade I nodded in polite agreement when people talked about how the tech bubble ruined the Bay Area, but Autodesk and CNET did all right by me. Until I got laid off in September 2001 after the bubble burst, those famously inflated tech salaries allowed me to pay for several thousand dollars of electrolysis, therapy, and hormones out of pocket at a time when I could not have afforded them otherwise. Thanks for the solid, dot-coms!

Baby Doll, Check Your Cheek

I had loved to dance since long before I came out as queer. Neil Young and Crazy Horse did a series of stealth gigs in a Half Moon Bay bar called the Old Princeton Landing in 1996, and while Tira and I only made it inside for one show, we stood about six feet away from Neil, so after that I was fine with listening through the walls. The Old Princeton Landing shows were a social event as much as anything else; we were already friends with many other Neil Young fans, collectively known as the Rusties, and we were closest with an old-school hippie named Burnout and his wife Janey. I spent many of those 1996 nights pleasantly stoned and dancing in the parking lot, as you do when your favorite musician is rocking out inside and your friends are close by and you're feeling wide open and happy to be alive.

But dancing to Neil Young at the Old Princeton Landing had been another life, and the goth scene became my respite in 1999. I was proud to score the email address *sherilyn@sfgoth.com*, and my favorite of the many clubs was Shrine of Lilith. It was in the basement of a large granite building at the corner of 1st and Harrison near the Bay Bridge onramp; designed by architect William Gladstone Merchant in the Streamline Moderne style and completed in 1950, the Harrison side of the building had tall front windows and the words SAILORS' UNION OF THE PACIFIC carved along the top. That was the building's official name, but it was colloquially referred to as Maritime Hall for the concert venue on the main floor. There was often a large crowd on the Harrison side for a Maritime show on Friday nights, while the entrance to Shrine was around the corner on 1st. It was a nondescript glass doorway leading into what looked like a narrow office building grafted onto the Maritime, with a series of portholes out of respect for the nautical premise. There was always a small murder of goths hanging out in front on Shrine nights, and a tall gentleman with long blond hair shaved on the sides checked IDs and stamped hands.

The music was muffled at street level, but as I descended the stairs it became louder and clearer, welcoming Babygoth Sherilyn like a raccoon-eyed Eurydice. I seldom recognized a given song, but familiarity was not the point. It was all about the sense of adventure and excitement as I entered this underworld, and as Coil's "The Golden Section" had predicted, my soul became smitten with Azrael's current form as Anodyne,

Flyer for the club Shrine of Lilith at the Maritime Hall, January 1999. Don't tell Fernando or Mopey Puppy that Perki was my favorite DJ!

the woman working the coat check. Anodyne's coat check led to the main barroom, which featured comfortable booths and more premise-respecting portholes. Some nights I was first on the dance floor after the doors opened, getting to spread out as I swirled and swooped, and some nights I was the last to leave when the house lights came on. There were some not-great nights, and there was plenty of disappointment and heartbreak, but the club felt like home. I made friends there who accepted me for the mess that I was, including a pair of young women named Helena and Phred and a Suicide Girl named Thora. Shrine of Lilith was also the first public place where I felt comfortable using the women's restroom, and I never stopped feeling gratitude for that. I also feel eternal gratitude toward c0g, a goth boy from Bolinas who was the first person to take me shopping for makeup. He also taught me how to apply eyeliner, and while c0g's personal makeup style had a 1972 Brian Eno grace, left up to my own devices my style was closer to Eastern Bloc Brutalism without the human warmth. My raccoon eyes were courtesy of the Tar shade of my favorite eyeliner, Revlon's Street Wear; I used the Flat end of the Tar for my eyes, while I often used the Frosty end as lipstick, because it stayed on well and completed my *corpse fished out of the hudson* look.

The one non-goth club I frequented in early 1999 was Trannyshack, which was Tuesday nights at the Stud on Harrison. I usually arrived around 10 p.m. and leaned against the wall next to the Stud's pool table under the blue light, both because it was a good place to see and be seen and because blue light is a dead girl's best friend. As I was bathing in the blue one night, I ruminated on the naïveté of my fantasy that if I worked twice as hard at proving I was a responsible and self-sufficient grownup, my mother would no longer diminish me as **the baby of the family**, and she would be halfway-willing to accept my queerness. Instead, she said she was currently grieving because she considered my coming out as trans to be the equivalent of my death. At least my makeup was on point! I'd had a rare feeling of *getting it right* earlier that evening when I untied my hair from the top of my head, which was always the critical moment; until then it's theoretical, an act of faith that the unrelated-seeming elements will come together as a whole, and the risk seemed greater because I was going less subtle even by my standards, lots of shadow around my already-sunken eyes and not sparing the white powder. But when I let down my freshly-blackened hair and saw it framing my face, I thought to myself, *this is how i'll look when i'm buried.* There it was: the only thing better than my usual goal of *corpse fished out of the hudson* had to be *both feet in the grave.*

Because I felt obligated to tend to my mother's feelings despite her refusal to acknowledge mine, I had recently explained at length over email that my being trans, let alone goth, had nothing to do with her.

(Going goth was inevitable ever since my best friend Conk had explained the slimming effect of black clothes when I was 13.) That I was trans was nothing my mother could have prevented; it was not her fault; it was not a rebellion against her; it was not a result of her breaking up with my seldom-mentioned father or the lack of a strong masculine role model; it was not a phase; and it was not a rash, impulsive, or otherwise unconsidered decision. None of that mattered, and when I tried to tell her about my life as a young urban professional in the most quotidian terms possible—I was out of the house by 4:15 on most mornings, at the gym by 5:30 for an hour of cardio, and at my desk at CNET by 8:15—her response was *i don't want to know*. But as I now looked to the large mirror on the other side of the Stud's dimly-lit pool room, I felt not the weight of my mother's disapproval, but a sense of wonder about the spectral, more-feminine-than-not creature in the reflection. I had died in my mother's heart, but at least I had a beautiful ghost.

Also present at Trannyshack were the Motherlode Girls, the transgender sex workers who operated out of the rough part of town known as the Tenderloin. They used to center around a bar at the corner of Post and Larkin called the Motherlode, which had picked up the slack after the 1991 closure of the Black Rose at Eddy and Jones. I had walked past the Motherlode a few times after I moved to San Francisco in 1994, and I admired the purple neon sign reading *The Motherlode* behind the bar when the curtains were open, but I was always too afraid to step inside. The Motherlode closed a few years later and was replaced by Divas down Post near Polk in 1998, and I hadn't yet set foot in Divas, either. The Motherlode Girls would now often congregate near me on these nights at the Stud in early 1999, because everyone looked good in blue light, not only dead girls.

The main event at Trannyshack was a drag show at midnight. I already found drag shows boring and a teensy bit problematic since their whole reason to exist was for cis men to caricature femininity, so I usually left the Stud around 11:45 p.m. and headed a few blocks down Harrison to the cavernous City Nights for my second-favorite goth club, Roderick's Chamber. It lacked the social aspect of Shrine, but the music was better than Trannyshack, the dance floor was bigger, and best of all, there was no freakin' drag show. I was also fond of Sanctuary and Bound, which were on various Saturdays at the 7th Note Showclub at the corner of Columbus and Lombard in North Beach, and I explored Bondage a Go-Go at the Cat Club on Folsom and Death Guild at the Manhattan Lounge on Market. Seeing a faded handstamp on my wrist from a recent night always gave me a boost during the day, and having multiple handstamps from multiple clubs was multiple times better. I was also glad I was getting out there, testing my limits, seeing new things, trying to find out what my boundaries were, experiencing what

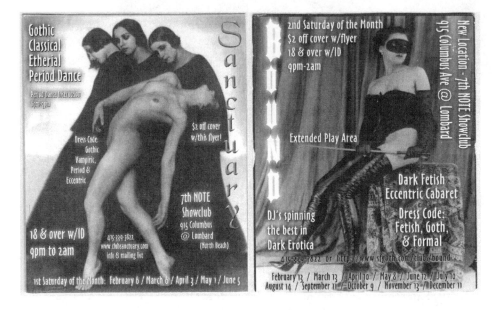

Flyers for the clubs Sanctuary and Bound at the 7th Note Showclub, February 1999. All dress codes should include "vampiric."

I could experience before the world definitely-for-sure ended on December 31, 1999. I was frequently reminded that I had done two very bad and wrong things, that I had fucked everything up and dashed the dreams of many people. None of those sacrifices would have mattered if I had just stayed at home, and no less important was that I was documenting it all.

Three things I knew by the time I was five years old was that I was not a boy, there was no God, and I wanted to be a writer. I lacked the language and courage to express those first two things until I was in my twenties, but I demonstrated an aptitude for the third thing from a young age. (For words about growing up Catholic and how my atheism and gender identity intersected, see my essay "The Permanent Prodigal Daughter" in Melanie E. Brewster's 2014 anthology *Atheists in America*. Would "The Perpetual Prodigal Daughter" have been a better title? God only knows!) My brother John was two grades above me, and he later joked that I became a strong reader and writer because he used to make me do his phonics homework. That early boost helped, and when I was in the first grade, I was placed in the Advanced Reading Group. It consisted of four girls and myself, and we would often be sent into the school library to do our advanced reading away from the rabble. The Advanced Reading Group was my first circle of friends, and being among them was the most natural thing in the world. I drifted away from them as external gender expectations took hold, and I never saw them again after the fourth grade because my mother and I moved to a different school district.

By the time I was in junior high I had an Atari 65XE computer, and I spent many hours plugging away at AtariWriter Plus. I was no good at making things up, so while I took the occasional stab at fiction, my arc bent toward nonfiction; the more intense the experience was, the more I was compelled to write about it. My first epic was about an emotionally brutal week at summer camp when I was 13 in 1986, and my second was about an emotionally brutal band trip when I was 14, so my themes were already in place. I was also already hustling to get my words into print. I won First Place for my grade level in the 1987 William Saroyan Festival Story Writing Contest—a true story about a classmate who had been shot and killed by a parent—and it became my first published piece when it ran in the *Fresno Bee*. I began contributing to the *Bee*'s Teen Tempo section a few years later, and I experienced my first backlash in 1990 over an essay about why I was not going to join the Army. I did not mention that a big part of it was that I was a girl despite all available evidence and I would have killed myself before suffering through the punishing masculinity of the military, but my unpatriotic pacifism during the Persian Gulf War still made many strangers angry. The backlash was scary, but I never regretted speaking my truth, even if the deeper truth of my queerness remained unspeakable. By the time I graduated from high school I was always carrying around a notebook, and when I got to San Francisco State University in 1994 and experienced a severe culture shock, typing it all out on my IBM clone was how I kept from going mad—or, at least, how I documented my descent into madness.

I sent long emails to friends about whatever recent adventure I'd been on whether the friend was interested or not, and then started an online diary in February 1999 after I came out as trans. It was raw, painful, and necessary while going through a dark period with what felt like little to no emotional support. It made people angry because I was angry and awkward and coming in hot, and I was defensive and quick to be offended because if I didn't defend myself against offense nobody else would, not when it had been made clear that I had done two very bad and wrong things. Rejection by family and friends was a possibility every queer person faced in those days, and I was prepared to be abandoned by everyone I loved. And if they did send me packing, I knew no jury on the planet would have convicted them.

Leave Your Expectations at the Door

Tira and I still did things together in those bleak early months of 1999, so long as we did them as casual friends. Sometimes it didn't work, like when we saw Jonathan Richman at the Make Out Room two weeks after we broke up. The show itself was great, heavy on songs I already knew by heart from his album *I'm So Confused*, but Tira and I were simmering before Jonathan came on, and he must have noticed the fighting couple near the stage as he debuted his brand-new song "Couples Must Fight." When Tira looked at me with burning in her eyes during intermission and said *i want to see you hurt as much as i'm hurting*, we went home because ya girl had herself a meltdown. (I have to sigh now.) And sometimes doing things together worked fine, like when we saw Hole and Marilyn Manson at the Cow Palace in March during their Beautiful Monsters tour. Hole's *Celebrity Skin* and Manson's *Mechanical Animals* were already the soundtrack of my second adolescence, with R.E.M.'s *Monster* and *Up* doing the rest of the heavy lifting, so Hole and Manson in concert together was the right show at the right time. I thought of Marilyn Manson himself and Hole's frontwoman Courtney Love as something of a best-case before-and-after scenario for my own journey, and it felt appropriate when their tour collapsed in a cloud of bruised egos a few days after the Cow Palace show because they couldn't get along.

Tira and I were accompanied to the show by our friend Howard. He used to work in the music industry and had schlepped Courtney around to in-store gigs during her druggier days, though his beef with her now was that she had **sold out**, and he also considered Manson's *Mechanical Animals* song "The Speed of Pain" too melodically similar to David Bowie's "Aladdin Sane." I didn't hear it beyond the phonetic similarities in the title, and

Ticket stub for Marilyn Manson and Hole at the Cow Palace, March 1999. This was a thing that happened, and I was there for it.

I thought "The Speed of Pain" was the better song. Besides, in addition to how much Manson's recurring themes of reconstruction and rebirth resonated with me, I liked how he wore his influences on his sleeve: when he sang "The Speed of Pain" at the Cow Palace, his outfit was clearly based on the character Jack Fairy from the opening credits of the recent Todd Haynes film *Velvet Goldmine*. Manson's previous costume during the concert was inspired by Fairy's outfit while singing "2HB" in *Goldmine*'s Death of Glitter Concert, which was itself inspired by Brian Eno's outfit from the inside of the 1973 Roxy Music album *For Your Pleasure*, because nobody works in a vacuum and all art is inspired by something that came before it.

As it happened, Tira had joined me for *Velvet Goldmine* at the Red Vic Movie House on Haight the week before the Cow Palace concert. It was Tira's first time seeing Haynes' poetic recreation of the early 1970s Glam Rock era in London, but I had already seen it at the Embarcadero Center Cinema on opening night in November 1998 with a friend who was a huge Roxy Music fan. One of *Velvet Goldmine*'s central themes would resonate with me in the years to follow: *the secret of becoming a star is knowing how to behave like one*. I also appreciated how it was structured like *Citizen Kane*, and I was happy to read in *Goldmine*'s companion book that Haynes owned the *Kane* influence, saying he didn't want *Goldmine* **to carry a notion of objective truth or ultimate psychological meaning** and that using the *Kane* structure **really allowed me to play with these elements**.

In addition to being an homage to the greatest film ever made, *Velvet Goldmine* contains the greatest representation I've ever seen of how it feels to want to get out of the closet, but not be able to. Teenager Arthur (Christian Bale) is watching Glam Rock star Brian Slade (Jonathan Rhys Meyers) in a televised news conference as Arthur's baleful Christian parents glare in disapproval. Slade makes no effort to act butch, saying **rock and roll is a prostitute—it should be tarted up**, and that if his fans were to get the impression that he's **a blinkin' fruit**, it wouldn't be **the wrong impression** in the slightest. Arthur is then on his feet, pointing at the screen and saying *that's me! that's me, dad! that's me!* But he only imagines it, it's only a fantasy, because Arthur knows he must never, ever admit who he is to his parents. And I had been there more times than I could count.

The magazine rack at the nearby Bullard Village Drug was full of cheapjack sci-fi news rags while I was growing up, and the month I turned 11, I was surprised that the latest issue of *Enterprise Incidents* devoted so many pages to a movie called *Streets of Fire*. It took place on Earth in the present, and most of the pictures were of a dark-haired woman named Diane Lane singing! Whatever indignation I may have felt at this genre-blurring was evened out by those pictures of Lane as rock star Ellen Aim, fully clothed in outfits which were sexy but not gaudy, and feminine

Flyer found at the Red Vic Movie House for the website Venus: The *Velvet Gold-mine* Fan Planet, March 1999. Venus was not my website, but I wish it had been.

without being a caricature, all of which was a wonderful rarity in the horrible soft-focus-and-shoulder-pads *Dynasty* era. Unaware that these sorts of pictures were historically called pin-ups, I was tempted to pin up a picture from *Enterprise Incidents* of Lane wearing a long dress while standing in front of a microphone in rock-star mode, but I didn't because I was afraid my mother would think I was gay. Hear me out: why else would I put a picture of a woman on my wall? The only reason I could think of was to admire how she looked and aspire to being like her someday, all of which meant the jig would be up and my mother would know I was ***gaaaaaaaaay!*** I did not understand what that word meant, only that it was bad, and it was what people would think I was if I didn't keep these feelings to myself. I went through a similar internal debate regarding the black-and-white cover of Olivia Newton-John's album *Soul Kiss*, which I could feel rewiring my brain (*this is important, this means something*) the first time I saw it in Bullard Village Drug's LP section.

If I had pinned up one of the *Streets of Fire* pictures, my mother probably would have been thrilled that I was showing a proper masculine interest in women, especially after my recent fascination with the not-great

April 1984 *Peanuts* special *It's Flashbeagle, Charlie Brown*. Inspired by the bad but high-grossing 1983 Adrian Lyne film *Flashdance*, the formless *Flashbeagle* was mostly a series of musical numbers which existed to fill out the soundtrack LP, but the centerpiece was Snoopy dancing at a disco while wearing a headband and legwarmers, even though Snoopy is a boy and only girls wore headbands and legwarmers and danced like that. I knew the music was terrible and the animation wasn't much better, but I was there for it as Snoopy did things only girls were supposed to do while wearing things only girls were supposed to wear, and I could tell my mother was troubled by my interest even though I was afraid to express aloud *why* I was there for it. I continued to not show a proper interest in many kinds of things teenage boys were supposed to be interested in for the next few years, and my mother could not have been more pleasantly surprised to come home one day when I was 16 and find me watching Woody Allen's *Annie Hall* with an unfamiliar 15 year old girl named Tira. Tira had recently broken up with her boyfriend so I thought *Annie Hall* might cheer her up, and I put a bowl of peanuts on the couch between us because I thought she might like a snack, and the way I was being friendly and hospitable while making no effort to get into her pants endeared me to Tira that much more. I was far from being a unicorn, for I was lonely and needy to an extent which was exhausting to her in the months to follow, but having sex with Tira was never my endgame in 1990, nor did I realize I was *expected* to try to have sex with her.

Growing up in the 1980s meant I saw countless comedies about teenage boys trying to fuck teenage girls, but I never saw myself in those characters—and when I did see a character who was queer the way I was queer deep down, it was never good. Though we had always existed, trans women started being referenced in primetime television a few years after I was born, the highest-profile example being the controversial sitcom *Soap*. Billy Crystal's character Jodie almost getting surgery to become a woman but then backing out and trying to commit suicide was a lot to unpack for a six-year-old who had one of her first *hey, that's me!* moments when she saw Crystal in a dress and wig, and the message the show sent was clear: **you do not exist**. When there was any hint of representation on the television shows my mother and I watched over the next decade, it always made me want to disappear into the recliner out of shame and embarrassment because what if she knew I was one of *those* people? (**"this week on night court, female impersonator jim bailey plays dan's college friend chip, now a transsexual who shocks dan with news of his upcoming sex-change operation!"**)

When I was 12, Paul Mazursky's *Down and Out in Beverly Hills* got a lot of buzz and controversy because it was Disney's first R-rated movie. I did not see it in the theater, but my mother did, and I overheard her telling a friend that of the film's many affronts, the one which bothered her the most was **the family's son didn't know if he wanted to be a boy or a girl!** *Down and Out* is sympathetic to Evan Richards' character of Max, laughing with but not at them in a way only possible because the film was designed to be provocative, and few things were more provocative in the 1980s than treating a trans woman with a modicum of respect. Max's queerness was eliminated in the short-lived Fox sitcom version of *Down and Out* because that dog did not hunt on primetime television, not even on the **aren't we sooooo naughty?** network of *Married with Children*.

I saw Peter Faiman's PG-13 *"Crocodile" Dundee* in the theater when I was 13 because it included the trailer for the fourth *Star Trek* movie. The trailer was okay, but it was not worth how *Dundee* kicked me in the teeth when the hypermasculine protagonist (some Australian asshole who also has story and screenplay credit) flirts with a trans woman (cis woman Anne Carlisle) in a New York bar. She is given the lovely name of Gwendoline despite only existing to be set up and knocked back down, and the protagonist is informed in the nick of time that Gwendoline is **a guy dressed as a woman—a fag**. The protagonist doesn't believe it until he grabs Gwendoline's crotch, a sexual assault which sends her rushing out while the barflies laugh harder than any Gotham audience has laughed since Martin & Lewis' final night at the Copa. Because I was thirsting for representation even though it was all poison, I watched that scene over and over when the movie came out on VHS, and my heart hurt for Gwendoline. She had the courage to be herself, only to be sexually assaulted and humiliated out of what was probably her regular hangout. I decided that after leaving the bar she took a deep breath, shook off what just happened, and then found someone who appreciated her, creating my own *Rosencrantz and Guildenstern Are Dead* in which Gwendoline was the hero who survives through the final reel and that macho shithead was a bit player. (As for Carlisle having played a dual role of both a human man and an alien woman in Slava Tsukerman's *Liquid Sky* a few years earlier, I cannot even get into that.)

When *Dundee* was released I was already spending many Saturdays at the Fresno State University library, doing research about what I was. Most of the relevant material was found in the Library of Congress' classification system under HQ77, specifically "HQ77–77.2 Transvestism" and "HQ77.7–77.95 Transsexualism," the latter of which was so distasteful that the LOC couldn't be bothered to conjugate the word correctly. Much of it was academic and dry, yet with a **look at the freaks / there but for the grace of god, right? / yeesh!** point of view which was hard to miss when you were one of the godforsaken freaks in question. I already knew not to believe everything I read, but the truth had to be in there somewhere, within and between the sums and remainders of the contradictions. As it happened, the closest thing I found to my truth was in a book which had been on our family's shelf since before I was born, Wardell Pomeroy's 1968 *Boys and Sex*. Pomeroy had been a researcher for the Kinsey Institute and was co-author of *The Kinsey Reports*, and God love him, Pomeroy namedrops Alfred Kinsey in *Boys and Sex* like a starfucker.

By the time I was nine I always looked in the table of contents and the indices of such books for the prefix *trans*, then skimmed through the book anyway to be on the safe side. While skimming the index-less *Boys and Sex*, I didn't see myself until the end of the chapter on homosexuality, and then I saw myself like I had never been seen before. After several boring, irrelevant pages about boys liking boys, Pomeroy wrote that **there are other aspects of homosexuality which are not quite so familiar,** which leads into a discussion of transvestism. According to Pomeroy it tends to start as young as four or five, and **sometimes it occurs in the common childhood game of "playing house," and a boy does so because he wants to get some sort of acceptance or affection from an older sister or playmate while he is dressed as a girl,** a sentence which made my nine-year-old heart ache. I already wished I had an older sister, but the thought of having *any* female friend or relative I could turn to for acceptance or affection while dressed as a girl was exquisitely painful because it would mean that not only was I able to achieve the impossible dream of dressing as a girl in the first place, but that the female friend or relative would accept me as a girl and would encourage me and love me and offer compassion and comfort and can you even imagine such a thing? How do you begin to imagine such a thing? I desperately wanted to live that life, but the warm fantasy Pomeroy described didn't produce the *hey, that's me!* feeling as much as the starker, colder scenario which came next.

> Some boys not only want to dress up like girls; they want to *be* girls. These are called "transsexualists." They want to dress like girls because they believe they *are* girls, in effect. This form of behavior also starts very early in life, even earlier than transvestism. As these boys begin to grow up, they think of all the worthwhile things about a girl's life, like not being roughed up, wearing pretty clothes, not having to earn a living (in the male sense). They do not think of the relative advantages of being a boy—that is, the relative freedom and independence boys have, the opportunities open only to them (a somewhat decreasing advantage these days, it's true), the lack of pressure to be married, and so on. Transsexualists are also homosexual, but because they think of themselves as females, they think of themselves as heterosexual. A few of these people have operations which, as far as it is possible, changes them from males to females. Some even legally marry males, as the newspapers inform us from time to time.

Much of that is reductive, and the admonition that transsexualists (!) ought to **think of the relative advantages of being a boy** misses the point in a spectacular fashion, but it was also as close to getting it right as was possible for 1968—such as the subtext that transsexualists (!!) are third-class citizens who will be treated as curiosities by the press, and I would bloody my forehead against the heteronormative myth that transsexualists (!!!) are attracted to boys and boys only countless times in the years to come. It's also hard to miss that he had to disclaim us from both directions, but while he was while reiterating that my people were a footnote to a footnote at best, that we were a variation so abnormal as to almost not be worth mentioning, my sexy boy Pomeroy was still fighting the good fight.

> The reason I am taking the time to talk about all these variations from what we think of as "normal" sexuality is that I hope the boys who read this will, by understanding what the variations are and how they happen, develop tolerance for people who may not be like themselves. A mature boy is one who can accept these differences as a fact of life and not be upset by them, who will not bully a sissy or sneer at homosexuals and try to put them down in one way or another.

So, I was learning the language for what I was by the time I was a tween, but I was also learning that it was language I must never use, and my mother made it clear that gender lines were inviolable. Growing out my dishwater-brown hair felt like the barest minimum I could do by the time I was 14, and when asking me nicely to get a haircut didn't work, she tried sneering at me by saying *your hair's getting so long, people are going to start thinking you're a girl!* Because I adhered to the Eleventh Commandment, my mother did not know that while she was trying to bully me out of being a sissy I had recently read her copy of *The Sensuous Woman*. (I didn't understand a lot of it, but I still felt myself in it more than in anything I ever read about male sexuality, which was not a subject I read much about in the first place because everything about it was gross and unappealing.) When my mother's dig at my inert masculinity failed, she pulled rank and forced me to get a haircut because my body was not yet my own. The last time she dragged me to Supercuts at 16 was my last haircut for years, but she never stopped giving me static, and on one occasion she pleaded with me to tie my hair back so its length wouldn't offend my niece Shandon's abusive, hypermasculine stepfather.

When I learned about the advertising technique known as the bandwagon (*everybody else is doing it, so you should do it too!*) in high school, my 14-year-old mind was blown. How could the bandwagon still work if the public knew about it, if we were aware that we were being manipulated? When I told my mother about this fascinating new thing I had learned, she said, *that's not true!* It did not matter that it was information I had learned in the high school on the other side of Fresno which my mother chose to bus me to because I tested well enough to be placed in the euphemistic

Gifted and Talented Education program. Because the information was now coming out of *my* mouth, she said it was wrong and not true. After graduating from high school, I attended Fresno City College because it was important to my mother that I go to college, but she never reconciled her belief in higher education with her anti-intellectual streak toward me, and she tried to discourage me from such talk by calling me *skewed*. One of my favorite classes was Political Science 2: American Government, but when I told my mother that I'd learned in class about the existence of for-profit prisons, she said, *oh, that's not true! you're just skewed!*

The net result was that our conversations had felt like Monty Python's Argument Clinic sketch since long before I came out, and when we had our in-person summit meeting in April 1999 after she finished grieving my Death By Being Transgender, my mother continued to automatically gainsay anything I said. *i'm doing it all by the book, mom.* **the book could be wrong!** *i went to a licensed psychologist who specializes in gender issues for the required twelve weeks, and i received her written approval to see an endocrinologist.* **psychologists are only in it for the money!** *i just got a raise and a glowing performance review at work.* **you don't know what people are saying behind your back!** And so on and so forth, though my favorite was when I said *my endocrinologist has prescribed premarin and provera*, and my 59-year-old mother responded *i take those! we call those old-lady hormones! did you know you're taking old-lady hormones?* I guessed she expected me to be so embarrassed about being associated with the occupants of the straight world's lowest rung—i.e., women who have the temerity to grow old—that I would decide to stop being trans.

I was aware that one of my mother's favorite songs was Rick Nelson's "Garden Party," and that its message of not sacrificing your own happiness by attempting the impossible task of making everybody else happy had resonated with her in the 1980s as she scrambled to put her life back together after breaking up with my seldom-mentioned father. She learned to prioritize her own feelings in a way she never could before, and as well she should have, because she deserved at least that much. The downside was that when my brother John and I tried to talk to her about our own difficulties, she brushed us off with *oh, everybody has problems*. Which was true, but it made bringing up my gender issues feel impossible. There was no way on Earth my mother would encourage me or offer acceptance or affection, and though she hadn't busted out the wooden spoon in years, I couldn't shake the feeling that she might resort to corporal punishment if I tried to tell her I was a girl. When I came out as trans—*if* I ever came out—it would have to be when I was far away, so she couldn't stop me from becoming myself.

The upside of my mother's emotional distance was that she let me enjoy whatever media I was inclined to enjoy whether age-appropriate or not, and she didn't monitor my viewing habits. It helped that I was always mature for my age, and as she later put it, I never gave her ***any real trouble***. In addition to my scholarly research at the library, I kept an eye on the television listings when I was a teenager, and I recorded any afternoon talk show which looked relevant. This was toward the end of the genteel *Donahue* era, but the shows still tended toward sensationalism, usually drag queens and female impersonators and transgender sex workers. I felt closest to the sex workers since they were doing what they had to do to survive as themselves, but it still hurt my heart when any of the guests was insulted or marginalized. I also noticed that when the guests were trans women who were not sex workers, the enforced narrative was always about how miserable they were, about their regrets, about how they wished they weren't trans or that they hadn't passed some arbitrary ***point of no return***. The message of ***being trans is a bad way to be and you should be thankful you aren't one of these bad people*** was loud and clear, and the all-important *status quo* was maintained.

I revealed my nonzero level of interest in crossdressing to Tira in January 1991, but it quickly became a bad year to be a closeted trans woman thanks to the February release of Jonathan Demme's *The Silence of the Lambs*, an eventual Best Picture winner which picked up the slack from Brian De Palma's 1980 *Dressed to Kill* by ensuring the public would equate us with serial killers for decades to come. Ugh ugh ugh, *Silence of the Lambs*. Fuck that goddamn fucking movie. Speaking of such things, want to know what Neil Jordan's 1992 *The Crying Game* did not do? Help. *The Crying Game* did not help one bit. David Cronenberg's 1993 *M. Butterfly* was an improvement since the trans-adjacent character Song Liling has a full inner life, is not a serial killer, and is never assaulted by the cis male lead. Song is a writer, even! But nobody besides me and Tira saw *M. Butterfly*, so it still didn't help.

The year 1991 started off determined to keep me in the closet, but my biggest *Velvet Goldmine* moment also came that year. The talk show *Sally Jessy Raphael* visited San Francisco in May, a month before I turned 18 and three years before I moved to the city. Raphael was interviewing performers from the female impersonator club Finocchio's; first up was a Dolly Parton and then a Cher, which, sure, fine. Later in the episode there was a Diana Ross and an Ann-Margret, which, again, fine. The questions tended to be about their daily lives, and the recurring theme was that they weren't gay and didn't want to be women, they were men who happened to do this for a living, that at the end of the day female impersonation was a job like any other and they were 100 percent male and the all-important *status quo* was maintained. Nothing new or startling to see, thank you, drive through.

The scale of my universe expanded exponentially in a fraction of a second after Sally Jessy Raphael made this introduction.

> Our next guest is probably the youngest female impersonator I've ever met: a twenty-year-old female impersonator. And some have said that this impersonator has taken the act too far, because he has had breast implants. Welcome Kelly Michaels as Madonna.

And there was Kelly Michaels, in a long black coat over a black bustier and fishnets, flipping around her own blonde hair as she danced down the aisle to Madonna's "Express Yourself." Everyone else on stage was wearing a wig and a costume, and while Kelly's hair and makeup had surely been leveled up backstage, this was who she was. At the end of the show the others would take off their *Dynasty*-hangover dresses and fake breasts and hip padding and put on their street clothes and merge back into the world as men, but I know Kelly was already wearing her street clothes. This was who she was, a trashy blonde Southern girl with a Madonna fixation.

I wasn't watching the show with my mother, but in a less broken world I would have pointed at the screen and said *that's me! that's me, mom! that's me!* Kelly was only two years older than me but was further along in becoming herself than I would get for another decade, and while I had no strong feelings about Madonna, I still wanted to be Kelly when I grew up. She was not a female impersonator (a straight man pretending to be a woman to entertain people who find that sort of thing entertaining) or a drag queen (a gay man pretending to be a woman for comedic value because aren't those gashes just so hilarious?). Kelly Michaels was a trans woman, and she was as close as I had ever seen to the best possible outcome to my timeline. Unlike myself, she had been openly queer from a young age and was rejected by her family long before she was on *Sally*, so Kelly had lived a more difficult life than I could imagine. I tried not to romanticize her suffering, but from where I was sitting, I couldn't argue with the results.

Kelly did a lot of porn in the 1990s, and her presence gave me a fighting chance at feeling represented. She had a distinct persona in her movies, young and energetic and *alive*, and every time Kelly was awkward and imperfect, it felt like she was being awkward and imperfect the way *I* would be awkward and imperfect in that situation. But identifying with Kelly's awkward imperfections also meant I shared in her moments of glory. She tended to be in scenes with cis men because everything in the whole goddamn freakin' universe was geared toward cis men in those days, but occasionally Kelly would be paired up with a cis woman. My favorite of her partners was Sharon Kane, who looked like Courtney Love's sister and who also had the large, tired eyes of my mainstream cis crush, Susan Sarandon. Just seeing Kelly kissing Sharon was the shiniest thing I could fathom, the

best of all possible couplings. I was also inspired by how Kelly did everything under her own name. The professional Madonna impersonator
Kelly Michaels was the same person as the porn star Kelly Michaels, and
she didn't try to hide who she was or what she did, not letting shame or
the disapproval of others interfere with her personal branding. It was a
form of self-acceptance which I hoped to someday emulate with my own
name.

A few weeks after Kelly Michaels appeared on *Sally Jessy Raphael* in
May 1991, Fresno held its first Lesbian/Gay Freedom Day Parade. The Ku
Klux Klan protested the parade in full robe-and-cone regalia, and some
of the nice white Christian Klansfolk held signs with slogans like *god's
answer to queers: aids* and *why does maggot sound like faggot?* while others shouted *long live aids!* and gave Nazi salutes. The Klan's spokesman
Jim Cheney lamented to the *Fresno Bee* that *we can't hang them or tar and
feather them anymore, but we can do other things*, all of which confirmed
that I could never, ever come out as transgender or tell anyone my name
was Sherilyn Connelly.

Love in the Dying Moments of the 20th Century

No matter how bleak things got in 1999, no matter how much my emotions were being stripped to the wire and my self-esteem was getting flayed,
I was determined to keep hope alive. I knew coming out would hurt, that
I would get static and blowback and that many people who neither knew
nor cared about how I felt would tell me that what I was doing was bad
and wrong. I knew those would be the consequences. I would have to get
through the next few months, the next few years, however long it would
take to get my shit together and chart my own course. There was so much
potential out in the world and within myself, and I wanted to explore it all,
to see what I'd been missing.

Not that I had been sheltered. In March 1996, I traveled into the Mis-
sion for what I would look back on as my first truly San Franciscan event:
Fuckorama, *a multiscreen showing of porn films* at the Artists Television
Access on Valencia as a benefit for the San Francisco Sex Information line.
I had been given a flyer by a fellow film student, a woman whose couch I
briefly surfed on before I moved into Lascaux West in May 1995. Tira was in
Fresno the night of Fuckorama so she did not join me, but she did not forbid me from going to this highly sexual event which another woman had
brought to my attention. I did not appreciate my good fortune as I walked
through the ATA and watched the various 8mm and 16mm porn film loops,
then witnessed a live demonstration of two women fisting. As tends to be

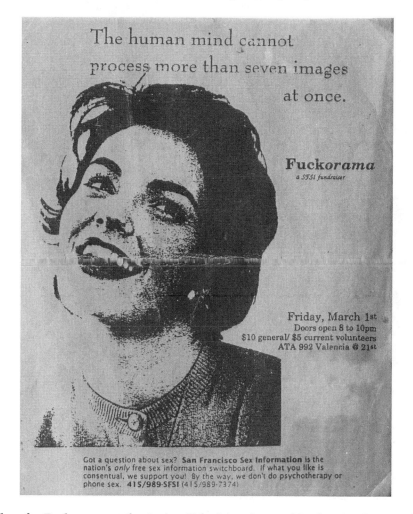

Flyer for Fuckorama at the Artists Television Access, March 1996. Seven still seems like a high number, doesn't it?

the case with freedoms, I would not realize how much I was taking this one for granted until someone else took it away from me.

An open acknowledgment and appreciation of sex was baked into my relationship with Tira from the start, even as I remained oblivious to the cultural expectation to try to have sex with her. The second movie we saw in a theater together was Peter Greenaway's *The Cook, the Thief, His Wife & Her Lover* in April 1990, after we'd started dating but before we officially became a couple in June. (It goes without saying that the first movie Tira and I went to together was Kenneth Branagh's *Henry V.* I mean, duh.) Everything about seeing the Greenaway picture was perfect: Tira was 15, I

Ticket stub for David Cronenberg's *Crash* at the Century Plaza, March 1997. I never did make it to the Geneva Swap Meet, though.

was 16, and the movie was NC-17; we got in for free because I was friends with the manager; and there were no paying customers because it was a controversial foreign film playing in Fresno, so us underage freeloaders had the theater to ourselves. *The Cook, the Thief, His Wife & Her Lover* would have been a revelation for its production design and cinematography alone, but the explicit sex and final-reel cannibalism made it no less of a bonding experience for me and Tira, giving us that wonderful feeling of *getting away with it*. It was not the first time I was underage in a movie theater, however; that was the R-rated double feature of Chuck Russell's *A Nightmare on Elm Street 3: Dream Warriors* and Alan Parker's *Angel Heart* at the Manchester Mall Cinema when I was 13.

Thanks in no small part to the Art Film Series at the UA Cinemas on Blackstone, Tira and I continued to go to all the NC-17 movies which played in Fresno when we were no longer underage, like Ken Russell's *Whore* and Philip Kaufman's *Henry & June*, and you'd best believe I'm bragging when I say I saw Abel Ferrara's *Bad Lieutenant* in its original 35mm release with Schoolly D's "Signifying Rapper" playing over the nun-rape scene. We fell out of the habit after moving to San Francisco because the fruit was no longer forbidden, but it was still a given that Tira and I would see David Cronenberg's *Crash* on opening night in 1997 because we were always first in line for Cronenberg's movies.

I had long been fascinated by stories about people who are changed by traumatic events and the way their loved ones are or are not able to follow them on their new paths; before *Crash*, my favorite example of the subgenre was Peter Weir's 1993 *Fearless*. (It's a bit overwritten and on-the-nose at times, but *Fearless* remains my favorite of Weir's American films by a wide margin.) Based on the J.G. Ballard novel, Cronenberg's *Crash* is about an underground community of people whose sexualities have been transformed and heightened by auto accidents. After protagonist James Ballard (James Spader) experiences his transformative accident, his wife Catherine (Deborah Kara Unger) tries to find her own fertilizing rather than destructive automotive event, her own capital-C Crash so she can join James on the other side. For as much sex as there is in *Crash*, and there is a whole bunch of sex, people tend to miss that the film is a love story. James has run Catherine off the road in the final scene, and as they cuddle next to her wrecked car, James asks **are you hurt?** The bloodied Catherine says *i think i'm all right* as her eyes brim and a single tear escapes—*all right* meaning that it didn't work, that this was not the transformative event they were hoping for. James tenderly replies, **maybe the next one, darling. maybe the next one.** They loved each other before the movie started, and they will continue to love each other and try to connect after the credits roll. It doesn't get much more romantic than that, and the scene would be just as powerful even if the film's costume designer Denise Cronenberg hadn't put Deborah Kara Unger into that certain long-sleeved, bruise-violet-colored cut velvet blouse.

I was a safe driver who respected traffic laws, understood how metaphors worked, and knew that nothing good came from real-life auto accidents, so my darkest, most improbable fantasy inspired by *Crash* was that central relationship. James and Catherine have impersonal sex with people they are not emotionally attached to on a regular basis, then tell each other about their experiences and work it into their own sex life. That degree of unfiltered communication was the film's most radical concept to me, but in the short term, I was trying to turn the life-changing, inevitable crash of the two very bad and wrong things I had done into a fertilizing rather than a destructive event. My sfgoth email signature line for much of 1999 was *the car crash is a fertilizing rather than a destructive event*, because email signature lines seemed as good a way as any to put an idea out into the universe in 1999.

Characters struggling with their potential queerness had been a theme in Cronenberg's work since the start of his classical period with *The Fly* in 1986. It was a subtext in the 1988 *Dead Ringers*, and the fear of what the word **queer** itself represents drives much of the story in the 1991 William S. Burroughs adaptation *Naked Lunch* (which is also one of the best movies ever about being a writer), while the political overtones in *M. Butterfly* almost make it easy to miss that Cronenberg considers Song Liling the film's hero in a way no other straight white cis male director would have.

But *Crash* felt like the first time he was rooting for his characters to queer up the joint, which was part of the reason it was so controversial, and at first Ted Turner refused to release the film in the United States for fear it would encourage kids to have sex in moving cars. Cronenberg expertly parried this in the newspapers:

> "I told Ted Turner he was off-base as soon as this got back to me," said director David Cronenberg. "'Crash' is an exploration, not an advocacy. Anyone who has seen any of my pictures will know my interest in exploring aberrant psychology and my habit of showing the consequences of taking an aberration too far," he said.

Fair enough. Sometimes you must tell the disapproving authority figure that it's okay, you're not 100 percent committed to being yourself, that you aren't advocating an aberrant psychology, that you haven't passed some arbitrary **point of no return** and that the *status quo* will be maintained, especially when your words are going out over the wire services and may impact your film's domestic distribution. But something which *Crash* as a cultural object helped me understand is that we study what few things wander into our light cones to find the metaphors which are so close to our truths that the equivalence principle kicks in, and once we recognize those metaphors we must roll with them, especially if we see ourselves in art which everyone else finds distasteful.

Getting cis people to understand what it meant for me to be trans was like a Sphere trying to explain what it means to be three-dimensional to a Square in Flatland, and my physicality didn't help. My family did not see a woman when they looked at my ridiculous, misshapen meat puppet—which, yeah, *exactly*, welcome to the dissonance that's been fogging up my own cognition, folks. If it was up to me I would have been born in 1983 rather than 1973 and my stupid skeleton would have topped out around 5'6" rather than 6'1", but I was not consulted on the matter. My family could no more empathize with me than I could understand what it feels like to be cis, the difference being that they had the whole of human history on their side, a history written by people who did not believe my people existed, and more recently my family had been marinating in the poisonously transphobic media of the modern era without realizing it was poison. I had managed to (mostly) expunge that poison from my system and had (mostly) accepted who I was and what I needed to do, and I was determined to be part of the first generation of trans women who were proud of who we were in spite of the best efforts of *Soap* and *Dressed to Kill* and *Sleepaway Camp* and *Night Court* and *"Crocodile" Dundee* and *The Silence of the Lambs* and *Soapdish* and *The Crying Game* and *Ace Ventura: Pet Detective* and other examples far too numerous to mention from a culture which told us we were bad and we should hate ourselves and we're deluded faggots who deserve to get punched in the nose by Stephen Rea.

I knew I was in it for the long haul, but the only thing I could say to set my mother at ease during our in-person summit meeting in April 1999 was to tell her I was not 100 percent sure about being trans, that I had not yet reached some arbitrary ***point of no return***. (Speaking in a hushed whisper with tears in her eyes from the depths of her knowledge of a subject she knew nothing about, she told me ***it's irreversible, you know***.) To say I was not sure about being trans was a lie, and it was not a lie I would feel comfortable with in the long term, but it was a lie which was necessary in the short term to comfort my mother. She was not obligated to reciprocate my efforts because emotional pain is a zero-sum game and my mother was the one who was hurting, not me, and I had forfeited any claim to compassion or comfort from her when I did the two very bad and wrong things.

Though David Cronenberg had to tell the comforting lie in the press, on his commentary track for the 1997 Criterion Collection laserdisc of *Crash*—which had fine cover art, making their 2020 Blu-ray cover all the more confounding—he spoke his truth in the way that you can when it will only be heard by people who shell out $50 for a piece of media which has already been rendered obsolete by the DVD. I listened to the commentary track many times in 1999, and this part always struck me.

> There are those strange characters, and those strange creatures who exist at the margins of society, and I am interested in that because I suppose I identify with them in some way. If you're a card-carrying existentialist, which I tend to think that I am, you feel that all of these things are in fact efforts of human will, that normality is just an effort of human will, a conceptual thing rather than anything that exists in nature, for example, as an absolute. So, these people are all embarked on a voyage which involves not just reinventing themselves, but reinventing their whole understanding of society and physicality, physiology, sexuality, everything else.

The one cultural advantage of being born in 1973 is that I am as Generation X as you can get—I'm so damn Gen-X, I agree with Neil Howe and Bill Strauss' argument that my generation should have been called the 13ers instead of Generation X—and Cronenberg's *Crash* commentary helped me realize I was also an existentialist. I was embarked on a voyage of reinvention, of defining my new normal through an effort of will, and if doing so meant I was destined to be one of those strange creatures who exist at the margins of society, I was okay with that.

All I had to do was not let myself be held back by fear … my own fear, or anyone else's.

2

Honor Thy Error
as a Hidden Intention

El Ritual de la Caja Para Gatos

Though they had known each other online for a few years, Ligeia didn't meet her friend Cally in the flesh until they were both in New Orleans in April 1999 for the goth convention Convergence 5. Ligeia then introduced Cally and me to each other over email, and we hit it off. I was desperate for someone to talk to about … well, about everything, and Cally seemed willing to listen. She lived in the Central Time Zone, and she was an erotica writer who was proud of the dozen sexy vampire fiction stories she'd had published so far. She also made many references to her **gutter mind** while we were chatting and emailing, often in the form of comments like **you've left yourself *very* open to a gutter-minded joke!**

Cally had left Her Abusive Alcoholic Husband around the time that I did my two very bad and wrong things, and in addition to telling me stories about the ways HAAH mistreated her both physically and emotionally, Cally spoke glowingly of a straight cis male Briton who helped her find the courage to leave HAAH. Cally said her **steamy** emails and letters with Her Briton were the closest she'd ever come to cheating and he was the inspiration for her most recent erotica stories, and Cally continued to wax rhapsodic about Her Briton after she and I declared ourselves a couple. Cally was also a Hole fan, and we both had pictures of Courtney up in our homes and workspaces; though Cally did not condone Courtney's drug use, she looked up to her otherwise, especially when Courtney was holding a guitar and being an Angry Rock Chick. Speaking of idols with drug habits, Cally and I also bonded over a probably-deceased, raven-haired writer named Danielle Willis. She was a self-styled vampire with aftermarket porcelain fangs whose lovers tended to be trans women, and Cally had first seen Danielle in an episode of the nonfiction HBO series *Real Sex* which

44

focused on sex activist and proud slut Annie Sprinkle. Cally and I both owned Danielle's book *Dogs in Lingerie*, which proved we were on the same wavelength.

My crests collided with Cally's troughs when I told her about Freyja and the Catbox.

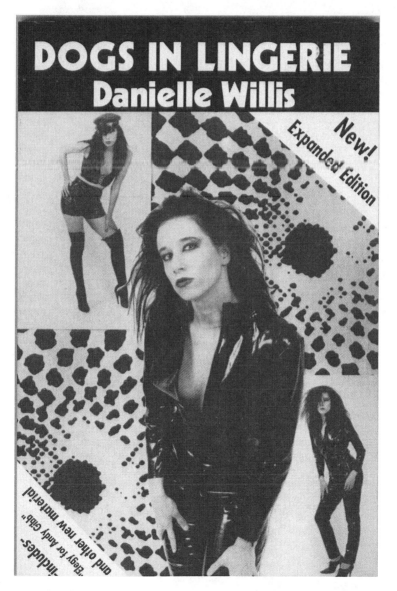

Cover of the 1993 edition of *Dogs in Lingerie* by Danielle Willis. Not pictured: Danielle's front teeth.

I had met Freyja in May at the annual goth picnic in Golden Gate Park—an event which was called the Gothnic, obviously—when she pretty much walked up to me and said *you look fun. be my friend!* I went to the Gothnic afterparty at Freyja's house that night, though it was at another party in late July when she invited me to participate in the Catbox Ritual: me, Freyja, Phred, and two other cis women standing topless in Freyja's small laundry room, admiring and then tweaking each other's nipples. Freyja exposited that the Catbox had nothing to do with sex, but was instead a form of female bonding, a way of seeing other kinds of breasts as valid and real and wonderful. And, best of all, it was silly. The silliness of the whole thing was part of why it was so great. It was also the first time I had been invited into a women's-only space, and that the space where we were doing the silly thing was Freyja's small laundry room did not make it any less of a wonderful, almost transcendent feeling: *this is what it means to belong.*

The gutter-minded erotica writer in the Central Time Zone was having none of this West Coast woo-woo about how the Catbox made a fledgling trans woman feel accepted. Assuring me twice that she was *not the insanely jealous type*, Cally was troubled that I had participated, since she herself had never *felt the need* to bond with her friends in such a manner. She did acknowledge that her anger toward HAAH was starting to spill over into our long-distance relationship, but that did not change Cally's proclamation that I should always prioritize her feelings over my own and never do anything that Cally wouldn't want me to do. Cally would later call her reaction to the Catbox *your fair warning*, and the short version is that mistakes were made, red flags on both sides were ignored, Cally visited San Francisco in September and I visited the Central Time Zone in October and both trips created more issues than they solved, and many things happened that should not have happened, the direst of those things being Cally moving into Lascaux West during the first week of December 1999.

While I was in Fresno that Thanksgiving, ten months after my life had been upended by the two very bad and wrong things I had done and ten days before my life was further upended by Cally's arrival, my mother told me how much she missed Tira and that she was still sad and disappointed in me for breaking up with the Daughter She Never Had. Knowing it was a terrible idea as soon as I opened my mouth, I said that as far as Tira's family was concerned, I no longer existed.

Without missing a beat, my mother replied: *well, can you blame them?*

I had already been reminded many times and from many directions over the past 10 months that I was unworthy of compassion, nobody was going to take my side, and I deserved whatever bad things happened to me. All the same, my mother's reply served as a reminder that I was unworthy of compassion, nobody was going to take my side, and I deserved whatever bad things happened to me.

The One to Walk in the Sun

I returned to Lascaux West from running an errand one day in January 2000 to find Cally fuming. This was nothing new, for Cally had thrown many temper tantrums since moving in six weeks earlier. They were often because I wanted to leave the house to do something fun at night, or go to the gym on Saturday morning, but sometimes I would be minding my own business and suddenly Cally would be crying and screaming at me with liberal doses of *fuck you!* and *i hate you!*, and if I tried to speak she would shout *shut the fuck up!* Since this verbal assault often led to me crying, Cally would then apologize for her tantrum, and she trained me well: if I did not console her while she was apologizing, she would get angrier than she had been during the tantrum she was apologizing for, creating the most toxic feedback loop, the most vicious of circles. But my training was not complete, for on this January day Cally discovered I had violated her Cardinal Rule: *sherilyn will not have any contact with tira.*

The rule went into effect when Tira came by Lascaux West a few days before Christmas 1999 to get her last box of stuff so she would be, per Cally's demand, *out of our lives entirely*. Tira seemed puzzled when I didn't invite her inside to meet Cally, but she didn't ask why, and because George Miller's *Babe: Pig in the City* had been one of my favorite movies of 1998 besides *Velvet Goldmine*, she gave me a set of pig magnets as a Christmas present. I suspected the thoughtfulness of Tira's gift would make Cally angrier, and I was correct: Cally was already vibrating with fury when I went back inside, and when I showed her the pig magnets, she screamed *those are not going on the fridge!* I had already cried out of fear and confusion many times over the past three weeks as Cally screamed *fuck you!* and *i hate you!* at me—in addition to not being allowed to speak above *sotto voce* during her tantrums, I sure as heck was not allowed to cuss back—but the banality of Cally forbidding me from putting pig magnets on the fridge hit me hard. When I could form words again, I tried to explain how much it hurt to not be friends with Tira, in no small part because of the (misplaced and unfair) guilt and shame I felt about how my gender issues had destroyed our relationship. Cally had denied this plea for clemency before, brushing off me being trans as *just a cop-out* and a cheap excuse to see the ex-girlfriend whom I obviously still wanted to fuck, so Cally doubled down: Tira was no longer to be spoken of or referenced in any way. Cally enforced this rule by throwing frequent temper tantrums and by occasionally hitting my arm.

Sometimes a strong flick, sometimes harder, but always to punish me out of anger, and I knew it wasn't mistreatment because I had been told so many times over the past year that I was bad and wrong, which meant I deserved what was happening to me because *pee cat gets the belt.*

When Cally visited San Francisco in September 1999, we spent a day poking through the shops in the Haight-Ashbury district, including the vintage clothing store Buffalo Exchange. Because I still thought of her as a gutter-minded erotica writer who appreciated a ribald tale, as we stood in line for the Buffalo Exchange dressing room, I told Cally about the time Tira and I had sex in the dressing room of an outlet store in Gilroy to drown out a loud family. That ribald tale became the post–Catbox Exhibit A of my disregard for Cally's feelings, and it launched her prohibition against me talking about sex—be it real or imagined, past, present, or future. When I posted something I had written in 1994 about bad sex on one bad night in college to my online diary in 1999, the gutter-minded erotica writer called it *information that had to be slowly absorbed and not taken lightly*, and while *it didn't make me think any less of you*, she said it was *insensitive of you to force the tale upon me without thinking how it might make me feel*, especially *in a public forum with no warning*. When I objected to Cally's implication that me posting something I'd written five years ago to the online diary which Cally had chosen to read was equivalent to me raping her, she acknowledged that it was *not as brutal as rape, but you are telling me things that i would rather not hear but really have no choice about hearing. is that not forcing?* That argument had been back in October when she still lived in the Central Time Zone.

On this otherwise fine January day six weeks after Cally moved across the country and into my home, she had logged into my email and discovered that not only was I communicating with Tira, which was bad enough, I had told Tira why I hadn't invited her inside back in December. Cally didn't want me talking to anyone about our troubles because she said it would give them *the wrong impression*, but going to her archnemesis was unforgivable. In her more lucid moments, Cally acknowledged that much of her anger toward me was because she was jealous that I had never been physically mistreated by Tira the way Cally had been physically mistreated by HAAH. She also said she knew she needed to learn to *not* stamp her foot and get angry whenever she felt challenged, and the way her tantrums resulted in me crying in fear and pain and confusion was a new experience, since HAAH never shed a tear. But I was still not allowed to be friends with Tira, and most of my female friends went on Cally's *never in a million years* list. Freyja was toward the top because of the Catbox, and because Freyja had kissed both Cally and me on New Year's Eve. Granted, Freyja had kissed everyone at her party for the most-hyped New Year's Eve of our lifetimes—if you weren't alive on December 31, 1999, it's hard to convey how big a deal it was—but Freyja had kissed me once before, so she might do it again.

One day in early March, Cally admitted that she was **perhaps subconsciously** keeping me on a short leash as a means of revenge against her family for having kept her on a short leash all her life, but since it was subconscious it was not her fault and I was not allowed to get upset about it. Later that night, Cally read my email over my shoulder and saw that I had received an invitation to Tira's housewarming in the East Bay. (Tira was moving in with her boyfriend, a sweet guy we had already known for a few years, and I was glad she was with someone who could make her happy in all the ways I could not.) Cally's response to me receiving the invitation was familiar: screaming and pounding every available surface before slamming the bedroom door behind her and pounding the wall and continuing to scream **fuck you!** and **i hate you!** I did not attend Tira's housewarming, and to get me to **shut the fuck up!** about the whole matter, Cally said I could be friends with Tira so long as I continued to have no contact with her. It was a win-win: I could tell myself I was still friends with Tira, but since I would never talk to her, Cally didn't have to deal with what she called **tira's shadow looming over us**. Cally did allow me to put the pig magnets on the fridge after a while, and she also told me in one of those lucid moments that she hoped if she fought me on it long enough, I would give up on remaining friends with Tira.

When Cally wasn't punishing me for the sins of strangers thousands of miles away, she often fussed over my makeup and told me how beautiful I was. Not only did her attraction to my femininity make Cally's Madonna/Whore complex about me all the worse, it also made me think of a song I had always found irritating, Cyndi Lauper's "Girls Just Want to Have Fun." I would never stop disliking the recording on a musical level, and the synth solo makes me feel like I'm covered in fire ants, but that final verse about how some beautiful girls get hidden away from the rest of the world by jealous boys? Yeah, I got that now. (I'll also admit the way Cyndi's voice is double-tracked on the words *hide her* is haunting, but the rest of the production? *Woof*.) As *She's So Unusual* Cyndi songs went I would have preferred to be one of the dialoguing stray cats in "All Through the Night" or to go south with the masturbators who roar like lions in "She Bop," but there was a law against those things so long as an angry biped was stepping on my tail.

Choking on the Dirt and Sand

Of all the red flags I ignored in 1999, the second-reddest was that Cally refused to dance. She had seemed to enjoy meeting my friends at Shrine of

Lilith when she visited San Francisco in September, but when Cally moved into my home in December, she didn't want me to go out dancing anymore because she said it made her think of when HAAH would go out and then come home drunk and force himself on her. When I told Cally how much it hurt when she compared me, a queer trans woman who rarely drank and who had never lifted an unkind finger against her, to the alcoholic straight cis man who used to beat and rape her, Cally would get angry and again brush off me being trans as *just a cop-out* and tell me that she had been *victimized* (her word) for 29 years and it was unfair of me to expect her to change overnight. Cally got hired at CNET in March, so we now drove to and from work together, but she still accused me of abandoning her when I tried to leave the house at night. It was enough that HAAH used to leave their house at night, but shortly after Cally moved into Lascaux West she'd had a nightmare in which Christina Aguilera lookalikes *fawned over* me and then stole me away, and Cally was afraid it would happen in real life if she let her guard down.

I convinced her to join me on a Friday night in March for a Shrine spinoff at the Manhattan Lounge called Cypher, and after sitting in a booth for a while as Cally stewed in her anger, I told her I was going to walk around. Which I did, but then the DJ started playing Siouxsie and the Banshees' "Cities in Dust" and I can't *not* dance to that song and it felt so good that I kept swooping for a few more songs until Cally ran up to me in tears and said that I'd told her I was going to walk around and now I was dancing and she was afraid something had happened to me and we had to go home right now. Though she had expanded it from Christina Aguilera lookalikes to any woman with a pulse, Cally still invoked the risk of me being *fawned over* as a legit reason to hide me away from the rest of the world.

When we got home from Cypher, Cally revealed her newest fear: I would declare myself to be a *100 percent real girl* and then leave Cally for a man because I would further declare that *100 percent real girls like boys and boys only*. Cally knew I had no interest in men, and what made her latest burst of cis heteronormativity more hurtful was that I lived in a city which was synonymous with queerness and where it was understood that women are sometimes attracted to women—it was why the ever-evolving LGBT acronym always led off with an L for Lesbian and why the Dyke March happened on Pink Saturday during Pride Weekend in late June, let alone why the Dyke March and the more corporate Pride Parade the next day were both led off by the Dykes on Bikes—and yet the concept of same-gender attraction broke down when it came to me as a woman. Upon learning that I remained attracted to women and not men, people sometimes asked me, *why are you becoming a woman if you're not going to date men?* Cally knew these things, and she knew how much it hurt to have both my gender identity and my sexual preference disregarded in one fell swoop, but she said she was still afraid I would declare myself to be a **100 percent real girl** and leave her for a man because **100 percent real girls like boys and boys only**—and like all the bad thoughts that popped into Cally's head, it was both my fault and my responsibility. I tried to break up with Cally that weekend. It did not work, and she warned me in no uncertain terms that I had better not ever try to break up with her again.

She did consent to seeing a therapist, who referred her to a support group for survivors of domestic abuse. I drove Cally to her first support group meeting, but as I was parking, she demanded that I take her back home because she had come to realize it was unfair that she was the only one in therapy. Cally's logic was that, yes, sure, fine, HAAH had beaten her and Cally's family had always pushed her around, and she was now taking out those years of pent-up anger on me in the form of frequent emotional mistreatment and less frequent physical mistreatment. She copped to all that, but since I had what Cally called **serious identity issues**—which was to say, my whole quote-transgender-unquote thing where I kept insisting that I was a woman despite all available evidence—that meant I needed to see a shrink far more than Cally did.

That shrink turned out to be the Nice Lady, and Cally and I had our first couples counseling session in early May. When we got back home, Cally flew into a tantrum because she had taken most of the blame for our problems during the session. She screamed that I should take more responsibility for her inability to trust me and that the way she had been treating me for the past five months was my fault as much as hers. I was and would always remain a deeply flawed creature but being told that I deserved what was happening, that the mistreatment I was suffering was justified, opened a new vein of hurt and shame. I collapsed into a sobbing heap, and by the time I was picking myself back up, Cally had tapped into her own new vein: she felt bad about how much her anger was hurting me, which made her that much angrier because emotional pain is a zero-sum game and Cally was the one who was hurting, not Sherilyn. Cally swore at me over and over, *fuck you!* being the most popular as ever, and she hit me on the head with a stuffed seal she'd bought at Pier 39. When I got more upset about that, she shouted that it was a stuffed seal so it did not hurt so it did not qualify as violence so I should **shut the fuck up!**

Good Morning, It's Possum Day

In addition to continuing to write in my online diary against Cally's wishes and trying to leave the house to do fun things against Cally's wishes,

I passed the time downloading music off the Usenet, about which Cally had no strong feelings. (Not even that I broke the First Rule of the Usenet by writing about the Usenet in my online diary.) My favorite newsgroup was alt.binaries.sounds.mp3.gothic-industrial, where I discovered a noise piece called *Rush Hour on the Event Horizon* by an artist named Durtro. It was ear candy which expanded my concept of what music could be, ranking up there with the Beatles' "Revolution 9," Negativland's *JamCon '84*, and Peter Gabriel's *Passion: Music for the Last Temptation of Christ*. Best experienced through headphones, Durtro's swirling cacophony sounded like what the title suggested: existing on the edge of annihilation and trying to generate enough momentum to break the laws of physics and escape an impossible situation. *Rush Hour on the Event Horizon* felt like a sonification of the chaos that was my life with Cally.

Since forcing me to pretend Tira did not exist was not making me forget Tira existed, Cally began an email correspondence with her archnemesis. The problem was that I bought myself a ticket to see Lou Reed at the Berkeley Community Theater in June, and it turned out that Tira and her boyfriend were also going. Worse, Burnout and Janey invited me to join them along with Tira and her boyfriend for a pre-concert dinner. Cally had described herself emailing Tira as taking **slow, sure steps**, but if I were to see Tira before Cally was ready for me to see Tira, I would be **turning up the treadmill**. Thus, Cally asked me to decline the dinner invitation while we were driving home from CNET a few days before the show,

Ticket stub for Lou Reed at the Berkeley Community Theater, June 2000. Don't be afraid.

and all hell broke loose in my lapis-blue Plymouth Neon when I told Cally I was going to accept Burnout's invitation. Cally wailed and pounded on my Neon's dashboard, destroying a brittle wildflower which had been sitting there since c0g gave it to me when we visited Bolinas in April. I was driving southeast on 1st between Mission and Howard a few blocks north of the Maritime Hall during Cally's tantrum, and as the particles of the pulverized wildflower were dispersing, she jumped out into traffic and ran down a side street. I drove in a circle until I found her, and after a little cajoling she got in the car. When we got back home, Cally used the Charles Foster Kane power move on Lascaux West, shattering the television remote and ripping a poster off the wall and tearing it to shreds while screaming through tears that I didn't love her, all before brandishing a large steak knife and demanding that I kill her since she couldn't bear the pain I was causing her.

The dinner was already going to be terrifying, since it would be the first time Burnout and Janey and heaven only know which other Rustics were going to see me in my nascent female mode. I was so nervous that before going into the restaurant I squatted and urinated in the corner of the parking garage since it felt less scary than using a women's restroom in the East Bay, and after dinner I hid in the Berkeley Community Theater's foyer until Lou took the stage. (I have no truck with regret as a rule, but I do regret not seeing Victoria Williams opening for Lou that night.) I was also admiring the merch I couldn't afford, including a shirt bearing three words which were not on Lou's new album *Ecstasy* but nonetheless spoke to my soul: *don't be afraid*.

i'm trying, lou. i'm trying. but what if i'm battling someone else's fear?

Tira soon entered the foyer, and while the Cardinal Rule **sherilyn will not have any contact with tira** was suspended because I was ignoring it, the rule **sherilyn will not tell anybody (especially tira) how desperately unhappy she is with cally** remained ironclad. I ignored the rule and told Tira how desperately unhappy I was with Cally, that things at Lascaux West were harsh and bad, and that when I needed to think of a friendly face Tira's always came to mind, at which point I collapsed into a sobbing mess under the ***don't be afraid*** shirt. Tira was beyond gracious, holding me and consoling me without ever suggesting that everything that was happening to me was my own fault.

Nine Inch Nails played the Cow Palace the following evening, and while Cally didn't like me abandoning her two nights in a row, it became less contentious when I confirmed Tira would not be there. I did run into my friend Helena, whom I hadn't seen since Shrine of Lilith in 1999, and I was happy to get to sit with her during the show. I wasn't always abandoning Cally to spend unchaperoned time with other women when I went to concerts that month; Cally joined me for Eels at the Great American Music

Hall and Alanis Morissette at the Fillmore, and Cally especially enjoyed the latter show when Alanis strapped on a guitar and became an Angry Rock Chick for "Joining You." Cally and I had bonded over our love for "Joining You" in June 1999, but she was tantrumming when we got home from the Alanis concert in June 2000, and by then, I was ready to jump into whatever fountain would bring forgiveness. (You know how us Catholic girls can be.)

I was not surprised when Cally accused me of abandoning her when I took the week of my 27th birthday off from work, and because she was staunchly anti-drug, I was also not surprised when she got angry that I used some of that time off to see Ron Mann's documentary *Grass* at the Castro. She had tantrummed on the Muni earlier in the year when I had suggested scoring grass from Burnout, which is not to be confused with her tantrum after I wrote in my online diary about taking mushrooms and acid for the first time when I was 16. We did have a breakthrough when I went to the Roxie Theater to see a new 35mm print of George Romero's 1968 *Night of the Living Dead* in May 2000 when I was 26; it was significant because Cally was afraid of the monsters which Romero had first called ghouls (we're not using the zed-word), and she would descend into an angry panic if I acknowledged the existence of those movies or the make-believe monsters therein. We did go to ghoul-free movies together, including anything with Courtney Love. Scott Alexander and Larry Karaszewski's Milos Forman-helmed Andy Kaufman biopic *Man on the Moon* was the first movie we saw in a theater after Cally moved in, and we managed to catch the few other movies Courtney appeared in (one of which co-starred Spalding Gray!) before her film career fizzled out.

Grass was not the only drug controversy during the month I turned 27, because I had an electrolysis appointment after work on the fourth Monday. I had only been zapped a few times since Cally arrived, and she now insisted on joining me to provide support. Her support collapsed on our way to work that morning when I mentioned my anesthetic cocktail: two prescription Vicodin downed with a chug of NyQuil. I called it the Green Death because I wasn't too proud to make a Denis Leary reference, and I had been using it for the past two years to deal with the pain of electrified needles being stuck into my face for two to four hours per session. Cally now nixed my cocktail, saying mixing NyQuil with Vicodin was too risky and I was in danger of overdosing. I told her the doctor who prescribed the Vicodin said taking it with NyQuil was fine and I had never come close to overdosing during several dozen electrolysis sessions thus far. Cally replied that I couldn't have known how close I came to overdosing because I had been ***under the influence of the vicodin***. My next argument was that I had been having electrolysis done since long before Cally knew I existed and I was tired of the pain, to which Cally snarled ***just deal with the pain***. When

I told Cally I was going to deal with the pain by continuing to alleviate it with the Green Death, she ran away screaming *just fuck me for caring! just fuck me for caring!* I had scraped Cally off the sidewalk during many public tantrums over the past seven months—including a corker when we walked into the vibrator store Good Vibrations and I picked up a classic Hitachi Magic Wand and turned it on and Cally burst into tears and ran outside and collapsed into a wailing puddle—but I felt a new level of mortification as *just fuck me for caring!* echoed through the Levi Plaza courtyard outside the CNET offices. We had managed to avoid this sort of thing at work, where it felt … well, the only word for it was *tacky*. It felt tacky. Cally apologized later that morning, and again that night after she saw the tears streaming down my cheeks as electrified needles were stuck into my face for two to four hours.

My last serious attempt at breaking up with Cally happened during the first weekend in July while she was housesitting for Ligeia. It did not work because Cally was afraid to stay at Ligeia's apartment up in Marin all by herself and Cally asked if I could please keep her company, so she wouldn't be afraid and alone? Wasn't that the least I could do for her?

3

eXistenZ Is unPauseD

Josie and the Vampire

Things improved thanks to the Nice Lady, who helped Cally understand what it meant for me to be transgender, that it was not just a cop-out
I was using as an excuse to see my ex-girlfriend. The Nice Lady did not
tell Cally anything I hadn't been saying since long before Cally decided to
move across the country and into my home, and it should not have required
professional intervention for Cally to believe that I was not just a boy who
looked good in eyeliner, let alone for Cally to understand how much it hurt
when she disrespected my gender and punished me for the sins of strangers thousands of miles away. But what mattered was that since Cally was
hearing it from someone who was not me, she was beginning to believe it.
She still threw tantrums, including a barn-burner on her 30th birthday in
which she exposited in no uncertain terms that her life was shit and everything in it was shit and I should return all the shitty presents I bought her
because they were all shit and everything about her life was shit, but the
tantrums now tended to lack the violence which had been retconned into a
single instance of throwing an adorable stuffed seal in the general direction
of my head. Acknowledging anything beyond the throwing of an adorable
stuffed seal was not allowed because doing so raised parallels between the
way HAAH treated Cally and the way Cally treated me, and whatever else
domestic abuse may be, it is not a cycle.

It also helped that during what was supposed to be our July 2000
breakup but instead turned into a Madcap Marin Weekend, a cover in the
Just Published section of a bookstore caught Cally's eye: Michelle Tea's
Valencia. She bought it on the spot, and it became her new favorite memoir.
Cally admired Michelle's honesty and bravery in writing ribald tales about
her sexual adventures in the 1990s San Francisco queer scene in *Valencia,*
and also about her gothier teen years back in Massachusetts in her previous book *The Passionate Mistakes and Intricate Corruption of One Girl*

in America. Cally met the intricately corrupted American girl in person at the 6th Annual Anarchist Bookfair in March 2001, though she had a tantrum that morning when her excitement about meeting her idol Michelle curdled into fear. I encouraged Cally to still meet Michelle, and her fear turned into anger at me for encouraging her to do a scary thing, which was part of Cally's routine. She later thanked me for encouraging her to meet Michelle even though meeting Michelle was scary, which was also part of Cally's routine.

Toward the end of her Anarchist Bookfair reading, Michelle implored women to write, arguing that the details of their lives should be recorded no matter how mundane they may seem at the time. I took it as a defense of what I had been trying to do for the past twenty-five months, since Cally remained unhappy with how much I wrote in my online diary. Several of her tantrums in 2000 had been because I wrote about something from before we met in 1999, which she called *living in the past and neglecting the present.* The present I was neglecting often involved Cally slamming the bedroom door and screaming about how mean I was while she pounded the wall, but I wasn't allowed to write about that, either.

Cally now went into groupie mode, and we started attending Michelle's shows at the El Rio on Mission, the open mic called K'vetch which Michelle co-hosted with Tara Jepsen at Sadie's Flying Elephant on Mariposa, and many other gigs at many other places besides, including dropping in on Michelle at the bookstore where she worked. There would have been hell to pay if I had fixated on another woman with a tenth of the intensity with which Cally fixated on Michelle, but equity was never the point of our relationship. What mattered was that we developed a social life in the queer literary scene, and my first time reading in front of an audience was at K'vetch on July 8, 2002. It was okay as virgin readings go, but things went downhill afterward when we joined an excursion to the Lexington Club, a dyke bar on 19th between Mission and Valencia. There was a benefit that night for the St. James Infirmary, a health clinic for sex workers, and the entertainment included strippers. I spent most of my time talking with friends outside the Lex, and Cally was livid when she found me, shouting *you left me alone during my first stripper experience!*

It took me a moment to do the math on my own first stripper experience. I was pretty sure the most recent time I had seen anything of the sort had been in August 1999, when I visited my friend Thora during one of her shifts as a topless dancer at the hungry i on Broadway in North Beach. I was happy to have a good reason to visit the hungry i because it was where Tom Lehrer had recorded his 1965 album *That Was the Year That Was.* To think, songs like "Wernher Von Braun," "The Vatican Rag," and my personal favorite "Smut" had been committed to tape within the same brick walls where Thora was now dancing! A few doors down from the hungry i at the world-famous corner of Broadway and Columbus was the Condor Club, where my seldom-mentioned father had fond memories of watching Carol Doda dance in the 1970s. My father and I were never close, but he was the only other person besides Shandon to not give me any static for breaking up with Tira, and he pretty much shrugged when I finally got around to coming out to him as trans in early 2000. Since my father had been the villain in the breakup due to him cheating on my mother, he lacked the clean slate which had allowed everyone else to excoriate me for doing the two very bad and wrong things. Me doing those things did my father no harm because it was my life and not his, and he did not grieve my death, for what he saw was me finally being *alive*.

I never went into the Condor Club myself, and my own first stripper experience had been at the Chez Paree on Mason in 1996, a few months after Fuckorama while I was still a film student at San Francisco State University. As a cultural exchange between the Cinema and Theater departments, we had to take a few of their classes and they had to take a few of ours, and I took Beginning Acting because I'd always harbored a secret desire to perform. (If my high school had had a theater department, my life would have gone in a different direction. Maybe. Probably.) The big project of the semester was a two-person scene, and I was pleasantly surprised when my classmate Josie agreed to be my partner. We decided on Edward Albee's *Who's Afraid of Virginia Woolf?*, and since Josie was a cis woman and I was closeted and the gender binary was still the law of the land, she was Martha and I was George. Though I was crushed out on Josie from the word go, I didn't know she was an exotic dancer until she made a passing reference to the Chez Paree while we were rehearsing.

Our *Who's Afraid of Virginia Woolf?* scene was from the second act— it's set in the parking lot of the roadhouse in the 1966 Mike Nichols film— and I added a clever new stage direction while Martha is making one last attempt to connect. She's talking about all the excuses a couple makes in a marriage, the way things can just *snap!*, and how she's tried with George, really, she's tried. And then the clever bit: Martha kisses George, who goes along with it for a few seconds before pulling away in disgust. They resume arguing, and Martha refers to *a second back there* in which she could have gotten through to George—clearly, the moment when they kissed! Not only did my stage direction signal the arrival of a bold new voice in the theater world, it meant I got to kiss Josie a few times per week for a few weeks, making her the third woman I had kissed in my 23 years. We kept our mouths closed, but they were real kisses, since that was the only way to sell the scene. It helped that simulated passion was what Josie did for a living, and I couldn't tell simulated passion from the real thing.

After the semester ended, Josie invited Tira and me to the Chez Paree. Tira was game and offered to buy me a lap dance; I wanted one with Josie, who politely but firmly refused. (I had the lap dance with a different dancer, and it was … weird. Still, as **sleazy achievements** and **new, dirty lows to sink to**, a Chez Paree lap dance is one for the books.) Josie suggested getting lunch together sometime, and I left a message once a month to set up that lunch, but she never returned my monthly calls until I invited her to a preview screening of David Lynch's *Lost Highway* at the Embarcadero. Josie then left a message saying she appreciated the offer, but she didn't have time to be friends with me, and I never saw her again.

Cally did not like the story which I titled "Act II: Walpurgisnacht" when I started reading it at open mics in 2003, and she continued to not like it when I included it in my third and final self-published chapbook *S (Unpronounceable Symbol)* in late 2004. (My first two chapbooks, *Substance* and *Sublimation*, were sold on commission at Modern Times Books and Dog-Eared Books on Valencia. Between them, I earned almost $4!) I realized there was a danger of me concluding many future stories with *i never saw her again*, but Cally's objection wasn't the bummer ending. Instead, "Act II: Walpurgisnacht" went on her **reasons sherilyn can't be trusted** list because she considered it a confession of cheating on Tira, and if I cheated on Tira I might do the same to Cally. It harkened back to the fundamental reason she distrusted me, something she had told me during one of my failed attempts to break up with her in 2000: Cally did not trust me because I had broken up with Tira in 1999. Cally and I never would have gotten together if I hadn't done the very bad and wrong thing of breaking up with Tira, but it meant I was also capable of doing the very bad and wrong thing of breaking up with Cally, *ergo* I could not be trusted, which I confirmed by trying and failing to break up with Cally. (Original Sin is harsh.)

What I found hilarious about Cally's fear of my ferality was that I could not have been more domesticated by the standards of the San Francisco queer lit scene. It seemed like everybody else had true stories about living on the street or squatting in abandoned buildings, about turning tricks that went awry, about suicide attempts, about being institutionalized, about having to kick bug powder or meth or just the demon booze, and I had no such things in my history. Watching Tom's struggle with addiction when I was a teenager had instilled a lifelong fear of addictive drugs, because it looked to me like the only two outcomes were either an unpleasant and humiliating death or a withdrawal period which felt worse than death, after which you would find yourself waving a towel at the corner of Palm and Bullard on the hottest day of the year to entice motorists to swing by your halfway house's pop-up car wash between the Union 76 and the 7–Eleven. Yeah, no thanks. My Happy Place was drinking free margaritas while playing nickel video

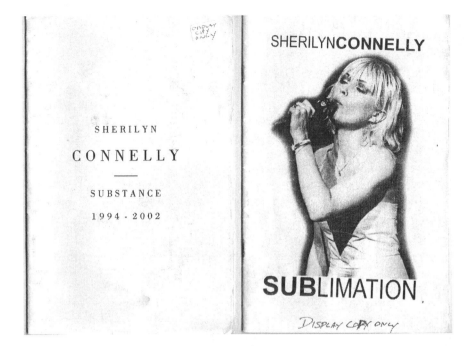

Display copies *only* of the self-published chapbooks *Substance* and *Sublimation*. No, that is not the author on the cover of *Sublimation*, but thank you for asking!

poker in the Las Vegas Hilton's Spacequest Casino, and when the hooch had loosened up my inhibitions, I might get saucy and bet quarters rather than nickels! But waking up in a pool of my own vomit when I was 20 had taught me to not drink to excess no matter how tasty mudslides are, so I only drank socially nowadays, and I seldom finished a given bottle of beer. Heck, I wasn't estranged from my family, which made me statistically aberrant among trans women in the early 2000s; my mother had started introducing me to people as her daughter, and though we weren't going to go the full *Grey Gardens* anytime soon, the introductions were still an important step. Abusive relationships were also a common topic, and writing about them was considered a means of healing, what my friend Jenn Cross would later call **writing ourselves whole**. But I couldn't be open about how Cally mistreated me until I was *not* in the relationship, and since one of the rules of the relationship was **sherilyn is not allowed to break up with cally**, writing myself whole was not an option.

Not only did I not attend an accredited School of Hard Knocks, I also lacked the formal education. When I joined the writing group the People's Literation Front of San Francisco in 2003, I was conscious that everyone else had, like, a Master in Poetry from Mills College or something equally highbrow. Meanwhile, I had a lowercase-u undergraduate degree in moving pictures from a public university, and I hadn't fit in there because I was the only film student on Earth in 1994 who did not worship Quentin Tarantino (the worst person named Quentin). I enjoyed *Reservoir Dogs* well enough when it played the Art Film Series, but the best part of seeing *Pulp Fiction* in the theater was the trailer for Kevin Smith's *Clerks*. That looked like fun, and part of it was set in a video store! But *Pulp Fiction* was already a miserable experience before Bruce Willis starts verbally abusing Maria de Medeiros and making her cry, at which point I began loathing that horrible movie and have never stopped.

Many of the writers Cally looked up to in the early 2000s wrote true stories about past or recent affairs, about infidelity, about the unique thrill of sex on the dark end of the street, about breaking the law and aiming to misbehave. It was what Cally's idol Michelle Tea did, and it was what erstwhile *Dogs in Lingerie* author and former stripper Danielle Willis did—and we could not have been more thrilled when, less than a week after Cally's traumatic *first stripper experience*, we met Danielle!

Though alive (yay!), Danielle was not well, *per se*. She was strung out from the bug powder habit that had been a part of her legend as far back as her 1989 play *The Methedrine Dollhouse*, and for as romantic as Danielle

The author (left) thrilled to be the little spoon to Danielle Willis, July 2002.

made being *junksick* sound in her writing, when you got up close and personal her state of semi-necrosis was unsettling. But the point is that Danielle was alive, and the point is also that by the standards of the San Francisco queer lit scene—or the graphic description of fisting in the first few pages of Cally's favorite memoir *Valencia*—reinterpreting Edward Albee to justify a consensual, closed-mouth stage kiss in an acting class six years ago was as transgressive as flagrantly ignoring the *one lollipop per customer* rule at a bank. But Cally didn't trust me with most lollipops.

Keep Circulating the Tapes

Cally and I were pleasantly stoned on some of Burnout's grass one night in December 2001 as we watched *Mindwrecker* on Access SF. It was one of my favorite kinds of *Mindwrecker* episodes, a close-up of a 45RPM record changer playing a stack of singles, and at one point Cally turned to me and said *we should do a public access show about cats!*

Spelled like it sounds, all one lowercase word with the numeral zero in

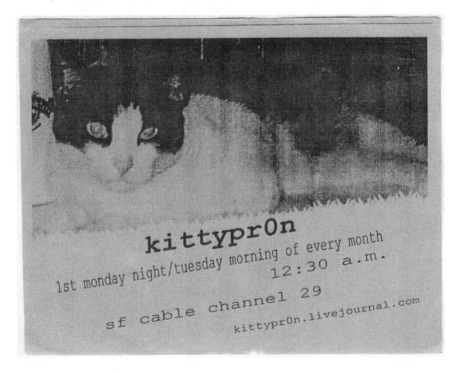

Flyer for *kittypr0n* on Access SF, February 2002. If this picture of Oscar doesn't make you want to watch the show, seek professional help.

place of the third vowel, *kittypr0n* was VHS footage of our cats Oscar and
Mina set to ambient/noise/experimental music of the sort which does not
tend to be associated with footage of cats. We stitched together Episode #1
("Pilot") using two VCRs, and the soundtrack was Zoviet France's *Vienna
1990*, though going forward I constructed the show in the editing suites
at Access SF. Sonically speaking, Episode #2 ("Catnipvision") was a mix of
Irdial's *The Conet Project: Recordings of Shortwave Numbers Stations* and
Stephen P. McGreevy's *Auroral Chorus II: Music of the Magnetosphere*, Episode #3 ("Boots!") used Coil's *Queens of the Circulating Library*, and Episode #4 ("This Is the Law of the Plague") was the most mainstream yet,
featuring Diamanda Galás' *The Divine Punishment*.

"Pilot" premiered on Access SF on cable channel 29 in February 2002,
and we made a point of scheduling *kittypr0n* at half past midnight on the
first Monday night/Tuesday morning of the month so we would come on
after *Queen Bee TV* and *S*P*L*E*E*N*. We also hoped *kittypr0n* would be
something pleasant for insomniacs and stoners to stumble across while
flipping channels. *kittypr0n* got a lot of silly buzz, which is the best kind of
buzz; many writers were happy to let Cally and me into their homes to vid-
eotape their cats to appear on the show, and I was proud that it got picked
up by a public access station in Portland, Oregon. We also heard from a
reliable source that *kittypr0n* had been used in the preshow for a DJ set
by the Canadian electronica artist Venetian Snares, which sounded good
to me. But one of the best things about doing *kittypr0n* was that I got to
know other public access television producers, who were some of the most
interesting and creative weirdos you could hope to encounter in the early
aughts, and I was proud to number myself among them. I was excited to
meet *Dee Dee TV* producer Dee Dee Russell at the afterparty for the 3rd San
Francisco Sex Worker Film and Video Festival in 2003, and for a brief shining moment the El Rio's dance floor was dominated by Access SF producers
in the form of Dee Dee, myself, and *Tranny Talk*'s Kitty Kastro.

When I attended the final night of the Beyond the Pale Festival at the
DNA Lounge in November 2002, I had already used music by two of the
featured artists, Sonic Boom and Stars of the Lid, and I was planning to use
the other two, Robert Rich and Tribes of Neurot. I wasn't able to speak to
Sonic Boom that night, whose Spacemen 3 recording "An Evening of Con-
temporary Sitar Music" was the backbone of Episode #6 ("Sleep #1"), but
the nice Texan boys from Stars of the Lid were pleasantly nonplussed as
I fangirled all over them about using "Requiem for Dying Mothers, Part
2" from *The Tired Sounds of Stars of the Lid* on Episode #8 ("A Saucerful
of Sirens") of this public access show they would never see. As for Robert Rich, he was in the studio of my favorite radio station KFJC one afternoon in December 2001, and I won tickets to his Alien Zoology concert

that night at the Morrison Planetarium when I called in to the station and defined Rich's neologism **glurp**. *kittypr0n* hadn't launched by the time of *Alien Zoology*, but I talked to him again at the merch table for his Sun Sets concert at Fort Mason's Cowell Theater in May 2002 after my show had been on for a few months. Rich gave me his blessing to use his music on *kittypr0n*, and he suggested his recent album *Bestiary*. It was a good suggestion! I already loved the glurpy, biological sound of *Bestiary*, which might as well have been titled *This One's for Sherilyn*, and I often used it as a temp track in the Access SF editing suite. But in doing so I had found *Bestiary* was *too* biologically appropriate for *kittypr0n*, too close to the sort of thing you might associate with images of cute animals, so I ended up using Rich's *Trances/Drones* track "Seascape" in Episode #18 ("Sleep #2"). As for Tribes of Neurot, Episode #11 ("El Gato del Chupa Cabras") featured their *Adaptation and Survival*, which was also biological but had more of a swirly, *Rush Hour on the Event Horizon* feeling.

The reason I could do any of this hobnobbing was thanks to the Nice Lady convincing Cally that she did not need to be threatened by me wanting to attend things that sounded boring to her, like ambient concerts at the Morrison Planetarium or noise festivals at the DNA Lounge. The Nice Lady next suggested that if I still wanted to go do a thing even though it sounded boring to Cally, like driving to Foothill College in Los Altos Hills to watch a bunch of ephemeral films, commercials, and Scopitone reels at the KFJC Psychotronix Film Festival, it was healthier for Cally to let me go do that boring thing by myself than for her to throw a temper tantrum to make me stay home. The Nice Lady did not tell Cally anything I hadn't been saying since long before Cally decided to move across the country and into my home, and it should not have required professional intervention for Cally to believe that it was better to let me walk in the sun than to hide me away from the rest of the world. But what mattered was that since Cally was hearing it from someone who was not me, she was beginning to believe it.

I made my way back into goth scene, and many old friends at both the 2002 Gothnic and then Club Smoke and Mirrors later that same April night asked where I'd been for the last few years. My self-esteem was only now starting to grow back after its turn-of-the-century flaying, and though true healing was impossible so long as the angry biped was stepping on my tail, it helped to hear the lovecats hissing **we missed you!** and to get to be so wonderfully pretty among them. Accepting compliments had never been my strong suit, but I was getting better at it, especially when Thora walked up to me at Smoke and Mirrors and said **you're skinny!** She was hardwired for absolute candor, so that one felt legit. I also felt legit proud when I took advantage of Smoke and Mirrors' **you bring it and we'll play it (unless it's abba, no fucking abba)** policy, marking what I suspected was the first

The slightly-dazed author about to go dancing at Club Smoke and Mirrors after having already spent all day in the sun at the Gothnic like a crazy person, April 2002.

time Negativland's "Christianity Is Stupid" was played in a San Francisco goth club. It cleared out the dance floor in seconds flat despite being Negativland's most danceable song because nobody else recognized it, but that was okay. That meant more room for me to swoop and stomp around, which I would have been happy to do from five o'clock in the morning 'til ten o'clock at night.

Earlier that same week I had hung out at Studio Z on 11th with Negativland's Peter Conheim (stage name: the Jet Black Hair People) during a show by sound-collage artist Vicki Bennett (stage name: People Like Us) and Conheim's Negativland bandmate John Leidecker (stage name: Wobbly). Conheim remembered me from when I occupied a front-row bean-bag chair during both nights of Negativland's brief residency at the DNA Lounge in August and September of 2001, and now at Studio Z, he asked if I'd like to hear about their upcoming project. It was an *i'm not worthy!* moment which I'm pretty sure I managed to play cool, though not as cool as the project itself, which Negativland released on CD in September 2002 as *Deathsentences of the Polished and Structurally Weak*. It came with a **64-page full color owner's manual** of photos of wrecked cars and the objects found inside those cars, and the music was described as **a meticulously-layered, ever-shifting electro-acoustic soundscape, created to accompany the pages of the book,** with **no bass lines, no melody, no dialogue, no singing, no beat—the sound of negativland's recording studio destroyed in a car crash.** Much like Robert Rich's *Bestiary*, it might as well have been titled *This One's for Sherilyn*, and Negativland's *Deathsentences* provided the soundtrack for *kittypr0n* Episode #10 ("Carnations and Petunias").

The cover of Negativland's *This One's for Sherilyn,* which was officially titled *Deathsentences of the Polished and Structurally Weak.*

Cally and I ended up making 22 half-hour episodes of *kittypr0n,* and our silly little cat show demonstrated how well we could work together on the rare occasions that we were anywhere close to being on the same page. We had no business being a couple because Cally should not have been with a restless queer woman and I should not have been in a relationship at all, and while the bad outweighed the good as it must when one partner is stepping on the other's tail, the best of the non-*kittypr0n* good was Cally's willingness to let Danielle Willis into my life.

A few weeks after we met Danielle in 2002, I visited the Single Room Occupancy hotel where she and her partner Sarjenka were staying, and the moment I set foot in the lobby the manager gave me the hairy eyeball and said **check-out day is tomorrow.** Sarjenka told me that their check-out day was indeed tomorrow, Danielle had left for the methadone clinic shortly before I arrived, and between my hair and makeup and glasses and jacket and boots and my whole deal I was a dead ringer for how she looked when she left the building. The manager thought I was Danielle! I was more than okay with that. A few weeks later I took Danielle to a literary festival called ForWord Girls while she was staying at a different SRO with someone who was not Sarjenka, and the slow, stretched-out drawl of Danielle's methadone-impaired roomie over the intercom was scarier and more powerful than a hundred PSAs of a hundred eggs breaking in a hundred frying pans. (**haaaaaaallloooo?** *i'm here to pick up danielle.* **whaaaaaaat?** *danielle! tell danielle that sherilyn is downstairs.* **ohhhhhhh.**) Danielle herself was distracted and fidgety as we sat in the ForWord Girls audience. She wanted to bum-rush the stage to read the poetic ramblings she had scrawled on the back of a flyer because bug powder is nothing if not a literary high, but I kept a hand on her arm and talked her back down. I was no longer starstruck by Danielle, but I was still happy to have her in my life, and I was determined to be as good a friend as I could be. And if that evolved into becoming her lover someday, so much the better.

That Halloween, Danielle got on a Greyhound to go to kick drugs in Cleveland. Her day of departure was coincidental but just as well, since Danielle tended to lay low on Halloween so she didn't have to deal with as many **what are you supposed to be? a vampire?** remarks about her aftermarket fangs. She told me that another downside of having fangs is that **you can't do trick-or-treat makeup anymore**, which I could see going either way: no trick-or-treat makeup sounds like a bummer, but what a timesaver the fangs are! Though I was fangless I got **what are you supposed to be? a vampire?** remarks now and then, and I always took it as a compliment. Strangers had also chanted **beetlejuice! beetlejuice! beetlejuice!** at me on a few occasions, which was a little dodgier—it was because I looked like Winona Ryder and not Michael Keaton, right?—but fine, sure. As misfired insults and/or backhanded compliments go, the best one ever was directed not toward me but Cally while we were eating at the Circus Circus buffet in Las Vegas. She was wearing a fetching black skirt with black-and-purple stripey tights, and a buffet employee walked up to our table and asked in all sincerity if Cally was one of the hotel's resident trapeze artists. I mean, c'mon! Getting asked if you're circus folk is high praise, and I could not have been prouder of Cally.

Spang of the Loathsome Dead

In January 2003, Cally and I attended a horror convention called SpookyCon, where we met the creators of a new comic titled *How Loathsome*. Though the title was a reference to Rozz Williams' song "The Beast (Invocation)" from the 1992 album *Every King a Bastard Son*, the comic's content was inspired by Danielle Willis' work, and the protagonist Catherine Gore was a vampiric, black-haired cis woman modeled after her. *How Loathsome*'s creators had been operating under the not-unreasonable assumption that she was no longer among the living, and when I mailed Danielle a copy of the first issue signed by the creators while she was in Cleveland that April (not) kicking drugs, they were relieved when she responded that *i had mixed feelings about the comic—a lot of it was lifted directly from stuff i've already published, but i was flattered as well as initially dismayed*. So that was a net win for *How Loathsome*, and it was no less of a win for me when I posed for the cover of the fourth and final issue as Catherine's transgender *objet d'amour*, Chloe. The *How Loathsome #4* shoot was my first time wearing a wig, in public or otherwise—and a blonde wig, no less, so I got a sense of how I would look when I took my inevitable deep penetrating dive into the peroxide pool. I also got to wear my favorite jacket, a long shiny black Formula X number with a faux-fur trim which became canon when it was incorporated into Chloe's wardrobe not only on the cover but in the pages of the comic itself.

Shortly after SpookyCon, I began attending the open mics Chick Nite and the Spang Bang at Spanganga, a performance space and art gallery on 19th between Mission and South Van Ness. I met many people there who would become an important part of my life for the rest of the decade and beyond, the most important being Spanganga's house managers Jim Fourniadis and Erin Ohanneson. Much like Freyja at the 1999 Gothnic, Erin walked up to me in 2003 and said *you look fun. be our friend!* In addition to open mics, sketch comedy shows, and stage adaptations of movies like Stanley Kubrick's *Dr. Strangelove* or the Worst Quentin's *Reservoir Dogs*, Spanganga was notorious for two sex parties: Darkness Falls and Splosh.

how loathsome

ted naifeh
tristan crane

The author near the corner of Castro and 16th Street during the photoshoot for the cover of *How Loathsome* #4, and the final cover, which was based on a different photograph. This was the first time I wore a wig in public.

The gimmick for Darkness Falls was that the 1,500-square-foot room was completely dark, so what you felt was what you got, though known relatives were required to wear glowing bracelets to avoid incest. For Splosh, the room was covered wall to wall with a tarp, and then with vast quantities of flour, oatmeal, cornstarch, confectioner's sugar, and so forth. It was a safe-sex, no-exposed-genitalia event, and afterward Jim and a few day laborers would roll the tarp into what Jim called a Splosh Burrito, because that's showbiz. I nodded in tacit agreement when Cally expressed her disgust about both events, and I did not tell her that I envied the people for whom Darkness Falls was a good time, nor I did tell her that Splosh sounded sorta possibly maybe a little fun in a full-sensory-immersion kinda way.

Down the street from Spanganga at the corner of 19th and South Van Ness was a bar called Sacrifice, which was a hangout for Spanganga folks, the queer lit scene, and people who wore leather motorcycle jackets even if they did not own a motorcycle. *kittypr0n* could sometimes be found playing on the television above the bar in late 2002, and the first literary reading

Flyer for the spoken-word show Back from the Dead at Sacrifice, July 2003. My whole showbiz career can be summed up by "dot dot dot and Sherilyn Connelly."

to be held at Sacrifice was when I shared the bill with Danielle Willis in July 2003 for her big comeback gig, Back from the Dead. The illumination came from candles and other indirect sources because we were all about creating a mood, which meant there was no direct light on the printouts which our myopic eyes were struggling to read from, but that was part of the adventure: if Danielle Willis and Sherilyn Connelly reading at Sacrifice isn't hella-spooky, then what was even the point of this whole exercise? Danielle wore a sparkly blue dress for the show, and as she put it on at Lascaux West earlier in the evening, she predicted the sparkles would get everywhere. She was correct, and seeing her blue sparkles embedded in my Neon's backseat felt like an antidote to the bad vibes emanating from the bits of pulverized wildflower which were still deep in the car's crevasses: that one bad night happened, but this one good night happened, too.

Many of Danielle's friends and colleagues were there on that one good night, including Zenyasha, legendary as the Violin-Playing, Roller-Skating Whore of the Tenderloin. She had a terrific energy, and the ***sherilyn! sherilyn! sherilyn!*** chant she started at the end of my set was pretty great. It was less great when Zenyasha gave Danielle some prescription downers, but to her credit she waited until after the show, and Zenyasha wasn't the only person who slipped Danielle drugs that night, making it clear Danielle would need to leave San Francisco again to get clean. I also learned that night that Sacrifice's owner was looking to sell the joint, and seven weeks later, Sacrifice was closed for good. (The bar soon reopened under new management as Bender's, a name I never made peace with.) Though the only reasonable conclusion to draw was that Danielle and I had cursed Sacrifice, Back from the Dead had been successful enough that a promoter approached me about putting on a monthly variety show at Jezebel's Joint at Turk and Larkin. The show didn't happen because most things end up not happening, but one of my ideas was to feature at least one sex worker per night, reading their poetry or playing an instrument or doing whatever their non-work talent might be. I pitched the idea to Zenyasha, who said she'd love to play her violin at my show, and then she added, ***ha! my life is so weird***. I was honored to have contributed to the weirdness of a violin-playing, roller-skating whore's life, and I was also happy there was plenty of weirdness in my own.

A few weeks after Back from the Dead, Danielle lip-synced to the Ramones' "I Wanna Be Sedated" at the 2003 Drag King Contest at SOMArts, where she was dressed from head to toe in denim and billed as ***joey hormone, back from the dead to sniff some glue!*** I was Danielle's stage mother that evening, and I was worried that she would find me too clingy because I didn't let her out of my sight, but she told me she appreciated my diligence. She said she needed it, she trusted me, and most importantly, I was eye candy. While we were backstage she tended to watch whoever was performing, but when one of performers used the Cars' "Just What I Needed" and I started dancing because I can't *not* dance to that song, Danielle lost all interest in what was happening on the stage. When I commented on her watching me dance, she said, ***well, yeah. it's almost pornographic.*** I couldn't have been happier to contribute to Danielle's spank-bank, but that was also the night I began to realize how much the Earth had been scorched around her. During the tech check I asked the soundperson to please not start playing "I Wanna Be Sedated" until Joey Hormone was all the way on stage and in position, and when the soundperson realized that Joey was Danielle Willis—like, yep, *that* Danielle Willis—they turned and walked away from me mid-sentence. Their job be damned, the soundperson could not feign civility toward me for another second! I wondered how many shitlists I was now on because of my association with Danielle, and if so, so be it. Something similar had happened when I became friends with c0g in early 1999, since he had stepped on many toes in the goth scene.

Danielle left town a few days after the Drag King Contest, and a few weeks later I auditioned for Spanganga's stage adaptation of George Romero's *Night of the Living Dead*. This made Cally angry both because she felt I was already devoting too much time and energy to pursuing my life-long dream of being a writer and because of her fear of the make-believe monsters in the title. I auditioned anyway, and I landed the role of Barbara. I wore a black hairfall to give my regular mane a little extra oomph, and in addition to looking good, having the line **they're coming to get you, barbara!** delivered at me by *Specious Species* editor Joe Donohoe as my older brother never failed to raise goosebumps. Getting to play the first of the major characters in every Romero *Dead* film who gets killed by ghouls (we're still not using the zed-word) but does not return as a ghoul themselves was also strangely satisfying. Like in the film, it happens off-stage: Barbara is pulled through the door by a pack of ghouls led by her now-undead brother and is never seen again. It was suggested that I come back at the end as a ghoul, but it was important to me that Barbara be not only dead but fully annihilated. If we didn't go all the way and have her consumed by her deepest fear, pulverized like a Bolinas wildflower that was in the wrong place at the wrong time, then what was even the point of this whole exercise? As for Cally, when she wound up being cast as the young girl who turns into a ghoul and kills her mother, her narrative changed from **sherilyn is mean for doing something cally is afraid of!** to **cally is brave for overcoming her fears!** Hey, whatever worked. Her freedom was my freedom—but she didn't like it one little bit when I treated that freedom as my right and not as her gift.

Cally got back in touch with Her Briton that August, and since she wanted to feel her squishy feelings for the boy without also feeling guilt, she asked how I would feel about opening the relationship. My answer was *i would feel fine about opening the relationship*, which was the wrong answer, and Cally screamed at me for wanting to fuck other women. Which was not what I said, but any hint of the desire for casual sex was a high crime in Cally's court, and she had told me more than once that she could never have sex with someone she wasn't emotionally attached to. Having sex with other women was never my endgame in 2003, though I kept a blue sparkle of hope alive about Danielle, who I had emotions about and whose body I wanted to explore even though I knew what it had been through.

While she was staying at Lascaux West in July, Danielle wrote a new piece for Back from the Dead about the horrorshow of kicking. She described the **bowlfuls of blackish shit that smelled like a mix of cabbage and uncleaned aquariums** while **my sweat smelled like sulfur** and **my pussy continually secreted gobs of acrid gluish discharge**, not to mention being woken up early in the morning by doctors who kept asking her to exposit upon the correlation between her fangs and being a Satanist and using drugs. Danielle also wrote

Night of the Living Dead

Spanganga Blue Room

Wednesday, Thursday, Friday and Saturday
October 22-25, 29-30
November 1, 5-8
8 PM

Program for the stage adaptation of *Night of the Living Dead* at Spanganga, October 2003. All the best things happen in Blue Rooms.

that in order to fall asleep without morphine, she would sometimes masturbate to the memory of the scene in Mike Leigh's 1993 *Naked* where **the girl with the black hair who looks kind of like me is getting fucked from behind, screaming**. I rewatched *Naked* every few years myself, and Katrin Cartlidge's Danielle-doppelgänger character Sophie always made me realize that my hair could never be dark enough and I could never wear enough black leather and fishnet and that sometimes it's quicker to take the escalator, but I would also never stop trying to achieve the dark sexiness which came so naturally for the fictional Sophie and the real-life Danielle.

It now struck me that how we each imprinted on *Naked*'s Sophie demonstrated the ways Danielle and I differed—or how we could complement each other, were we ever given the chance. It was on-brand for Danielle to masturbate to Sophie getting raped by Greg Cruttwell's clean-cut character Jeremy, but I was all about that early sex scene between Sophie and David Thewlis' scruffy character Johnny—you know the one, where they're first topless on the couch with Johnny on top of Sophie and then they move to the stairs and they're still both dressed in black below the waist and Johnny slaps Sophie's ass and they briefly make out and Johnny does that weird headshake and then it cuts to a close-up where you can't tell if they took off the rest of their clothes but Sophie is on top and is starting to laugh while she's orgasming and the hypernihilistic Johnny seems on the verge of cracking a smile? That scene was on-brand for me, as was the fully-clothed, far rougher sex scene between them on the couch 10 minutes later—you know the one, after Johnny has gotten tired of Sophie following him around like a needy little sister and as if that isn't bad enough she then says *i really like you* and he replies **you don't know me** and she says *i think i do* and that irks Johnny more and he grabs her hair and twists her arm behind her back and asks if she still likes him and she says *i love you* and Johnny gets angrier and he grabs her hair harder and twists her arm harder but Sophie says *i understand you, johnny, i do* which results in him fucking her as he grips her head and slams it against the arm of the couch? Straight sex scenes seldom did anything for me because even if I could see myself in the woman I would be put off by the man, but the pairing of Katrin Cartlidge and David Thewlis in *Naked* was one of the few non–*Crash* exceptions to that rule.

But Danielle was elsewhere, and every time I saw her might be the last. In any event, my deepest, most unspeakable fantasy during the Arrangement in Q3 2003 was not to fuck other women or to have a go with David Thewlis at his most vitriolic. My deepest, most unspeakable fantasy was to share simple, fully-clothed warmth and affection with a woman who wanted to be warm and affectionate with me, and—this part coming up right here, this was the bottleneck in the aqueduct—a woman who had never screamed **fuck you!** or **i hate you!** or **shut the fuck up!** at me.

One August night during the Arrangement while Cally was at a concert with a friend, I went to the 12 Galaxies on Mission for a queer variety show called In Bed with Fairy Butch. My original plan was to attend c0g's mother's annual all-night Garden Party in Bolinas, but Cally nixed that because she knew that when I attended the Garden Party in 1999, I snacked on some of the local mushrooms and slept fully clothed next to c0g on his bed and overall enjoyed myself in ways that scared Cally. **sherilyn might enjoy herself in ways that scare cally** was a common reason to nix my plans, but her official objection was that she had never spent the night alone at Lascaux West, and me spending the night in Bolinas at the Garden Party was not a good enough reason. *Ergo* I went to the much closer In Bed with Fairy Butch instead, and because the terms of the Arrangement allowed me to kiss another woman, I shared a brief transactional kiss with no emotional component at the Tingle and Mingle Table with a woman who agreed to participate because brief transactional kisses with no emotional component were why the Tingle and Mingle Table at In Bed with Fairy Butch existed, *QED*.

Since I had enjoyed myself in a way that scared Cally, she altered the terms of the Arrangement to nix further spontaneity: I could now only kiss another woman if Cally was present and if I had cleared it with Cally beforehand. A few weeks later we made plans to have dinner with friends, and when I told Cally in accordance with Arrangement protocol that I found one of those friends attractive and would be open to kissing that friend if they were interested in reciprocating, Cally threw a tantrum and screamed that I was *taking a mile* and canceled the dinner plans. She soon ended the Arrangement and stopped talking to me about Her Briton—though I hoped for her sake that she stayed in touch with him, that Cally would allow herself that much happiness.

She Gets to Sing Just Like a Bird

One of my first name-on-the-flyer readings after Back from the Dead was at the Voodoo Lounge on Mission in early August 2003. The show was a fundraiser for Camp Trans, an alternative music festival held down the road from the Michigan Womyn's Festival, which was famous for its *womyn-born-womyn-only* policy. Trans men of any hormonal or operative status were welcome at the Michigan Womyn's Festival, as they tended to be in San Francisco's women-only spaces such as the Osento bathhouse, but trans women who hadn't had bottom surgery were not, and we were still looked at askance if we'd had surgery. (Original Sin is harsh.) I was honored to be asked to perform at the Camp Trans benefit, and more honored when I was asked to open the show with a 15- to 20-minute set. Can do! The centerpiece of my set was a new essay called "V.I.C.E." about the adversarial relationship between my gender and the size of my body, and how if I couldn't do anything about my altitude, then I would at least rein in my circumference. Aware that acknowledging a desire to be thin was controversial, I disclaimed beforehand that the essay was only about me and my anxieties and did not reflect on anybody else.

It was my first time performing under a spotlight, and though I did not suffer from a fear of the stage—quite the opposite, for after a lifetime of stifling self-consciousness I loved getting my Ellen Aim on at the microphone stand and feeling like I was at long last controlling how and why people were staring at me—in terms of visibility, it was *très* Rick Danko facing the void as he sings "Stage Fright" in Martin Scorsese's 1978 *The Last Waltz*. I

Flyer for a Benefit for Camp Trans at the Voodoo Lounge, August 2003. The phrase "an erotic kissing booth!" still makes me laugh.

couldn't see which fancy people were drifting by at any given moment, so it's unclear when the walkouts happened, but I suspect this was when the moment of truth was at hand:

> My stomach is the gauge, the eternal reminder of my past vices, my past indulgences, of my *past*.
>
> I think we can all agree that I'm shallow. More than that, I want to be physically shallow. I want to hardly exist at all. I take more space than I deserve. If

you can't see every one of my ribs, I'm doing something wrong. I want to fucking disappear. Intellectually, I know how dangerous and unhealthy an attitude this is. Emotionally, though, it can be overwhelming. I'm not anorexic, though sometimes I wish I was.

After my set I stepped outside to enjoy my post-performance endorphin rush, and a few minutes later a stout cis woman walked up and said she decided it would be *safe to talk to you* since she was leaving town soon. As I was digesting this stranger's unbidden implication that I posed a threat to her safety, she informed me that her burlesque troupe had walked out of the Voodoo Lounge *when you said real women can't be fat*. Which was not what I said, at all, and the burlesque dancer went on to inform me that her own femininity was often denigrated because *i'm not as tall as a supermodel like you are*. Ugh, the S-word. I had been called *as tall as a supermodel* on many occasions, and it was meant as a compliment, but it was also a pandering sugarcoat of one of my biggest hurdles.

The great disillusionment came in my 14th year when I discovered that if the largest of the dresses which I bought shame-facedly at the Salvation Army on Blackstone would fit around my huge body, and most of them would not, they sure as hell wouldn't zip up all the way. Now at 30 I was still reeling from when I was 24 and preparing to present as female in public for the first time under the aegis of the StopAIDS Project's Drag Outreach, and a friend told me I would always have trouble finding women's clothes because I was *barrel-chested*. I already knew I was too freakin' big but hearing it phrased that way knocked me for a loop because being barrel-chested is a good thing if you see yourself as William Holden in Joshua Logan's 1955 *Picnic,* but a bad thing if you see yourself as Susan Strasberg in *Picnic.* (The film itself makes no sense anyway, predicated as it is on the patently absurd notion that Kim Novak is prettier than Susan Strasberg.) Despite the slashing to my emotional heel, I soldiered on through the Castro District with the StopAIDS contingent that night in 1997, a night which was already memorable because the world in general and the Castro in particular was mourning the death of Princess Diana. I did not wear a wig because I was a trans woman and not a drag queen, though I adopted a Southern twang as a tribute to my wigless spiritual role model, Kelly Michaels.

I knew there was about a nil chance that the burlesque dancer berating me outside the Voodoo Lounge in 2003 was ever called *him* or *he* or *sir* because she was short and wide the way I was still called *him* or *he* or *sir* because I was tall and wide, but I said nothing as she scolded me that I did not exist in a vacuum and that I should take care to not say anything that might trouble anyone else. There it was! At an event which was about the right of trans women to be included in the conversation, I was being told there were things I should never say about being trans. The dancer and I should have felt solidarity because we were battling the same problem from different directions, but emotional pain is a zero-sum game and the dancer was the one who was hurting, not me. (For more about my early struggles with finding gender-congruent clothes that fit my ridiculous, misshapen meat puppet, see my essay "The Slimming Effect" in Michelle Tea's 2007 anthology *It's So You: 35 Women Write About Personal Expression Through Fashion and Style*. It did not get me into any trouble when it was first published, and it is full of words and ideas which have all aged well!)

I went back inside the Voodoo Lounge and tracked down my cis friend Meliza Bañales, both because I respected her opinion and because I was now afraid that I had offended her as well since she was not ***as tall as a supermodel***. I had not offended Meliza, and she told me what I needed to hear: I had the right to speak my truth, and I should never censor myself. Meliza said she and Michelle had often received negative feedback when reading their own seditious words, both in the forms of walkouts and other reactions which were less passive. So, I was in good company.

4

Dead Cats and Cab Drivers

For Rent: Black Sheets, Never Reported

In early January 2004, I read at Perverts Put Out!, a **long-running and ever-popular literary smut salon** at the 848 Community Space on Divisadero. Perverts Put Out! was a fundraiser for the smut publisher Black Books, which had evolved from a 'zine launched by Bill Brent in 1993 called *Black Sheets*, which in turn lead to a recurring sex party called Black Sheets, which was scheduled to recur on the third Saturdays of even-numbered months in 2004 at Marty Kahn's Faery House on 14th. I was honored to read alongside Bill Brent that January 2004 night at Perverts Put Out!, and I debuted "The J.C. Scrolls," my contribution to one of my favorite subgenres: Judas and Jesus as human beings with relatable, human emotions. I could trace my fondness for those stories back to the original 1970 record *Jesus Christ Superstar* (though not Norman Jewison's 1973 botch job of a movie) as well as Martin Scorsese's 1989 *The Last Temptation of Christ,* and it didn't hurt that Peter Gabriel's *Last Temptation* soundtrack album *Passion* was one of the first times I had a spiritual reaction to instrumental music. "The J.C. Scrolls" was a series of diary excerpts from a crushed-out Judas whose intimate, blood-oriented relationship with Jesus continues after the Crucifixion. Taking advantage of the rumors of his own suicide as well as Jesus' own last request, Judas removes the Christ's body from the Garden Tomb before the third day and goes into hiding and never stops loving Him.

The piece went over well at Perverts Put Out!, which had a reputation for nakedness in the audience. There were people in various stages of nakedness that night but only one totally naked person, which Bill Brent told me was a low number of totally naked people by Perverts Put Out! standards, though the presence of one totally naked person was enough to send Cally into a panic which evolved into a full-on tantrum when we got home. Despite this and many other times Cally had panicky reactions to nakedness or anything too sexual, we attended the Black Sheets party in April 2004, during the eon between the First and Second Arrangements.

Cally was okay with the people of various genders and legal ages wearing little or nothing at Black Sheets, and though she kept a death-grip on my arm, she didn't get too scared by the undulating terrain as we wound like hellbenders through the orgy in the main fuck room. So far, so good! Our destination was the basement dungeon, and the nook therein known as the Medical Room, where I was going to be play-pierced. Play-piercing triggers endorphins by penetrating under the skin and back out again with hypodermic needles, and before we entered the Medical Room I was told to not write about any of it in the online diary which some people were starting to refer to as *your goddamn blog*. Because it was 2004 and I was already in the habit of clicking Agree without reading the Terms and Conditions, I agreed. As Cally straddled the table behind me so I could lean into her, the piercer asked for permission to hit me in the chest to bring the blood to the surface. I nodded, and the piercer socked me a half-dozen times, which got me into the right frame of mind:

> this **pound** is **pound** not **pound** going **pound** to **pound** be **pound** gentle.

I kept my eyes closed until the piercer had put eight needles into my breasts, four around each nipple, and I felt the tiny pool of blood gathering on my stomach before I saw it. I opened my eyes as the piercer was wiping up some blood with their fingertips. They smeared it on my chest like they were writing their initials on a frosted window and then put the rest on my lips and then they removed one needle via what they called **the easy way** which was quick and painless and then removed another needle via what they called **the hard way** which caused me to squirm with dark pleasure and the piercer asked which way I preferred and I responded *the hard way* because if not what was even the point of this whole exercise and that was when Cally said **i'm overheated and i need to lie down right now** and I stood up because if anything had been screamed into me over the past four and a half years it was that Cally's needs were always always always more important than mine at all times and in all situations or *pee cat gets the belt* and after I got onto my feet the last thing I saw was Cally lying on the table with the back of her hand on her forehead—*(everything is black and dreamlike, i am somewhere else entirely, and i have no idea how i got here or what's going on)*—colors swarmed in, dots of tone and hue crowding each other as they took the form of the piercer, who was standing over me. They looked troubled, so I asked if they were all right. Also, my ass was cold. Why was my ass cold? Because I was crumpled in the corner of the room. Why was I crumpled in the corner of the room? It dawned on me. *(did i black out?)* *(i* *blacked out!) (how cool!)* I realized I must have only been out for a few seconds, and after a few more seconds passed the piercer painlessly removed the remaining six needles from my breasts. Wow. That was quick. I had requested the hard way, and I guess I got it.

When Cally and I went back out into the party, I had the adrenaline shakes. Worse, I felt *incomplete*. I was on the verge of discovering something new and wonderful, a heretofore unknown capacity for sensation, and it was cut short because Cally got a case of the vapors. For as much as I had imprinted on Deborah Kara Unger's Catherine Ballard in *Crash* I was now Holly Hunter's Helen Remington when she's watching a crash test video with the Seagraves and the picture freezes right before impact because the tape player's fucked, it always does that, and the twitchy *why did it go away bring it back bring it back BRING IT BACK* expression on Helen's face was where I was living in that moment at Black Sheets and where I had been living ever since the angry biped started stepping on my tail. My soul ached, and I mourned for what I almost had, but I was too amped to cry. At first, anyway; a little while later I said something too sexual to Cally while we were at a sex party which was famous for all the sex people had there, and I had to escort her back to my Neon during her sudden but inevitable tantrum as she screamed that I had violated her boundaries and ruined the whole night and that she was now in a bad mood and it was my fault. Cally's bad moods being my fault was the defining narrative of our relationship, but she was expositing that point harder than usual, that I had ruined the whole night, and I was crying by the time we got to the car. I cried in the driver's seat for another ten minutes as a confused Cally told me she wasn't *that* upset and that I was overreacting and I needed to get over it. When I could see again and my breathing was mostly steady, I drove us back home, though a second wave hit as we arrived, and I went fetal on the kitchen floor.

At least I'd get a funny story out of it! I've always believed in doing a timeskip straight from tragedy to comedy, and I already found the whole incident to be as empirically hilarious as that one shot of the burly men in lederhosen dancing on a pub table in Dario Argento's *Suspiria*. Though they tended to lean more dramatic than comedic, such stories were known as **scene reports** and could often be found in the smut anthologies by publishers such as Black Books as well as in the original *Black Sheets* 'zine from which the party got its name. Except, no: in addition to having clicked Agree before going into the room, I was informed that I would violate the privacy of the other people who were in the room if I wrote about the scene. I had been the one with needles in her breasts, and I had been the one who blacked out because the pleasure-averse biped stepping on her tail panicked, and everybody in the room knew going in that I was a scorpion, but none of that made it my story to tell.

Whether or not things I experienced were my stories to tell was already a source of controversy. A week after I read "The J.C. Scrolls" at Perverts Put Out! but a few months before my own dark comedy at Black Sheets, Cally and I participated in a photoshoot for an illustrated memoir by Michelle Tea titled *Rent Girl*. It was about Michelle's experiences as a sex worker, and we volunteered to be photographed as prostitutes, photographs which would be turned into the illustrations. I got a few *wow, you're as a tall as a supermodel!* comments at the shoot, though I did not need a verbal reminder of my height as I towered over the other (all cis) women who, unlike myself, were able to mix and match the available clothing. I was like a supermodel who can't model anything because nothing fits her! I brought my own clothes to the shoot and wore my black *Night of the Living Dead* hairfall, but my stupid Women's Size 13 ~~clown feet~~ supermodel feet were a problem, since my daily footwear of Fluevog Lucky Angel 16-eye lace-up boots (*"resists alkali, water, acid, fatigue and satan"*) was not appropriate for this theme. I did not own theme-appropriate high heels for the same reason I did not own a wig: my size was already a barrier to people accepting me as a trans woman, and wearing heels and/or a wig would tip the scales into *drag queen*, which was one of my deepest fears. (Some cis people got angry at me about that, since they considered the difference between drag queens and trans women to be splitting hairs, and I had been informed more than once that I needed to lighten up and stop putting everyone into boxes.) So, I remained barefoot except for my fishnets, and I stood on my tiptoes so shoes could be added to my feet in post—and, as the photographer put it, to give me *the illusion of an ass*.

Our main scene was the Hooker Party, wherein Lil' Michelle and her Raggedy Dyke Friend watch prostitutes acquiring patrons on the dance floor of a Bostonian in-hotel nightclub which was named either Chances, Faces, or Wishes. There were four prostitutes and three johns at Chances-Faces-Wishes, so I flew solo, the eternal Wallflower Hooker. The shots were composed so I was always interacting with someone just out of the frame, the practical reason being so that my supermodel height wouldn't block the non-supermodels, but my brain kept whispering *putting you on the edge of the frame means you can be cropped out.* When the book was released in July by the Bay Area publisher Last Gasp I was not cropped out of the frame, but I did get cropped out of many people's lives because *quel scandale!* There had been some concern about bringing me on because of my goddamn blog, worries which came true when they read my entry about what an emotional rollercoaster the shoot had been. I had thought of the entry as being akin to a story about a gravedigging cat who pretends to be a courtesan princess, but since I expressed the common showbiz fear of getting left on the cutting-room floor, people who weren't Michelle accused of trying to make the shoot and thus *Rent Girl* all about *me me me*. Because I wasn't Spalding Gray, my anxieties about being cropped out due to my Otherness were not viewed as a *Swimming to Cambodia*-style voyage of discovery but instead as an *ad hominem* attack on the photographer. This made me all the gladder that I hadn't written about how much it hurt when the photographer referred to me using male pronouns, as in **move *him* a little to the left** or **nope, *he's* still blocking michelle**. Most any other trans woman in San Francisco would have gotten away with writing that she had been misgendered, but I knew it would only backfire on me. And though my goddamn blog got upwards of ten hits on a busy week, I was scolded that what I'd written would hinder the sales of the book.

So, the whole *Rent Girl* foofaraw lost me some friends, which was not great. What was great was that when I featured at Kirk Read and Larry-Bob Roberts' open mic Smack Dab at Magnet a few months later, I gave them my favorite behind-the-scenes photo for the flyer, and they

The author staying inside the frame on page 14 of Michelle Tea and Laurenn McCubbin's *Rent Girl.*

captioned it ***sherilyn connelly, goth superhero***. That's right up there with being asked if you're circus folk.

Or maybe it was like the bumper sticker says: *well-behaved women rarely have comic books written about them.*

You Probably Think This Book Is About You

After *Night of the Living Dead* at Spanganga wrapped in November 2003, my trans male friend Frankie Tenderloin and I launched a variety

Sherilyn Connelly
goth superhero

Roger Pinnell
literary troubadour

SMACK DAB

Open mic in the Castro hosted by Kirk Read and Larry-bob Roberts

Wednesday April 21, 2004
7:30 signup, 8 pm show

Magnet, 4122 18th Street between Castro and Collingwood

Bring five minutes of words, music, comedy, etc.
or just come and watch and cheer folks on.

Free, all ages,
all genders

Flyer for Smack Dab at Magnet, April 2004. Though I am wearing a hairfall, my bangs are my own, and the rest of my hair is in danger of being cut by my sharp shoulders.

show at the El Rio which we called Wicked Messenger. The name was Frankie's suggestion in honor of Patti Smith's version of the Bob Dylan song "The Wicked Messenger" and was coincidental to the popularity of Gregory Maguire's novel *Wicked* and the Stephen Schwartz musical adaptation, the latter of which opened at the Curran Theatre in San Francisco in June and then on Broadway in New York a few weeks before our show debuted. For Frankie and me, it was all about our love of Patti Smith; we also tossed around doing an act for the 2004 Drag King Contest in which I would be *Easter*-era Patti performing "Because the Night," Frankie would be Tom Verlaine, and *Godspeed* author and Tribe 8 lead singer Lynn Breedlove would be Lenny Kaye, but it didn't pan out.

Speaking of things not panning out, while the first Wicked Messenger in November went well, the El Rio cancelled us after Wicked Messenger 2 in December, Wicked Messenger 3.0 in January, and wickedmessenger-foür in February all failed to attract an audience. Still, we lasted two months longer than Negativland at the DNA Lounge in 2001! wickedmessenger-foür got trounced by the Grammys and *The L Word*, which was a shame because Danielle was back in town and killed during the open mic with new material she had typed up at Lascaux West the night before, and Spanganga's Jim Fourniadis performed a terrific set. Among the many things I envied about Jim was his musical talent, and we bonded over the spooky drones he created on his blood-red Roland SH-101 analog synthesizer for *Night of the Living Dead*. Jim's wicked-messengerfoür set was him on his acoustic guitar, and heavy on songs he'd written for his old band Rats of Unusual Size, including "Math Brain" and "Macho Shithead." Except for the low turnout, it was a good night all around.

Flyer for wickedmessengerfoür at the El Rio, February 2004. It's hard to believe that lower-case text on a black background didn't compel audiences to attend, but there you go.

When Spanganga announced its impending closure in early 2004, Jim and Erin opened a new performance space called the Dark Room at the corner at 2263 Mission. It had most recently been Mission Records, but 2263 Mission had been home to many disreputable watering holes over the decades; in the 1940s it was the V & J Club, and by the late 1970s it was called Jug of Punch, because why not? The bar itself was still installed along the north side of the main room, and between that and the glass block wall facing Mission, a rumor circulated that the scene in the country bar Torchy's in Walter Hill's 1982 *48 Hrs.* had been filmed there. The glass block wall was considered proof, but setting aside that anyone with a basic understanding of film production can tell the scene was shot in a space several times larger than the Dark Room, the more boring truth was that director Hill and production designer John Vallone liked the way glass blocks looked. (Hill and Vallone's next collaboration *Streets of Fire* featured more glass blocks, though they mixed it up a bit in *Fire* by calling the bar Torchie's instead of Torchy's.) I debunked the *48 Hrs.* rumor out of general principle when it came up over the years, but I was also proud of it. I was no less proud that Wicked Messenger 4.11 became the Dark Room's inaugural show on Easter Sunday 2004, and the series' final installment, Wicked Messenger Forever, took place at the Dark Room in June.

The word *wicked* continued to follow me: when I organized a reading for my 31st birthday with two of my poet friends at Modern Times Books, the bookstore titled the reading Wicked Words, which was coincidental to it taking place two nights after Wicked Messenger Forever. Wicked Words was my second birthday reading, my first having been at Adobe Books for my 30th birthday. Since the secret of becoming a star is knowing how to behave like one, organizing a public literary event to celebrate turning 30 when I didn't start reading in open mics until I was 29 was an act of unearned confidence which made me feel like I was living my best *Velvet Goldmine* life.

Jim encouraged me to mount a play at the Dark Room, and the impossible production I kept coming back to was *Crash* told from Catherine Ballard's point of view, possibly as a solo piece. My *Crash* play never happened because most things don't, but it was still an intellectual exercise which took my brain in interesting directions, which is always the point. Another idea which was unlikely to happen but was fun to imagine for the casting possibilities alone was *Cabaret*. I wanted to be Sally Bowles, because another secret of becoming a star is believing you're beautifully tragic enough to be Sally Bowles (*cf.* the Replacements' "Achin' to Be"). Lynn Breedlove also wanted to be Sally, which surprised me at first because Lynnee was male-identified, but he knew a good role when he saw one, and he wasn't as hung up about how people perceived his gender as I was. Our queer cis friend Cindy theorized that Lynnee and I could do a dual–Sally production, and I would have been happy to let Lynnee take "Mein Herr" and "Life Is a Cabaret" so long as I got "Maybe This Time," which Kander & Ebb wrote for me as surely as I was on Stephen Sondheim's mind when he wrote "I'm Still Here" for *Follies* two years before I was born. Cindy would have been the Emcee in our hella-queer production, though both Danielle Willis and Lynnee's Tribe 8 bandmate Flipper also called dibs on the role, which opened a new world of possibilities. In truth, I would have been content to be that one Kit Kat Girl you saw in pictures of regional productions of *Cabaret* if you were the kind of person who spent time looking at pictures of regional productions of *Cabaret*, you perv: the one who's taller and bulkier and not as attractive as the others, but who gives it her all and puts an extra swish in her tail. You can't miss her because she tends to be paired up with the objectively sexiest Kit Kat Girl, the one who is of a normal height and who is curvy and symmetrical and classically attractive in all the ways her taller, probably-wouldn't-want-to-see-her-without-makeup counterpart is not.

Shortly after Wicked Messenger Forever, Jim cast me as Karen Carpenter in the Dark Room's original stage production *Zippy the Pinhead in Fun: The Concept*, adapted from the Bill Griffith comic by Denzil Meyers and co-directed by Jim and Denzil. Karen was the guardian angel and life coach to Zippy, played by an actor I'd first met at Shrine of Lilith named Bryce Byerley, and also to Griffy, Bill Griffith's avatar played by poet and artist Mikl-Em. Most of my scenes were with Mikl-Em, and it was my favorite role of my spotty acting career, though not only because I was portraying the world's most famous anorexic, or because Karen Carpenter as a guardian angel was a role nobody had ever played before, or because I got to wear angel wings, or because I was already a proud owner of a bootleg VHS copy of Todd Haynes' *Superstar: The Karen Carpenter Story*. It was all those things, plus I got to sing the chorus of the Carpenters' "Superstar" every night, and because Mikl-Em was always present in the moment and generous and made me seem more talented than I was.

Best of all, the role was controversial. Much like the source comic, the *Zippy the Pinhead in Fun: The Concept* script was full of strange characters and bizarre situations and meaningful non-sequiturs. When Jim sent it to the real-life Bill Griffith, who had given the Dark Room the legal rights to mount this play based on his comic and thus made our show an official part of the Zippy the Pinhead multiverse, he only had one quibble:

> Off the top of my head right now, I'm thinking Zippy deserves a better "Guardian Angel/Life Coach" than Karen Carpenter ... images of Leona Helmsley, Julia Child and Joan Rivers come to mind.

Who else can say they played a Zippy the Pinhead character that the creator of the original comic thinks is too square a peg? (Are we having fun yet?) Thankfully, Griffith was cool with it after Jim's response:

> I'm kind of locked into Karen Carpenter (my idea), cause we've already cast, and Karen actually works quite well, and the person we have playing her is simply off the map. My idea was that she was such a false icon of goodness, that being a guardian angel was her "community service" in heaven.

I was off the map! One night during *Zippy* rehearsals in June we went for drinks at the Mission bar Doc's Clock, where I met Denzil's spouse Pamela Holm. She was *Zippy*'s set designer, and my ears perked up when Pamela mentioned that she'd been doing readings and radio interviews for her new

Lobby card featuring Mikl-Em as Griffy, and the author as Griffy's guardian angel Karen Carpenter singing "Superstar" in *Zippy the Pinhead in Fun: The Concept* at the Dark Room, July 2004. This was the second time I wore a wig in public.

book *The Toaster Broke, So We're Getting Married*. It was a memoir about marrying Denzil, and she used their real names, which blew my mind. You mean, you can do that? You can write about your own life, your experiences, and tell the truth about things that happened while other people were present? Pamela assured me it was possible, and Denzil told me his philosophy was that ***becoming a character is an occupational hazard when sleeping with a writer***. I liked how Denzil brought individual responsibility into the mix, considering that Cally was still angry at me about the *Rent Girl* backlash, some of which spilled onto her. Cally didn't like how people assumed that being my girlfriend meant she had my back and always supported what

I wrote or said, since nothing could be further from the truth. (I was obligated to have Cally's back and always support what she wrote or said, but equity was never the point of our relationship.) Her latest stab at getting me to dial back on my lifelong dream of being a writer was to tell me **nobody else will ever want to be with you because nobody wants to be written about.** The headgame of **nobody else will ever want to be with you because (you are a scorpion)** was considered bad form by 2004 San Francisco standards, but Cally doing it to me was not the same as when HAAH used to do it to her, because whatever else domestic abuse may be, it is not a cycle.

I told Pamela about the *Rent Girl* brouhaha and how that evolved into more recent accusations of **namedropping** and **starfucking.** The big example was that Danielle Willis and I drank Cally's blood the night before wickedmessengerfoür, but I was told that I was being a namedropping starfucker when I mentioned Danielle in the story I wrote about the thing the gravedigging cat and the vampire princess did together while the vampire was a guest in the cat's home. The real criticism should have been that the story's title "Plasma and Poultry" was lazy and first-draft, but then again, there were pieces in Danielle's book *Dogs in Lingerie* titled "Psychic Powers and Suicide," "Navane and Baloney Sandwiches," and "Autism and Eroticism." I figured if the "Thing and Unrelated but Phonetically Similar Thing" title formation was good enough for Danielle it was good enough for me, and I used "Plasma and Poultry" to open my sets during my July 2004 Southern California tour with Lynn Breedlove. Though I was the acknowledged starfucker, that tour only happened because Lynnee was a big enough star in Cally's eyes to suspend her otherwise ironclad **sherilyn must be home every night** rule.

It also raised some **what if the mogwai gets a caraway seed stuck in its teeth while in an airplane crossing the international date line?**-type questions, like, was it still starfucking in the pejorative sense if the star in question wanted to fuck me as much as I wanted to fuck them? Here's a random example from late 2003: after an unsuccessful stint in a Christian rehab clinic in Ohio, Danielle had been moved to a Bay Area clinic based on a system called Rational Recovery, which was light on the Western religion but heavy on West Coast woo-woo. I visited her there on Thanksgiving, and since I knew she would be starved for eye candy I wore my shiniest black PVC pants and goth-tarted up more than might be considered appropriate for visiting a rehab clinic on a major holiday. Danielle spent much of the time I was there soaking me in for the shiny object I was, and I was happy to reciprocate. She looked healthier and lovelier than ever as her body healed from the ravages of bug powder, and even better, she was now wearing glasses. I also thought back to the description of Danielle in David McCumber's 1992 book *X-Rated: The Mitchell Brothers—A True Story of Sex, Money, and Death*:

She is a stark, imposing twenty-five year old, easily six feet tall in her spikes. Whippet-thin. Flowing black hair and pale white skin. High angular cheekbones, big strong unapologetic nose and a set of teeth like a quarter horse, huge pretty swollen red-painted mouth stretched over them, snarling, laughing, giving you a look at them, big bright white straight ripping teeth that could really do some damage—have done, you get the feeling.

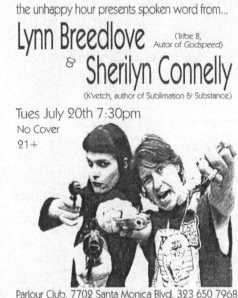

the unhappy hour presents spoken word from...

Lynn Breedlove
(Tribe 8, Autor of *Godspeed*)

& Sherilyn Connelly
(K'vetch, author of *Sublimation & Substance*)

Tues July 20th 7:30pm
No Cover
21+

Parlour Club, 7702 Santa Monica Blvd. 323 650 7968

Flyer for the author's appearance with Lynn Breedlove at the Unhappy Hour at the Parlour Club in West Hollywood, July 2004. Guinevere Turner attended the show and bought my chapbooks! That deserves an exclamation point!

That Danielle's teeth could really do some damage was indeed a feeling I had gotten more than once. McCumber probably meant *a set of teeth like a quarter horse* as a snark, and I sensed a bit of self-consciousness in the way Danielle kept her mouth closed in the four, count 'em, four photos of her on the front and back cover of *Dogs in Lingerie*, but in person I found her overbite deeply sexy. As the Thanksgiving table was being set, one of Danielle's fellow Rational Recoverers looked at me and said, *danielle, can you give me a hand with this?* After having been mistaken for the addled Danielle by the SRO manager, now being mistaken for the far-cleaner Danielle by someone with whom she regularly broke bread was all the more of a boost to my self-esteem and made this whole peculiar scene all the hotter.

Danielle had been open about sticking her figurative fangs into me on a professional level, to use my fledgling career to help resurrect her own, and I was happy to be used in that respect. Something I did not include in "Plasma and Poultry" was that on the same night as the blood-drinking, I had mentioned to my houseguest Danielle that I was planning to make a chapbook about meeting her, and she immediately sat down at my computer and wrote an introduction. It was her idea, and

I couldn't have stopped Danielle from engaging in this act of what she called ***productive procrastination*** if I had wanted to. So, who was fucking whom? Who was the parasite, and why did either of us need to be? Besides, another *Velvet Goldmine* edict was ***nothing makes one so vain as being told one is a sinner***, and since I kept being told that the way I translated my thoughts and experiences into words was a sin, I was now embracing my sinful vanity.

"Plasma and Poultry" was published in the tenth and final issue of Loren Rhoads' magazine *Morbid Curiosity*, and the story was mentioned by Peter Carlson in his June 2006 *Washington Post* review. Carlson wrote that the tenth *Morbid Curiosity* was tame compared to the previous nine issues, with one exception.

> Nobody admits to killing anybody or sleeping with a corpse. The most shocking thing in the issue is "Plasma and Poultry," Sherilyn Connelly's account of sitting around with a couple of friends and drinking each other's blood, which was, she reports, "an odd sensation."
>
> Sipping blood from a syringe inspired Connelly to contemplate vampires, and she concluded that she isn't one. "Vampires don't exist," she writes. "But, by gum, you willingly drink blood and your weirdness factor can't help but shoot through the roof."
>
> So true! And only in *Morbid Curiosity* would a story about recreational blood-drinking include the phrase "by gum."

I appreciated Carlson's appreciation of my authentic Gabby Johnson–style frontier gibberish, but he didn't mention that Danielle was one of the friends, goldarnit! I dropped her famous name, and my blatant starfuckery went to waste. It was almost as though few people knew who Danielle was, and fewer gave a damn about my literary sins.

The Midnight Sisters Convene in Kopenhagen

When the Second Arrangement began in late September 2004, Cally and I had a newer circle of friends who were happy to onboard us into their complicated flowchart of relationships. Cally suggested I ask Lynnee to teach me how to cruise for women, and things got off to a promising start when Cally got drunk and makeup-smearingly snoggy with a cis goth boy named Eldritch at the Folsom Street Fair. I couldn't attend because I was taking a self-defense class called Girl Army which met on Sundays, but Cally happily showed me photos of her and Eldritch dancing and swapping spit at the Cat Club and then at a house around the corner from the Cat Club known as Castle Funkenstein. Having overcome her fears of ghouls and dancing, Cally was now proud of herself for being so bold and allowing herself to have a good time at what she described as ***the best folsom ever!*** I was proud of her, too.

Danielle had been wanting to take me into the Mitchell Brothers O'Farrell Theatre since the first night we met, and it finally happened in early October, a few days before I was going to start having my hair bleached blonde. For as much as she enjoyed me being mistaken for her, Danielle approved of my impending blondification, since she had always said that if I was blonde I would look like Stephanie March as Assistant District Attorney Alexandra Cabot on one of Danielle's favorite television shows, *Law & Order: Special Victims Unit.* I was surprised at first that she would be hooked on a network procedural, but then I got past my snobbery and realized it was a network procedural about sex crimes, so for Danielle it was the next best thing to tapping into the *Videodrome* signal.

Danielle had participated in many fascinating sex crimes herself over the years, but she would always be most famous for sending O'Farrell Theatre co-owner Artie Mitchell to the hospital in the summer of 1988. Artie was a notorious rapist who, as Danielle put it, thought the world owed him a blowjob. She was the first dancer to successfully resist Artie's rape attempts, and when he wouldn't take ***fuck off*** for an answer, Danielle attacked him with a steel-heeled stiletto and knocked him down a flight of stairs. When she lost her job at the O'Farrell shortly before *Dogs in Lingerie* was first published in 1990, however, it was not because of her act of self-defense against Artie's rape attempt, but because Danielle was a weirdo. She tended to wear green wigs and strip to songs like Alice Cooper's necrophilia paean "I Love the Dead" long before her own flesh started to necrotize, and Artie's brother and O'Farrell co-owner Jim Mitchell called Danielle ***a fucking novelty act***, which was not the ***are you a trapeze artist?***-type compliment it sounds like at first. After getting fired from the O'Farrell, Danielle spun fantasies about killing both Artie and Jim, fantasies which were derailed when Jim killed Artie for her in February 1991.

Well, not *for* her; Danielle Willis was surely the furthest thing from Jim Mitchell's mind when he pulled the trigger. But his act of fratricide did remove an item from Danielle's to-do list, and she made sure her assault on Artie was an official part of her legacy by making it the climax of Act I of her play *Breakfast in the Flesh District.* Meanwhile, the Expanded Edition of *Dogs in Lingerie* printed in 1993 included evidence from one of her most fascinating sex crimes: an SFPD Incident Report Form from May 9, 1991, when Danielle attacked both an events promoter and a police officer at the DNA Lounge during Jennifer Blowdryer and Veronica Vera's touring show *This Is Not a Smut Fest.* The incident was reported as ***sexual battery / battery on a police officer***, though the form doesn't go into much detail about what Danielle did to whom, beyond noting that there were ***photos taken*** *of human bite to ankle*, one of the two victims *refused medical treatment for trauma to genitals and face*, and most importantly, Danielle's ensemble that evening included *black coat, green pants, black boots*. (Were the green pants made of leather, though? Green snakeskin? Suede, perhaps? Was she wearing the pants over the black boots or inside them? So many unanswered questions!) There's no other reference in *Dogs in Lingerie* to the event; it was just a bit of ephemera from a thing Danielle was proud of and wanted to be remembered for.

San Francisco Police Incident Report Form from May 9, 1991. But what kind of black coat was it? And were the boots Doc Martens?

My first stop with Danielle at the Mitchell Brothers O'Farrell Theatre in October 2004 was New York Live. It was a stage surrounded by comfy seats which were like the connected rows of a movie theater, though Danielle informed me that it was not the room in which movies used to be shown. Indigo sparkles orbited from the mirror ball as spotlights bathed the dancers in blues and reds, and Danielle told me she always asked for blue light for the same reason I gravitated toward it at the Stud: blue light is a dead girl's best friend. Neatest of all at New York Live was the circle of light high up on the wall behind the stage. I couldn't quite figure out the source, but I found it mesmerizing, like the prominences during the eclipse of a purple sun.

Next was the Green Door Show, which was a bit disappointing. I was expecting more from it because it has *the* name—y'know, *Behind the Green Door!* *Rabid*'s Marilyn Chambers and Ivory Soap and all that! What happened was, a curtain parted to reveal a large, round platform, and behind it was the Green Door. On the platform were two pairs of women who fulfilled the O'Farrell's promise of Live Sex Acts as the platform rose a couple feet, then went back down, and *ta-da!*, end of Act I. Danielle said she could tell the pair on the left had the giggles and were trying hard to not burst out laughing. I was surprised by how sparse the audience was, and I ruminated that things would probably pick up in a few days with the start of that nauseating display of dick-waving known as Fleet Week, when the military descends and weapons of mass destruction fly laps over San Francisco. Danielle said that Fleet Week was usually slow at the O'Farrell, while the strip clubs and titty bars up in North Beach got all the extra business. Yeah, that figured.

Whenever she could, Danielle chatted up the dancers. Not just because she was a pig, though Danielle was as proud of being a pig as I was proud of being a cat, but because she used to work there. None of the dancers gave a hoot about her being an alum, so the solidarity she tried to establish never happened. One dancer did say she had been there since 1990, the year Danielle was fired, and they missed each other by a few months. Fourteen years, though. Damn. (I could scarcely imagine doing any one thing for that long.) When Ratt's "Round and Round" started playing, Danielle told me the metal band Slaughter and their attendant groupies came into the dressing room one night while she was getting ready to go onstage, and she was proud that she got the groupies' attention. *i wanted to be the rock star*, Danielle said. *don't we all*, I replied.

The Jedi Danielle and her Padawan Sherilyn breezed past the Ultra Room, slowing only to inspect the hair and makeup of their beautiful ghosts as they walked down the dimly-lit mirrored hallway toward the ever-mysterious Kopenhagen Room. It was between shows, so the

Kopenhagen was empty and dim, but not quite as dark as I'd hoped. Three of the walls were lined with a long couch, and what looked like the hand-held lights used by ground crews to guide airplanes were scattered about. Like much of the rest of the O'Farrell, there had been some remodeling in the Kopenhagen since Danielle left; here it was in the form of bars above the couches for the dancers to hold onto, which Danielle demonstrated as she straddled me. There were also individual curtains for privacy, but we kept them open as we made out. *(breathe, breathe)* Her teeth were sharp, as I'd hoped they might be. Not only the aftermarket fangs which she didn't get until years after *Rated X* was published, and damn if McCumber hadn't hit the nail on the head about her natural-born masticators: Danielle's front teeth felt like they could rend anything in their path, and I imagined them lacerating my tongue, her mouth filling with my blood. I wanted it to happen, but it doesn't happen because we can't let it happen.

Every few minutes the music from New York Live changed, and the announcer would encourage the deadbeats in the audience to tip the dancer. Danielle always looked up at the sound of the voice, making sure nobody else had come in. We were squatting, after all, and she was respectful of the fact that the dancers were on the clock. Satisfied that we were alone, Danielle sighed and said it was weird to be back in the Kopenhagen. I asked if she used to work in here a lot, and she nodded, saying this was where she had once done Mötley Crüe's Vince Neil, who complimented her clit. Danielle laughed at the memory, then kissed me and said **but this is the first time i've ever wanted to be in here, just to enjoy myself,** and my heart skipped a beat.

My fingernails were not long or sharp enough. I didn't think so, anyway, as I ran them down her back. I kept them short, and normally that was fine, but I knew they wouldn't leave marks on her back as I so wished they would. Her teeth were sharp enough to leave marks on my neck, but they didn't. *(you are a force of nature and i am an abhorrent vacuum)* She was going easy on me, and I wanted to tell her not to hold back, but I couldn't. We both knew she needed to restrain herself. I was ready to blow everything up, to break every rule that my current partner had ever placed on me or would ever try to, but Danielle didn't want that on her conscience. There was also the problem that while Danielle had kicked the bug powder—and this sober, lucid Danielle was far and away the sexiest creature I had ever come into intimate contact with—there were still communicable things in her blood which we had to make sure did not get communicated to my blood. When a couple of men walked in, we left the Kopenhagen Room and then the O'Farrell. Our first stop was the market across the street; Danielle and the owner went back as far as her dancing years, and he was happy to see her. I had always wondered what the people who ran the store thought about having the most notorious strip joint in town across the street, and now I knew. If the O'Farrell ever closed, it would surely hurt the market's business.

After strolling through the Tenderloin for a bit, we went into Divas. It wasn't a part of my world yet, but Danielle was a regular, and she reveled in the fact that many people refused to believe she was cis. Danielle was now telling people I was her girlfriend, and I was there for it as she showed me off. After she got the necessary schmoozing out of the way we were able to sit down and talk, occasionally indulging in kisses across the table which were more charming for their awkwardness. It was gratifying to hear that my friendship and advocacy had helped her get on her feet, particularly when I'd taken her to ForWord Girls. As we now sat holding hands at Divas two years later, she told me that night had been a turning point, making her realize how much she needed to get her shit together. We talked about her current writing projects: she was collaborating on a comic, was working on a potential gig with *SF Weekly*, and had a solid lead on a literary agent. The thought of her writing career getting back on track pleased me to no end, and I was cautiously optimistic. I would help Danielle in any way I could, but it wasn't up to me.

I never saw her again. (Gah! That right there, that's what I'm talking about.) But a hardcover compilation of the four-issue run of *How Loathsome* was published several weeks later, and it included a new introduction by Danielle.

> My first reaction to "How Loathsome" was a total freakout.
> I was lying on a couch in Cleveland waiting for my drug dealer to fucking show up, when my lover tossed a manila envelope in my lap. It was from my friend Sherilyn in San Francisco and contained what I was fairly certain was a comic book version of my life, written and illustrated by people I'd never met. Either that or I'd gone totally delusional and was indulging in the sort of bitter old drag queen "Madonna wrote that song about me" bullshit I've always found incredibly tiresome in bitter old drag queens.

Danielle went on to praise *How Loathsome* like you do when you're introducing something, and I was already familiar with the introduction since she had sent me her early drafts in 2003, but there it was: *now i am part of danielle willis' print canon*, in a hardcover book with an ISBN number and all. The thing is, I knew I was nothing unusual or unprecedented or all that interesting in the arc of Danielle's life. I knew there were many precedents for me, all manner of Brigits and Bambis and a Sarjenka or two. I knew Danielle had far sexier and bloodier fun with them than she ever had with me, and I would be a footnote to a footnote at best. But even for the substellar object that is the failed starfucker, there was no better feeling than seeing Danielle Willis referring to me as *my friend sherilyn* in print.

Were You Jerking Off to Her or Were You Jerking Off to Me?

The night before I went out with Danielle, I launched a weekly ambient/noise/experimental show on Pirate Cat Radio, an unlicensed broadcast station which had moved into a closet at the Dark Room. I titled my show *Rush Hour on the Event Horizon*, after the Durtro piece; I had been in touch with him ever since using his original *Rush Hour* as the soundtrack to *kittypr0n* Episode #14 ("Leash"), and he was honored that his work inspired me so much. The last five years had taught me to expect a tantrum when I told Cally I was going to be out of the house every Monday night—let alone for something on the radio, since she did not share my passion for the medium—but she was fine with it so long as I came straight home afterward. The tantrum occurred when I told her I was also going to spin danceable platters that mattered once a month at the new Club Pirate Cat at the 12 Galaxies. Cally ended up attending opening night in January 2005 and she enjoyed herself, but her initial response to the Club Pirate Cat news was anger, as tended to be the case when I behaved as though I had the freedom to make these decisions for myself. My desire for freedom was always a problem for Cally, and it would soon be personified by Ivy, a cis woman who was part of the relationship flowchart which included Eldritch and his partner Taos.

On the Friday of the same busy week that I launched *Rush Hour on the Event Horizon* and visited Kopenhagen, we all gathered at a friend's house to celebrate Cally's birthday. The tipsy birthday girl spent the first few hours making out with Eldritch; I had always had a thing for Taos, and she was politely receptive, but I happily changed course when Cally learned that Ivy liked me and told me as much in accordance with schoolyard rules. Ivy and I spent the rest of the night buzzing with absinthe and making out like teenagers who were learning to mesh their bodies while remaining fully clothed, and Taos stayed close, not participating but happy to see two of her friends making each other happy, because that was the point of it all for her: finding a bit of warmth in this stark, cold world. When Cally saw me with Ivy, she did not get the same warm fuzzy feelings as Taos about human connection. She instead detached herself from Eldritch and sat alone for the rest of the evening, and she later said she regretted telling me about Ivy.

Cally still trusted Taos enough to let her to start bleaching my hair the next day. Taos focused on my three-month growth of roots, which survived

Flyer for Club Pirate Cat at the 12 Galaxies, January 2005. I figured Kelly Michaels wouldn't have used a DJ name, so I didn't, either.

the process without getting too fried. I rather enjoyed the spiky, burbling feeling of the peroxide doing its thing, and I chose MC MAX Wicked Blonde as a toner for the shade and not just for the name, honest. As my scalp burned in October 2004, Cally fiddled with the Second Arrangement: we could now only be affectionate with people we already knew and who Cally had pre-approved at big parties we both attended, like the upcoming Halloween soiree at Castle Funkenstein. On paper, she approved of me being with Ivy at Funkenstein since Cally herself would be with Eldritch.

The evening started off with Cally between me and Eldritch on Funkenstein's living room couch. Cally and I took turns kissing Eldritch, and Cally said watching me snogging him was *very hot*. I did not find it hot, instead considering it a means to an end since seeing me kissing Eldritch put Cally at ease because it alleviated her guilt. It was unthreatening to Cally for the same reason the play piercing had been unthreatening at first: I found the piercer attractive, but they were not offering gentle affection, so it only ticked one of the two threat boxes. Eldritch was offering gentle affection, but though I liked him as a person I was not attracted to him, so it again left one of Cally's two threat boxes unticked.

Me being with Ivy ticked both threat boxes, which was why everything dissolved when Ivy and I went into another room by ourselves. Not *by ourselves* in the sense that we were alone, for we were just able to eke out some space on the edge of a bed which was already occupied by two other couples, but in the sense that after a few minutes Cally came in and shouted that she had been looking for me and couldn't find me and we needed to go home right now because I was being mean and unfair and breaking her heart and putting her through the emotional wringer and we needed to change the rules of the Second Arrangement again because tonight proved for the nth time that I could not be trusted.

Speaking of peroxide-blondes who could not be trusted, Courtney Love played the Fillmore the following Tuesday. In a pre-show *San Francisco Chronicle* interview with Neva Chonin, Courtney described her backing group the Chelsea as *a crazy horse of a band*, referring to Neil Young's longtime band which Tira and I had seen up close and personal at the Old Princeton Landing in 1996. Cally and I scored a cherry spot at the foot of the Fillmore stage in 2004, putting us as close to Courtney as I had once been to Neil, but everything else about the Courtney show was off-kilter. It was seven months after the release of her solo debut *America's Sweetheart*, a so-so album in which the best version of the best song—the shoulda-been-a-classic statement of purpose "Sunset Strip," which picked up where "Celebrity Skin" left off—wasn't on the domestic CD. (The bad album version of "Sunset Strip" is 5:31 long and starts with acoustic guitar, while the best version is 5:53 and starts with electric guitar and is often labeled as a demo version though it is not.) Courtney herself was a mess, and she made several references to having just gotten out of rehab, but what I saw as I looked up at her was a mess who was making a go of it.

After *America's Sweetheart*'s "I'll Do Anything," Courtney apologized for how much it sounded *like a fucking nirvana song*, then declared, *this is an onanistic fucking career—i do this for myself*. Right there, that was it. I knew *onanistic* would be a kind word for my career, and I would always be doing it for myself. Courtney went on to add, *you're seeing a fabulous*

show during the fabulous quote "down time" of an artist! fuckin' feel lucky.
Which I did, and I soaked it all in, imprinting on Courtney like a big sister
who was teaching me the most important lesson of all: charting your own
path is going to be a messy process and if you aren't prepared to crash and
burn in public and accept that people are going to say vile things about you,
then there's no point to starting.

Cally was disappointed because Courtney did not play the guitar,
which meant Courtney did not fulfill her duties as an Angry Rock Chick.
(Just to make the occasion more special, the concert was on the fifth anniversary of the bad night in 1999 when Cally had described me posting
a story from 1994 to my online diary as *forcing the tale* upon her. Toxic
relationships grow up so fast!) The *San Francisco Chronicle*'s cis male pop
music critic was also disappointed, and he fired off some heckles which I
suspected had been in his chamber for a long time.

> She sounded horse. Not hoarse, but like an actual horse after it had been run
> through the glue factory. On top of that she kept clutching at her crotch. But,
> again, not in the boastful manner that someone such as Nelly normally does;
> more like someone who might be suffering from a raging case of something
> nasty.

When Nelly grabs his crotch he's a stud, but when Courtney does it
she's a diseased skank. Oh, we do have fun! This sort of slut-shaming was
starting to go out of fashion in music criticism by 2004, but it was understood that it would always be open season on Courtney Love. Cally and I
got many a look up at the oft-clutched crotch in question because Courtney
was often crouching directly in front of us, and though we had to duck her
thrown cigarettes, we remained a smidgen out of toe range after she took
off her shoes and socks. It was all glorious, but as far as Sherilyn's Fillmore
Starfucking went, getting a stirrup's-eye view of Courtney Love was not my
most intimate.

A week before my thirtieth birthday in June 2003, my dear friend
Horehound Stillpoint took me to see the Cramps at the Fillmore. The Buzzcocks had performed there the previous night, and Horehound was still
sore from a moment of rock 'n' roll synchronicity: as the Buzzcocks played
their signature "Ever Fallen in Love (with Someone You Shouldn't've),"
Horehound fell in love with the boy he was bodyslamming with in the
moshpit though he knew he shouldn't've. My Hore nevertheless insisted
that we be at the front of the stage and thus in the moshpit zone so Cramps
singer Lux Interior would see me. Lux was in *Fiends of Dope Island* mode,
wearing makeup and tight salmon-colored snakeskin pants and a match-
ing shirt with long black PVC gloves, and he did notice the tall goth girl at
the front. Lux sang in my general direction quite a few times, and I had his

ass and crotch up in my grill on at least one occasion each. For all that transcendent sleaziness, the true blessing came when the Purple Knif kneeled down, took my face into his sweaty, PVC-clad hand, and looked into my eyes as he sang the opening lines of what was already my favorite Cramps song, *Flamejob*'s "Let's Get Fucked Up." I leaned into Lux's glove and nuzzled, non-verbally expressing my consent and agreeing that I would indeed like to do some stuff, to strap on a little of that abnormal delirium, and that feeling like I got hit by a truck tomorrow would be worth getting *fuuucked up* tonight. So, yes, let's!

Though I never got *fuuucked up* with Lux Interior in 2003, I was more than a little honored to be mentioned in Beth Lisick's *SFGate* column a week after the Courtney Love concert in 2004. Beth was writing about Suspect Thoughts Press' new anthology *I Do / I Don't: Queers on Marriage*, which contained my essay "Two-Sixteen-Ought-Four." The piece was a stylistic experiment which didn't quite work, but I had been published in a real book! It was a doorstop of a book with 139 contributors, and yet I was among the five, count 'em, five writers Beth named along with Horehound, Mark Ewert, Mattilda Bernstein Sycamore, and Margaret Cho—so, y'know, no big whoop. In that same column, Beth wrote about the Courtney show, which she loved as much as I had.

> Sure, some songs were more together than others: "Miss World," from Live Through This, sounded like she was channeling herself 10 years ago, but the drama and the suspense of how a song was going to turn out was plenty for me. Maybe she's tragic, but she's a hell of a performer.

I emailed Beth and thanked her both for mentioning my presence in *I Do / I Don't* and for her non-snarky review of the Courtney show. In the long term I should be so lucky as to have someone write *maybe she's tragic, but she's a hell of a performer* about me, and in the short term, seeing the names **sherilyn connelly** and **courtney love** within a few paragraphs in the same showbiz column was no small rush. Speaking of rushes, on the Friday before Thanksgiving, Beth asked if I could perform in a mere 72 hours at her monthly Porchlight Storytelling Series at Café du Nord. The premise of Porchlight was that six people told unscripted, seven- to ten-minute stories on a given theme, and November's theme was "Imposter! Tales of Identity in Crisis." Everything about it was terrifying, so, *challenge accepted!* To ensure that I did not squander this opportunity to flame out at Café du Nord as spectacularly as Courtney had at the Fillmore, I told the story of the still-radioactive *Rent Girl* ruckus. Speaking extemporaneously to a mostly straight audience about something which many queer people were angry at me about was more intense than I expected, but the response in the moment was overwhelmingly positive.

Porchlight on Monday was only one element of what I came to think of as my Blaze of Glory Week. Though I had no piercings or tattoos, on the night before Porchlight I hosted a show at the Dark Room called Pins & Needles: Writers on Body Art. One of my favorite things about being on the theater's staff over the next ten years was getting to step in and host shows I wasn't otherwise involved with, both because I was good at it and because I was there. Though not just hosting, nor just at the Dark Room: a few weeks after Pins & Needles, Alicia Dattner asked me at the last minute to run the soundboard for her neo-mini-quasi-circus the Latest Show on Earth at a Pirate Cat Radio Listener Appreciation Party at the 12 Galaxies. I was happy to help, and not only watching Dattner's velcro-wrestling, lightbulb-chewing madness unfold but getting to participate behind the scenes gave me a renewed sense of gratitude for the privilege of being involved in this world of artists and performers, of instigators and creators, of sluts and goddesses. It made me sad to think of all the things I'd missed over the years because I was either too lazy to leave the house or because my tail was being stepped on, but what mattered was that I was out here now, and I was mindful that I would someday be like Mandy Slade, looking back on this as a gorgeous, gorgeous time when we came as close as we could get to living our dreams.

The brightest fire during my Blaze of Glory Week was the night after Porchlight, when Horehound and I were among the half-dozen performers at City Lights Books for a reading from JT LeRoy's *Harold's End*. It was being published by Last Gasp, whose rep said that I, Horehound, and the other four had been chosen for the reading because we were all good at it and because we all ***play well with others***. The trans-adjacent JT didn't show up because not showing up was their big *Velvet Goldmine* star move, but we began an email correspondence a few days before the show, and the following day they asked: ***how'd the reading go in your opinion? i was sick, chills and everything, couldn't go. but i heard you were great!!! which passage did ya read?*** I had no idea why they were calling in sick *ex post facto*, let alone to me, but since they asked I told JT that I chose to read the climactic scene in which the protagonist panics after accidentally killing their pet snail Harold because *i've been there, submerged in loss and panic and self-recrimination and the overwhelming sense that the one good thing in your life is gone and it's ALL YOUR FAULT*. As I typed that out, it hit me how tired I was of carrying that misplaced burden. I also knew I would never be able to lay down that burden so long as I was in my current relationship.

The punchline is that the news soon broke that JT LeRoy was not a person who existed in the real world, that they were a fiction created by a cis person. (Which was already what most cis people thought about trans people, so, thanks for that!) Far more famous and respectable writers were up in arms, but I had the luxury of laughing: I read at City freakin' Lights, which wasn't bad considering my first time at an open mic was only two years earlier, and I did so in the context of the silliest literary hoax of the first decade of the 21st century, thus putting me in the company of people including but not limited to Carrie Fisher, Madonna, Susan Dey, Rosario Dawson, some guy from Dashboard Confessional, Nancy Sinatra, Tatum O'Neal, Shirley Manson, Michelle Tea, and Lou Reed. Not only had I been the final reader at the City Lights event right after Horehound, it turned out to be the final LeRoy reading before the scandal broke, so me and my Hore snuck in just before the door closed, making us a footnote to a footnote. Also, Mark Mardon wrote in his *Bay Area Reporter* review of the *Harold's End* reading that **sherilyn connelly blew me away she was so gorgeous and dynamic and a real star presence**, and that did not suck.

What did suck was that Cally and I spent the last few weeks of 2004 processing and fighting and rewriting the Second Arrangement. Every thing under the sun remained the same when Cally told me I needed to communicate with her better—unless I was trying to communicate anything having to do with sex, in which case she said *i shouldn't have to hear about that sort of thing from you,* 'twas ever thus. When I tried to communicate my point of view or otherwise speak my mind, Cally stormed out of the room, 'twas ever thus. Worn down by it all, I agreed to go monogamous until the end of the year—with the condition that on New Year's Day of 2005, the Third Arrangement would begin. I was unhappy, and I wanted out, 'twas ever thus.

A Large Room, Full of People

Famed in Connelly legend is the story of how my big sister crawled into my brother Jim's closet and disappeared before I was born. Jim's closet was messy enough that the story seemed plausible far longer than it should have, and like all myths, it has an element of truth. My mother was hoping for a daughter after Jim's birth in 1962, and if their second child had been a cis female they would have stopped right there, but the next two to emerge were my brothers Tom and John. My parents gave it another shot while Nixon was on the campaign trail, and during the annual Connelly family drive from Fresno up to the Pacific Northwest in August 1972, my mother splattered the tasteful pink décor of her sister-in-law's bathroom with the alien red of my big sister's miscarried fetus.

Nothing has ever convinced me more of the biological drive to reproduce than the fact that my parents continued trying to do so. Not just because three children are more than enough, or the way they breezed right past what some might have interpreted as the warning sign of the miscarriage, but because they did so during the ugliest month on record. The decade is famous for its tackiness, but I maintain that the month I was conceived was the nadir. This is nothing against my parents, who were inoffensive enough by suburban Fresno standards; with the exceptions of Persis Khambatta and Brian Eno, who were both in the United Kingdom and whose paths probably never crossed, everybody on the planet was hideous in September 1972.

But the species continued to propagate, and on June 16, 1973, I was born at St. Agnes Hospital in Fresno. I was misgendered right out of the parturient canal, and though my mother was disappointed to not get the daughter she would have named Jennifer, my parents decided to end the experiment. (That's correct: I would have shared a name with *Labyrinth* star Jennifer Connelly, so that's one bullet I dodged by being born trans.) I was still going to be a lot of work because my legs grew crooked during gestation, causing my feet to point inward. The pediatrician's best guess was that I was cramped in my mother's womb despite being its fourth full passenger, which goes to show I was already too freakin' tall as a fetus.

When five years of leg braces and physical therapy and petitioning the Lord with prayer and putting my shoes on the opposite feet did not fix my legs, my parents took me to Stanford Medical Center. The condition had already been diagnosed as Internal Tibial Torsion, and the Stanford orthopedist said I would likely suffer from crippling arthritis in my legs as a grownup if the problem wasn't corrected right away. So, in October 1978 I spent ten days at Valley Children's Hospital, where the doctors performed the little-known, seldom-used Bilateral Proximal Tibial &

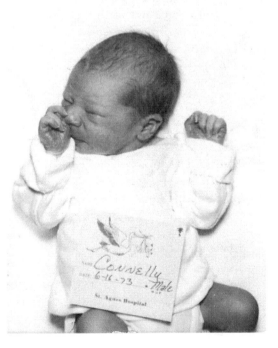

The author's first day in her ridiculous, misshapen meat puppet, St. Agnes Hospital, Fresno, California, June 1973.

Fibula Derotation Osteotomy. In simpler language, they broke and re-set my legs. I was asleep during that part and woke up with my legs in casts, though I was wide awake and unanesthetized a few days later when the doctors sawed a square out of one of those casts to see how my leg was doing, thus setting my first baseline for searing physical pain. I had experienced pain before, and I remembered some of it at the ripe old age of five, but I had no idea it was possible for pain to hurt that much.

Though I had many books at my bedside, the one I most associate with my hospital stay is the paperback version of the February 1978 *Peanuts* special *What a Nightmare, Charlie Brown.* After Charlie Brown shames and humiliates Snoopy as a sissy for leading **a prima donna life** compared to sled dogs in the Arctic, and shouts **you know what's wrong with you? you're overly civilized!** at him, Snoopy has an indigestion nightmare in which he is forced to be a sled dog in the Arctic. Though there were the usual sight gags and digressions which tended to fill out the running time of the *Peanuts* specials, it was all quite dark, and would be without the emotional subtext that Snoopy deserves the bad things that are happening to him. When Snoopy finally acknowledges in the third act that he is alone and unloved in a cold, hostile world and he will starve to death so long as he continues to stand up straight and be a person, he shoves himself into the closet by getting down on all fours and adopting the aggressive, hypermasculine behavior of the other sled dogs. There is no more heartbreaking moment in the entire Charles M. Schulz catalog than Snoopy's conscious descent into brutality and violence in *Nightmare,* the manufactured tearjerkiness of *Snoopy Come Home* be damned. *What a Nightmare, Charlie Brown* was quickly forgotten by the culture and wasn't rebroadcast for another 10 years, but I read the heck out of the book when I was five in the hospital. (A few years later I read Marjorie Flack's *Walter the Lazy Mouse,* which became the *ur-text* for my fears of being abandoned by my family and having to start over in an unfamiliar world.)

After several months in waist-high, bent-knee casts and using a wheelchair and then crutches, I had to learn to walk from scratch. By the time I was able to stand up and get around without crutches when I was seven, people were already telling me how tall I was and would continue to for the rest of my life. But for as much as I've hated towering over other people, and as much as I've hated people pointing out that I was towering over them, as I write this sentence at the age of 47 without a hint of arthritis in my legs, I feel nothing but gratitude toward my parents and toward medical science that I was ever able to tower at all.

5

The Epoch of Recombination

Mechanism of Occupant Ejection

The Third Arrangement did not begin on the first day of 2005 because Cally screamed at me enough to get me to drop it ('twas ever thus) and ya girl had herself a meltdown, a hard and heavy crying jag which was not just about the angry biped stepping on my tail like she would never stop doing until I escaped from her, but also about the pain of the past 12 months, the things I'd lost, the friends who had gone away because I expressed feelings of an almost human nature, the new sensations which evaporated before I had a chance to experience them. We were out of tissues and I didn't have any hair ties and I was just a big sobbing mess and that was okay. I needed to bathe in the feelings, to sense everything my body was producing, to connect on a physical level with the emotions, to confirm that it was a true experience. To *feel*.

Part of it was from knowing what was ahead, as I worked up the nerve to do what needed to be done. As I wrote in my goddamn blog on January 1:

> I suspect this year will bring great disapproval, demonization far worse than coming out as trans. I will endure.

I also realized I needed to change tack. Most of the stories and essays I'd written had been reactive, about things that happened and how those things made me feel. I was proud of most of those stories and essays, especially the ones that got me into trouble or had the potential to. I met a visiting Québécois named Lenore in early 2004 at an open mic which I soon started hosting called Lit at the Canvas, and after we corresponded for a while, I sent her an early draft of the Black Sheets story which I had been told not to write. (Someone should see it, I figured.) I would continue to accept the consequences for my words because getting in trouble for writing was better than not writing at all, and like Sinéad, I would no longer live by someone else's policies. But to get to a place where I could sleep peacefully and with a clear conscience, I needed to write about who I wanted to be, which meant it was time to weaponize the thing which scared Cally the most.

No, not weaponize. I was a writer, so it was time to *manifesto* my desire.

The perfect opportunity manifested itself when Lynn Breedlove and I were invited to participate in the 2005 UC Berkeley V-Day production of Eve Ensler's *The Vagina Monologues*. (The V in V-Day stands for Victory, Valentine, and Vagina.) Ensler had written a new trans-specific piece, but like most things written by cis people about trans women it was not good, so the V-Day producers asked me to write and memorize a thousand-word monologue in a week and a half and asked Lynnee to do the same from a trans male perspective. *challenge accepted!* The event took place over three nights leading up to Valentine's Day; the first two shows were in UC Berkeley's 350-seat Dwinelle Hall, and the final night, the only one Cally attended, was in the 650-seat Wheeler Hall. I monologued about how I do not equate gender with sexual organs, that if I could snap my fingers to change my flesh I would give myself a flat stomach, and that the most important change needed to happen within myself. So, the usual, but since I was putting a message out into the universe, I erred on the side of being overwrought.

> Maybe I fear my *potential*.
>
> See, I want to take on the world. I want to be Yoko Ono crossed with Courtney Love, to bear the sins of humanity, to take the blame for the weaknesses of men, to go too far because *someone* has to. I want to feel the sexual pleasures which I have allowed myself to believe I do not deserve. I want to find my moan. I will pound nails into the coffin of my old life and blow it straight to hell. The ruins of the old covenant will be drenched in the blood which my body will never produce, and I will not care anymore. Anyone who stands between me and what I desire will be cast aside as I open my legs to the heavens and cry out, *LONG LIVE THE NEW FLESH!*

My energy level was strong on the third and final night, and I was becoming what I had always wanted to be when I grew up, but the moment I stepped offstage I began to feel an illness which had been held off by performance adrenaline. When the show ended twenty minutes later, I was sniffly and snuffly and as stupid as a second coat of paint. Twenty-four hours after that I had a fever of 101.5F, which was soon joined by a shotgun cough. When I finally dragged my carcass to San Francisco General Hospital in early March, X-rays revealed that I had **posterior basilar segmental consolidation consistent with pneumonia**. But there was also **a lack of pleural abnormality**, so yay for that! My mother said she wasn't surprised I got sick considering my *lifestyle* and I needed to take better care of myself. When I clarified that the doctors called it *community acquired pneumonia* and that several of my *Vagina Monologues* castmates had also fell ill, it only proved her point, and she did not take the bait and congratulate me for being in *The Vagina Monologues*. Enh, it was worth a shot.

Though my mother had heard of *The Vagina Monologues*, I had never heard of the holiday of Purim when I learned that the Beyt Tikkun Synagogue was looking for someone to perform a queer revision of the Book of Esther which would consider *culturally ascribed gender roles, notions of masculinist sovereignty, feminist reclamations of power, "coming out" politics, and getting drunk*. Queer revisions of the Scriptures were in my bag, between "The J.C. Scrolls" and a more recent story called "The Face of the Field," written from Jezebel's point of view right before she gets defenestrated for being a slut. My new story was told from Esther's perspective, though the most important character was Queen Vashti, who fakes her own death and returns in disguise as the eunuch Harbona to help Esther navigate the violent anti–Semitism of King Achashverosh's court. Vashti and Esther become lovers, and Vashti says that while nobody ever trusted her because she descended from Nebuchadnezzar, she always considered herself to be more of a student of Jezebel. After all, what are the Scriptures if not the original shared universe?

When Esther is heartsick at the end about the fact that 75,000 people got slaughtered on her watch, Vashti encourages Esther to write herself whole.

> "When I last saw Uncle Mordy," I said, "he was writing in the Book of Chronicles, proclaiming this to be a day of celebration for future generations. He said my name will be forever associated with the events of the last two days, with the Purim."
>
> "History is written by the winners," Vashti said, "and you are the winner, thank G-d. Is it such a bad thing to be remembered as the savior of your people?"
>
> I sighed. "I suppose not. I'm just afraid that my own story will never be told."
>
> Without saying a word, Vashti got up and left the room. She returned with parchment and a stylus.
>
> "Then tell it," she said.
>
> So I did.

Not subtle or artful, but sufficient for a piece with the title "Impurim," which was almost as lazy and first-draft as "Plasma and Poultry." Beyt Tikkun's Purim Party was held the night before Easter Sunday in a performance space on Folsom near the Cat Club, and as she did for most of my gigs, Cally stayed home. Ivy had a DJ set at Castle Funkenstein that same night for a Dr. Seuss-themed party called The Flat in the Hat, however, and she was happy to swing by the Purim Party for my reading. Though she had been Cally's archnemesis since October, Ivy was not the reason I broke up with Cally the next day.

I'd had a solo therapy appointment with the Nice Lady on Good Friday, and she got her equivalent of angry at me. The Nice Lady knew better than anyone how unhappy I was and how much I wanted to get out of the relationship—to be precise, the Nice Lady knew better than anyone other than Cally, since Cally knew how unhappy I was and how much I wanted to get out of the relationship—and yet I was continuing to *not* get out of it. Yes, I had come at the King before and missed, but that was back in the futuristic year of 2000 when dinosaurs rode jetpacks to their jobs at pets dot com because pets can't drive. It was now 2005 and the Nice Lady said she wasn't sure there was any point to continuing our therapeutic relationship, since we would keep going in circles and wasting each other's time so long as I stayed with Cally.

Being told by your shrink to defecate or vacate the receptacle is a strong motivator, but I also knew this was my big *Age of Innocence* moment, my time to Wharton it up. The usual had tasted like cinders for years, and I felt buried alive under this future, so on Easter Sunday 2005, I broke up with Cally.

I already had plans for Easter night: Jim Fourniadis had invited me to perform at the premiere of a new weekly Dark Room show called Bad Movie Night in which we would heckle a movie *Mystery Science Theater 3000*-style. The inaugural movie was John Milius' hypermasculine 1985 *Red Dawn*, which I hadn't seen in years but knew was ripe for heckling. Cally wasn't interested in Bad Movie Night so she had already gotten angry at me for agreeing to do it, 'twas ever thus, but now she argued that it would be mean to break up with her and then leave the house. Wouldn't I stay home one last night? Wasn't that the least I could do for her?

I did not stay home with Cally.

Keep Your Tracking Knobs Properly Adjusted

The first part went fast: we broke up on Sunday, Cally found a new apartment on Monday, did the walkthrough on Tuesday, and signed the lease on Thursday. Cally was angry that I couldn't join her for the walkthrough on Tuesday, but she soon got over it. She observed that we were getting along better now than we had in the past several months, her personal metric for us ***getting along*** being how long it took Cally to get over a given burst of anger at me. Though her most violent tantrums in 1999 and 2000 were thrown to enforce her philosophy that one should never remain

impossible productions presents

Bad Movie Night

We've taken all the guess work out of the age old question, "Will this movie suck?"

It will suck.

Every Sunday for a measly 5 bucks you can put your feet up, enjoy a crummy movie, scarf down free popcorn and yes, you too can yell at the movie screen, and we promise to have you in bed by 11pm.

SUN March 27th: "RED DAWN"

Special Guest Hosts include Bucky Sinister, Mikl-Em, Lynnee Breedlove, Sherilyn Connelly, and more to be announced...

What more could you ask for of a Sunday night?

When: Sundays March 27th - April 24th 8pm
Where: Dark Room Theatre
**   2263 Mission St. (Btwn 18th & 19th St)**
Tickets: 5$ at the door
Info: www.darkroomsf.com
**   wsup@darkroomsf.com**
**   401-7987**

Flyer for the inaugural Bad Movie Night at the Dark Room, March 2005. Little did I know I would have to watch *Red Dawn* **every damn year for the next decade.**

friends with one's previous partners, Cally now declared that we would put the past behind us and move forward in unity as Best Friends. One of the parameters of our new Best Friendship was that if she needed someone to perform some task, like waiting for the plumber at her new apartment, that someone would be me. Being her Best Friend also meant that I would not do anything which made Cally feel like I was moving on with my life before she was ready for me to move on and that after X years I should not expect her to change or get used to anything new overnight. It wasn't worlds different than before Easter Sunday, except that now we didn't live together, though she insisted I spend the first several nights at her new apartment so she wouldn't have to be alone.

Our awesome new Best Friendship was of no consolation to my mother when I called to tell her about the breakup. All my mother's anger and disappointment was directed toward me; she didn't want details, and as far as she was concerned, Cally was blameless. My mother's tears of rage did not subside when Cally herself chimed in on the call and confirmed that the breakup had been the healthiest thing for the both of us, and the gnashing of Fresnan teeth continued for several weeks. My mother said she was praying I would come to my senses and take Cally back and she wished she could be there in person to comfort Cally, whom she considered to be the new Daughter She Never Had ever since I had ripped Tira out her life (though my mother still dropped references to how much she missed Tira and how she was still sad about the very bad and wrong thing I'd done). After that initial phone call in March to my mother, however, my new bestie had notes for me: I must always phrase it as *i broke up with cally*, never *cally and i broke up.*

My friend Sister Edith Myflesh was the Abbess of the Sisters of Perpetual Indulgence, an organization of nun-attired queer activists who were dedicated to (among other things) promulgating joy and preventing the spread of venereal disease. Edith also worked for a gay porn website called NakedSword, and I landed a job there in mid–April. I was going to be a librarian, sorta! Among my duties was to maintain the Naked-Sword Tape Library, the room of DVDs and VHS tapes they digitized and put online; the official language was that in addition to doing web programming I would **oversee management of all physical movies (vhs/dvd/ mini dv)**, and my initial title was the hella-sexy Tape Librarian/Associate HTML Producer. The stars continued to align for me after breaking up with Cally, for on the same day I received the good NakedSword news, Lenore wrote to say she was going be in town next week for the Alternative Press Expo.

After the second day of APE, Lenore came to the third Bad Movie Night: Menahem Golan's *The Apple*, presented in glorious Betamax. Jim Fourniadis asked me that night to be his regular Bad Movie Night co-host going forward, and I happily accepted. Cally was also there, and she never let me out of her sight, so Lenore and I kept our conversation brief, just making plans for her to join me the next day for *Rush Hour on the Event Horizon*. My fellow Pirate Cat Radio DJ KrOB had covered *Rush Hour* the previous Monday since I was helping Cally move into her new apartment, which was why I had also skipped the second week of Bad Movie Night and canceled one night of a two-night gig with the Tranny Roadshow in Berkeley. My bestie told me to cancel both nights of the Tranny Roadshow, as well as my new monthly gig hosting an open mic called Retool & Grind at the Eros bathhouse, but I refused.

After *Rush Hour* on Monday, Lenore and I went to the Lexington Club. This was going to be the first night in over a week that I wouldn't be sleeping at Cally's new apartment, and I was continuing to explore and savor these new textures of freedom: I didn't have to go straight home after shows anymore! I could stay out! I could do things without having to ask Cally for permission to do those things and without fear of being punished for just wanting to do things Cally did not want me to do! (I had no idea how naïve I was being!) After we had a few beers and made out for a while, Lenore invited me to a play piercing class being taught that Wednesday by Fetish Diva Midori. I was hesitant because the class was $25 and I was broke and in debt to my bestie, who assured me she was going to collect every penny I owed her for the last several months of Lascaux West's rent. Lenore offered to pay my fee because she had enjoyed my forbidden Black Sheets story and was excited by the thought of piercing me, and I was excited by the thought that *she* was excited to do something with me—and it was because of my writing, no less. Besides, I was single now, right? Sorta: my bestie wanted me to drive her on errands that same evening, and without going into detail I told her I was going to hang out with Lenore, emphasizing that it was Lenore's last night in San Francisco. Cally admitted to being jealous that I was spending time with another woman and that it felt like I was already moving on, so Cally asked me to please cancel my plans so she would no longer have those feelings.

The piercing class was held at Madame S, a leather-and-fetish-gear store which had spun off from the more masculine Mr. S, and I didn't recognize Lenore at first when she arrived after the class started. She usually presented butch with buzzed hair and well-scrubbed face, but she was now wearing dark makeup and a short red wig. There weren't any seats near me, so Lenore spent most of the lecture and demonstration portion sitting across the room. When it was time to practice with the needles on oranges before we used them on each other, Lenore gave me an *i'll be right back* gesture and stepped out of the room. She returned a few minutes later in a long black wig which made her look all the more like a rare and radiant maiden whom the angels would agree had the perfect name. It was also uncanny how much she looked like a vampire I had once known, and her teeth looked a little sharper.

After the class we had dinner around the corner at BrainWash, a café featuring a laundromat, a handful of pinball machines, and a Wednesday night open mic which was just ending as we arrived. I showed Lenore a few more San Francisco sights on the drive back to Lascaux West. Most of the furniture was gone, so we spent an hour making out against the kitchen counter. Lenore took off my top and went after my breasts, the first proper attention they'd received in the seven years I'd been on estrogen and spironolactone, and she mostly attacked my right nipple, all teeth and menace. I drove her back to her crash pad after midnight, and Lenore apologized that it couldn't be an all-night fuckfest, but I was okay with that. The next time I had sex was going to be a lot like losing my virginity, and for as hot as being with Lenore was and as much as I wished we had more time together, she was ephemeral. I would need to be with someone I already felt comfortable with, someone who I knew had my best interests at heart. Someone who, for want of a better way to put it, I was emotionally attached to.

I had two missions the following night: one was helping Cally set up her computer, and the other was returning the vacuum I'd borrowed from Ivy to use at Cally's apartment. Cally told me to return the vacuum first and come straight back, but the timing didn't work out because Ivy wouldn't be home from work until late. Cally seemed suspicious, but she let it go, and we had a pleasant time. I arrived at Ivy's around 11:15 p.m., and we sat for a while on her couch and talked, which led to making out, which led to going into Ivy's bedroom where she turned on her purple fairy lights and put *Figments of Emancipation* by the Doctors of Madness on her stereo, and below Ivy's poster of Baz Luhrmann's 2001 *Moulin Rouge* featuring Nicole Kidman bathed in blue light and bearing a tagline which I wanted to apply to my own life now that I was finally free, *this story is about beauty*, we had wonderful and revelatory sex which made me feel like I was finally and properly losing my virginity.

And Ivy went after my right nipple even more ferociously than Lenore.

John Calvin, He's Long Dead (We Gotta Get That in Our Head)

I saw the Nice Lady the next day. She approved of me cutting the cord with Cally, and she also approved of my dalliances with Lenore and Ivy over the past 72 hours. When I would see the Nice Lady on and off over the next decade, she was the only person with whom I could be completely open about what had happened. She was also the only person who would always tell me without reservation that my feelings mattered, that she was sorry I'd had to go through all that, that it had not been karma or cosmic justice or in any way excusable when my bestie had mistreated me and diminished me and punished me for the sins of strangers thousands of miles away, that I had not deserved any of it, that I was not damned for all time, that the answer to the question **well, can you blame them?** was *yes, i can absolutely blame them for denying my humanity just because i'm queer.* It helped that simulated sympathy was what the Nice Lady did for a living and I couldn't tell simulated sympathy from the real thing, but her words were always warm enough to feel like a much-needed hug.

I continued to help Cally move on Saturday, and all was well until we went shopping for housewares in a harshly-lit dollar store. After picking up a measuring cup, Cally glanced at my neck and announced that I had a hickey. Her eyes starting to water, she asked if it was from Lenore. I wasn't sure because I hadn't been aware the hickey existed, and Lenore later confirmed that it had to have been Ivy, but it was just as well for Cally to think it was the sin of a stranger thousands of miles away, so I said *i guess so.* Cally beaned me with the measuring cup and ran out of the store. She was wailing by the time she reached my Neon and continued as I drove her back to her apartment, my amygdala sparking to life as she screamed *slut! slut! SLUT! i can't believe how hurtful and inconsiderate you're being, you slut! the bed isn't even cold yet, sherilyn! you're already fucking other women! slut! slut! i thought you were my friend! slut! you SLUT! the bed isn't even cold yet! slut!*

I realized this Slutburst was the frozen moment when I saw what had been at the end of Cally's fork since the Catbox: all her fear of *slash* anger about *slash* disdain for my sexuality, revealed and unfiltered. Every tantrum over the past half-decade, even the worst in 2000 when she was screaming *i hate you!* and *fuck you!* and destroying random objects, all had a certain schematic quality. Which made sense, because Cally's tantrums were rhetorical devices, and the reddest flag I had ignored in 1999 was the way she talked about the strategic times she chose to cry and pout, and she joked that *i wouldn't want to have to subject you to one of my temper tantrums *grin** as though temper tantrums were a healthy thing which healthy grownups did. But this was the genuine article, and as I drove away after dropping her off at her apartment, I thought about how I hadn't heard anyone other than Cally use *slut* as a pejorative in years. All I had done was some brief piercing and topless, toothy snogging with one woman and then had sex with another, and the only visible evidence of any of it was a middle-school hickey, so I didn't feel like I'd earned what Cally had meant as her darkest of condemnations. On the plus side, Cally was using a misogynistic and thus feminine term to reflexively shame me, so maybe that meant she accepted me as a woman and didn't think I had *serious identity issues* anymore! That was progress.

The phone was ringing by the time I got back to Lascaux West, and I let it ring for the next five minutes. When I answered, my bestie asked: *is there anyone else?* She kept asking this for a while, and I kept not hanging up. I glanced at my 2005 *Extraordinary Chickens* Calendar and noted to myself that ~~Cally and I broke up~~ I broke up with Cally exactly 20 days earlier. When I told her it was none of her business, she rephrased the question: **have you done anything with ivy?** I did not say *we had the best sex i've ever had, better than i thought it could be.* I did invoke the Fifth Amendment, saying that I was not obligated to answer her questions about my private life. Cally rephrased the question: **but you're pursuing ivy, right? you plan to court her?**

I told my bestie that I didn't know if I was going to court Ivy or not, marveling to myself about how Cally kept busting out the old-timey heteronormative terminology. She cooled down after an hour or so, and the final item required her presence, so I drove back to Cally's apartment and picked her up and brought her to Lascaux West, where it had not occurred to me to remove my 2005 *Extraordinary Chickens* Calendar from the wall because why should it have occurred to me? When she saw the names of two women written down for the following week, one of whom was my platonic friend Lilah and the other being Ivy, Cally's tantrum began anew. It was also then that I decided that part of moving on was to rename my home.

One day back when Tira and I were not yet a couple but were hanging out and going to movies like *Henry V* and *The Cook, the Thief, His Wife & Her Lover* as young people did in Fresno in 1990, we visited my brother John. He was living in the Tower District, which was Fresno's official Cool Part of Town, and he'd recently had a tenant who'd lived in a walk-in closet, as young people did in the Tower District in 1990. The tenant had painted the walls of the closet black, created patterns with day-glo paint, installed black lights, and pinned up black light-reflective posters of Jimi Hendrix and Led Zeppelin purchased from the Blackstone head shop Kaleidoscope (**the gifts of tomorrow ... today**). John kept the closet as it was when the tenant moved out, and I showed it to Tira that day because I'd always thought it was neat, closing the door behind us for the full effect. We were silent for a minute, and then Tira put her hand on the back of my head and kissed me—not a chaste peck, but the real, fully-immersive deal. It took me a moment to process what was happening, and once I did, it was an exhilarating experience which opened the floodgates of affection between us. Tira later said she had been **somewhat overwhelmed** by the room, and while I had not been angling for my first kiss, I couldn't argue with the results. Ever since then I'd always had at least one naked black light bulb in my bedroom, and in more recent years I installed black light bars in the living room and bedroom at Lascaux West. I put black sheets on the walls of the bedroom in 2000 because I'd always hated white walls, and while Cally nixed me also putting black sheets on the living room walls (much to *kittypr0n*'s visual detriment), I was now free to do so.

I was also free to rename my home. It was now the Black Light District.

"Someday, This War's Gonna End"

Cally took the *kittypr0n* stars to her new apartment, and I adopted a black longhair cat who had recently given birth. The agency was trying to adopt out the kittens, but I knew the mamacat was mine when I learned her name was Perdita, just like Isabella Rossellini's peroxide-blonde character in David Lynch's *Wild at Heart*. It also felt appropriate that her name translated from Spanish as *lost little girl*, since my Perdita had been rescued from the street while pregnant. Though she would cuddle next to me and purr up a storm, she refused to stay on my lap for more than a few minutes. I could relate to Perdita's anxiety, because I had recently mentioned to Ivy that my schedule was filling up, and Ivy said she hoped that I would have some time for her, an innocuous statement which triggered alarms in my scarred little brain: *oh no, not again, too soon too soon toosoon....* I liked Ivy and I knew she had my best interests at heart, and I wanted to make time for her, but my skittishness was strong. I needed to believe that my destiny was mine and mine alone, that nobody got to tell me or hint strongly at what to do, because if I let that happen it would lead to them screaming horrible things at me until I was broken again. I knew that wasn't how Ivy rolled, because putting on the DVD of *Velvet Goldmine* and then stripping down to our shiny black pants and having at each other like Sophie and Johnny on the stairs was how Ivy rolled, and I couldn't have been happier to come down like water with her, but I was deathly afraid of someone stepping on my tail again.

Much like the last time I went through a breakup which was messier and more adolescent than it needed to be, I was crushing it as a grownup. Nobody had created a catalog of the NakedSword Tape Library, so that kept me busy, showed initiative, and gave me an excuse to find the few movies we carried which featured trans and/or cis women. (Cis women only appeared in movies with *Bi* in the title, and many of the women in those movies wore glasses on camera. It was like there was a nerd-fetish streak running through the bisexual porn industry.) Ivy was my date for my first company party, which was in early May at a Tenderloin joint called the Olive Bar. As we watched my coworkers dancing and drinking and carousing and living like there were no rules and only fun, I wondered aloud if this was all real, if this was my life now. Ivy assured me that, yes, this was all real, and this was my life now, if I wanted it. Sister Edith had an inkling of what I had gone through over the past six years and was thrilled to see me and Ivy out in the world, and so blessed us with the wisdom of the Sisters of Perpetual Indulgence: ***go forth and sin some more***.

The problem with me going forth and sinning some more had not changed since 1999: Cally did not want me to sin at all. She asked me on the day of the Slutburst to not date Ivy for three months, an arbitrary number she later increased to six months because after X years I couldn't expect Cally to change overnight, 'twas ever thus. When I ignored my ex-girlfriend's request, she launched a public relations war which I came to think of as Operation Archangel. As all effective propaganda campaigns must be, Operation Archangel was based on a simple idea: ***sherilyn hurt cally by breaking up with her, and the fact that sherilyn does not feel guilty for how much she hurt cally makes cally's pain even worse.*** There were variations on the theme, often interpolating how much I was hurting Cally by moving on before she was ready for me to move on, but the core was what Cally described me as her ***"my pain is deeper than yours" stunt.*** Just as an effective propaganda campaign must be simple, it must also be relentless, and Taos warned me after a few weeks that I was losing this PR war by not engaging: Cally was writing a half-dozen LiveJournal posts a day about how much I had hurt and betrayed her, while I wasn't saying much in public about the breakup, not even in my goddamn blog. Because we still talked every day per Best Friend regulations, Cally kept me informed of the many times she burst into tears in public because of how much I hurt her by breaking up with her, and she also told me whenever so-and-so agreed that I was being hurtful and mean by moving on before Cally was ready. She admitted in private that our breakup had been necessary, that it was a cord which needed to be cut—she had said as much to my mother, for all the difference it made—but in public, Cally made sure the loudest narrative was how much I had hurt her by breaking up with her and how betrayed she felt by my lack of guilt and by how I was trying to move on.

It was considered bad form to trash-talk someone's ex in public without that someone's consent, and in early June my bestie gave that consent by calling what became known as ***open season*** on me. Like so much of Cally's own venting it was initially aimed at a small group of people on LiveJournal, but the Velvet Underground Effect was at work. While ruminating about the low commercial potential of his new album *Ambient 4: On Land* in a 1982 interview with *Musician* magazine, Brian Eno said that Lou Reed had recently told Eno that ***the first velvet underground record sold 30,000 copies in the first five years***, meaning the acknowledged classic *The Velvet Underground and Nico* was a commercial failure; Eno then mused that ***i think everyone who bought one of those 30,000 copies started a band***, and in June 2005 people I had never wronged stopped feigning civility toward me in real life, complete with turning and walking away from me mid-sentence.

Cally refused accountability for the way I got hurt when she lashed out at me, 'twas ever thus. The closest she came was telling me during a chat in late June that she felt ***conflicted*** about how effective calling ***open season*** on me had been, because *it's good to feel that my friends love me so much, but it hurts that they're treating you almost as if you have no feelings of your own—which, yes, i've been guilty of too*. Only a few people knew of the ways Cally had treated me as if I had no feelings of my own over the years, especially those first several months when she would scream profanities and disrespect my gender and punish me for the sins of strangers and sometimes hit me. I also knew nobody would believe me if I brought it up now, and it would be spun as my latest and greatest betrayal of Cally. Instead, I tried to be amused by the way she made me the Courtney to her Kurt: Cally/Kurt was the tender soul whose crying can be heard all around the world, while Sherilyn/Courtney was the nasty bitch who is blamed for the good person's pain. Even worse, after breaking Cally/Kurt's heart, Sherilyn/Courtney has the nerve to try to move on with her life instead of crumpling into a ball of shame and guilt and disappearing the way Sluts/Angry Rock Chicks should.

I was struck upside the head in a figurative sense in late July when my bestie told me how frustrated she was about a mutual friend who was not snubbing Ivy. Worse, Cally was frustrated that she had tried to **do the right thing** by expressing her frustration about the lack of a snub in a calm and rational manner, but when the mutual friend continued to *not* snub Ivy, Cally was further annoyed that the result didn't seem any better **than if i'd thrown one of my usual temper tantrums**. Though it helped that she now explicitly framed them as her preferred alternative to doing the right thing, I was embarrassed that it had taken six years since the first time Cally had talked about her tantrums as just a thing she did for me to realize that Cally knew. She knew what she was doing. She always knew what she was doing. All those times Cally had screamed *fuck you!* and *i hate you!* and would storm out of the room when I tried to speak up for myself? She knew what she was doing. She knew it was wrong. She knew how much it was hurting me. She just kept doing it. I now knew that I was done with it all, and I would no longer abide her emotional abuse.

The week after I decided to forsake our Best Friendship and stop talking to Cally, Ivy and I went to see the last original 70mm print of Francis Ford Coppola's 1979 *Apocalypse Now* at the Castro. I had not cared for Coppola's 2001 remix *Apocalypse Now Redux*, so I was doubly glad this 70mm print of the original was still in circulation. Unfortunately, it had started to fade to magenta as aging 70mm prints are wont to do. It was already showing its age when Tira and I had seen it in the late 1990s, but I hadn't expected it to get this bad so soon. (You never do, do you?) Even as the print decayed before my eyes like a William Basinski loop, something new spoke to me every time I saw *Apocalypse Now*. Not only was the name Operation Archangel just sitting right there waiting to be repurposed for a truly pointless feud, I was struck by Kurtz's anecdote about the pile of arms and his realization about the genius required to do something like that, the will.

Cally did not have to put so much effort into alienating me from a significant swath of the community, did not have to put so much effort into scorching the Earth around me. Real talk: Cally was a cute cis woman whose physicality triggered the human instinct to protect small, defenseless-looking creatures, while my ridiculous, misshapen meat puppet put me in the Uncanny Valley for most people, that mental space where the human mind reacts with disgust and confusion to a simulation of a person which comes close to resembling the real thing but ain't ... quite ... right. I was not sympathetic or charismatic or easy to get to know, the *Rent Girl* squall was continuing to not help my reputation, I would never be how the trans community wanted to see themselves, and though I cleaned up nicely, my face was not pretty enough to compensate for my awkwardness. The humane thing would have been for Cally to step back and let me move on with my life after the breakup, but her default stance toward me had always been cruelty; her punishments had never fit my sins, not even on those less-common occasions when she was punishing me for my own sins and not the sins of strangers thousands of miles away.

All I could do now was hold my head up, walk unafraid, and try to keep Cally's darkness out of my own heart.

Bleeding Like a Polaroid

For all the doors which slammed in my face during Operation Archangel, there were some windows I could defenestrate through like my girl Jezebel. When a group called SF in Exile asked me to perform in their 2005 National Queer Arts Festival program called the Bad Date Show, I decided it was time to tell my Black Sheets story. You can't get any sexy scars without first getting a few sexy lacerations, and I also knew I was living out an important lesson from the best Monty Python movie, *Life of Brian*: when you're surrounded by an angry mob which is going to stone you as a blasphemer, you may as well dance in the dirt and sing *jehovah! jehovah!* What was I going to do, make things worse for myself?

All the same, I knew I was not and never would be Pamela Holm, so I kept my deniability plausible: I did not mention Black Sheets in my Bad Date Show remix, and I replaced the piercer with a bespectacled fantasy redhead whom I named after Marilyn Manson's *Mechanical Animals* song "Coma White," which also became the name of the story. Fictionalizing the forbidden fruit did not prevent the folks who forbade the fruit in the first

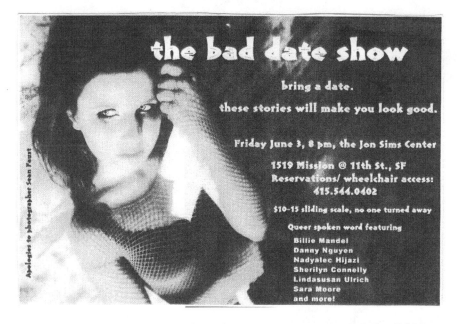

the bad date show

bring a date.

these stories will make you look good.

Friday June 3, 8 pm, the Jon Sims Center

1519 Mission @ 11th St., SF
Reservations/ wheelchair access:
415.544.0402

$10-15 sliding scale, no one turned away

Queer spoken word featuring

Billie Mandel
Danny Nguyen
Nadyalec Hijazi
Sherilyn Connelly
Lindasusan Ulrich
Sara Moore
and more!

Apologies to photographer Sean Feast

Flyer for the Bad Date Show at the Jon Sims Center, June 2005. Why did I keep being in shows with the word "bad" or "wicked" in the title? It's a mystery which may never be solved.

place from getting furious all over again, and during the resulting censure I was asked to leave the People's Literation Front of San Francisco for being an untrustworthy splitter. It also proved that requests both for permission and forgiveness would be denied, so no matter what my words may bring I was going to live by my own policies and sleep with a clear conscience. Besides, this kind of Onanistic fucking career was what it meant to be an Angry Rock Chick, *n'est-ce pas*? (I had recently acquired a bootleg of Courtney Love's Fillmore show from the previous October, and though it was no great shakes musically, I continued to be inspired by her between-song banter.) The Bad Date Show's host called "Coma White" one of my best pieces yet and asked if I would be interested in curating SF in Exile's show in the 2006 National Queer Arts Festival. (That was the thing about doing the work: it led to more work.) And while it didn't have the same indie cred as reading at City Lights, a few days after my 32nd birthday in 2005, I participated in an *I Do / I Don't: Queers on Marriage* reading at the Barnes & Noble near Pier 39.

There were many respectable queer events happening all over town as Pride Weekend approached after the Barnes & Noble reading, but Operation Archangel was putting me into a transgressive mood. When listening to Alice Cooper's "No More Mr. Nice Guy" on repeat wasn't enough,

I Do I Don't
(an anthology on queer marriage)

A benefit for Femina Potens   2pm FREE

June 19th

Raffle w/ Dildos

books

videos

& more

Featuring Charlie Anders, Sherilyn Connelly,
Carol Queen & Patrick Califia

reading @ Barnes & Noble
2550 Taylor @ Fisherman's Wharf

Flyer for the *I Do / I Don't: Queers on Marriage* reading at Barnes & Noble, June 2005. Oddly enough, this probably was *not* the first time there was a dildo raffle near Fisherman's Wharf.

on Thursday night I decided to go to the most transgressive place I could think of: the Power Exchange. Many people called it filthy and dangerous and filled with leering men jerking off at ugly crossdressers, which I noticed was the only context in which it was still acceptable to use the word *ugly* in the body-positive queer sex community. There was also a minor hubbub at the time surrounding the club's Lezbi Inn event since trans women were excluded, and my bestie kept me apprised of the good work she was doing to fight that policy, mainly writing a strongly worded email extolling the rights of trans women to go where they want to go and do what they want to do. But she had also made this trans woman a pariah for going where she wanted to go and doing what she wanted to do, so why not go to the pariah's sex club?

I went, I saw, I took notes, and I wondered how much cooler *i went, i saw, i took notes* would look in Latin. I fashioned my notes into a story which I read the following evening at a queer open mic called the Queer Open Mic, known informally as QOM. It was hosted by my friend Cindy in the Three Dollar Bill Café in the Lesbian, Gay, Bisexual & Transgender Center, itself known informally as the Legbutt. QOM at the Legbutt was part of the National Queer Arts Festival on this fine Pride Friday, and it was also my first time as Cindy's new co-host.

On the first Saturday of July, I received a forwarded email saying Annie Sprinkle needed emergency assistance with her website, and I was at Annie's house by noon. I ended up being no help whatsoever, but Annie could not have been more gracious. She paid me for my time and fed me, and as I sat at her kitchen table having lunch with Annie and her partner, I felt like I was receiving an organic and most yummy Communion. Annie and I were also aware that we were both featuring at a smut show called Sizzle at the performance space Femina Potens in August, and I would always consider the event flyer which gave me billing over Annie to be a misprint because there was no universe where I deserved billing over Annie Sprinkle. It had to have been a *puppet show and spinal tap* moment for her, but I speak for all my fellow puppet shows when I say, let us have this one, okay?

Before I left her house that day in July, she gave me a mountain of merch out of her closet, an instant Annie

QUEER OPEN MIC

come on over and hang out with sherilyn connelly and cindy emch for a hot and hilarious good time with poets, performers and true rox star action at the June Queer Open Mic!

7:30 sign up
8pm show
$3 Bill Cafe

1800 Market @ Octavia

threedollarbill

an official part of the National Queer Arts Festival

Flyer for the Queer Open Mic at the Three Dollar Bill Café at the LGBT Center, June 2005. It was truth in advertising, for Cindy and I did bring the hot hilariousness.

collection of books, videos such as her classic *Sluts and Goddesses* and a comic called *Legends of Porn, a Cartoon History #1: Annie Sprinkle*. Being a mature grownup who had recently turned 32 and who already owned *Sluts and Goddesses*, I read the comic as soon as I got home. A full page was devoted to a New York sex club in the early 1980s called the Hellfire Club, where Annie wrote that she could **experiment freely and not be judged, but actually be appreciated for my sleazy, slutty ways.** Not being judged for expressing desire? To, like, *not* get beaned with a measuring cup and slut-shamed for having a hickey? What a wonderful, alien concept! Annie went on to describe all manner of wide-open, occasionally Splosh-tacular mayhem, and ended the page with **some nights when i had a lot of sex, i would actually hallucinate, without any drugs—i often think that drugs are just the lazy person's sex.**

Now I knew my fate, or my destiny, or whatever the word was for *something i really really really wanna do*: to be Annie Sprinkle at the Hellfire Club. No matter what had been screamed at me for having a hickey, I wasn't slutty or sleazy, but I *wanted* to be. The big problem was that a lot of what Annie described involved cis men, which, *ewww*. Kissing Eldritch at Funkenstein back in October had confirmed that several years into my transition to female, I remained as unattracted to cis men as ever. Trans men, too; masculinity was just a turnoff across the board. But at least if I didn't like men after this, nobody could accuse me of knocking it before I tried it. And if I did find it within myself, my sex life would explode like a supernova. Nay, a Sprinklenova!

The bit about hallucinating without drugs sealed the deal. Though my first orgasm was profound, I was always more

Flyer for Sizzle at Femina Potens, August 2005. There is nothing of visual interest about this picture other than my name being above Annie Sprinkle's. Stop looking at it!

interested in recapturing the feeling of the first time I did mushrooms and then acid the summer I turned 16, that wonder of discovering whole new states of consciousness. The notion that sex could produce similar effects ... *dingdingding!* That. Right there. *That* was what I wanted on my slate. Transcendent, hallucinatory sluthood. To achieve what I had only been accused of. What I needed was a place to experiment, to find that part of myself, to let loose, to discover my own capabilities.

But I was in Gavin Newsom–era San Francisco, not Ed Koch–era New York, and there was no Hellfire Club. There was only the Power Exchange, so I returned ... and it was still just okay. I walked around some more, wrote about everything I saw, and I read some of it at Sizzle the next month with Annie in the audience. But these initial visits were more about acclimating to the environment of this new world, like Allegra Geller taking the time to feel the textures after the smooth interlacing from place to place. Or, to put it in monomyth terms, I was still refusing the call to adventure. It was not my time yet.

I'm Not an Angel, But at Least I'm a Girl

Which is not to say I wasn't seeking out adventure, and in the latter half of 2005 I felt a sense of momentum which I'd never thought possible, propelled by escaping from my bestie. I danced without fear of ever again getting in trouble for wanting to dance in the first place, I had sex in locations where one is not generally supposed to have sex—including the NakedSword Tape Library, which ticked a lot of my pleasure boxes— and I did fun, non-addictive drugs in interesting places with friendly people. When I saw Negativland at the Great American Music Hall I ran into *Dee Dee TV* producer Dee Dee Russell, who told me that she and many other Access SF producers were still fans of *kittypr0n* and talked to each other about it, which was the highest praise I could imagine for my silly little cat show. I met Durtro in person while I was on a whirlwind tour of the Pacific Northwest with Jennifer Blowdryer and Alvin Orloff for Jennifer's new nonfiction anthology *Good Advice for Trendy Young People of All Ages*, and I bonded from afar with the bulkiest Kit Kat Girl during the Shotgun Players' production of *Cabaret* at the Ashby Stage in Berkeley.

Because the opportunity arose, I auditioned for a new network procedural called *The Evidence,* just a few lines as a transgender sex worker named Desiree who referred to herself in the third person because of course she did. The cis male they cast as Desiree did a fine job, and he didn't tower over the show's lead actors the way I would have. I'm not saying my height is the only reason I did not get the part; I did not get the part because I'm not good at acting and because the camera does not love me, and I wouldn't have been surprised to learn that my audition was so bad it was included in the gag reel at the casting agency's holiday party. My only regret about not getting the part was that the scene was filmed in front of the worker-owned North Beach peepshow the Lusty Lady, and the main source of illumination was the Lusty Lady's red neon sign. It's a brief scene, but it looks damn good, and I would have looked damn good in it.

I auditioned for *The Evidence* because I was full of unearned confidence, which is the only kind of confidence that makes interesting things happen. It also means the potential for failure, and I returned to Neva Chonin's 2004 interview with Courtney Love which focused on the commercial failure of *America's Sweetheart* as well as her personal tribulations.

> She lights another cigarette. "I've had tons of failure; failed marriage No. 1, failed marriage No. 2, failed family life. But I've never had a professional failure like this. Ouch! But I've not partaken of the bitter pill yet. This is America. I get to have a third act. I get to come back."

Exactly. And my own first act was just starting.

I had collected a number of Hole VHS tapes over the years, and I now found myself returning to three shows in particular: the 1995 MTV *Unplugged* episode, their professionally-filmed set at Perth's Big Day Out in January 1999, and most crucially, a bootleg video of the Cow Palace show I'd attended in March 1999. On an aesthetic level I was pleased to be reminded that I'd been doing variations on Courtney's looks all along, like the black dress with the lace sleeves over the black tights and boots in *Unplugged*—oh, the way she gripped onto the microphone stand for dear life during "Old Age," her left leg stretched behind her for support like I had done a million times when I'd had to crouch like a slam poet at open mics to compensate for a too-short microphone stand!—or the black leather pants and sheer top that she wore at the Cow Palace show while she was arguably at her thinnest, which was similar to my own frequent ensemble of boots and shiny black PVC pants with a sheer fishnet top over a black sports bra. Watching the Hole videos in 2005 after I turned 32, I did the math and was relieved to find that Courtney had been 31 when she shot *Unplugged* in 1995, and thus was 35 at the Cow Palace show in 1999, which meant nobody could accuse me of youth fetishism. Besides, these images were aspirational, and I knew I would never be a categorical fox like Hole bassist Melissa Auf der Maur, so I kept my aspirations achievable.

At 32 I was the thinnest I'd ever been, and seven years on estrogen and spironolactone had redistributed the still-ample remaining fat into a more appropriate silhouette, and you could see my ribs and my clavicles— hot damn, my clavicles were visible, just like Venus Xtravaganza's were in the interview segments in her bedroom in *Paris Is Burning*!—but my skeleton would never, ever get smaller. So I worked with what I had, and in my most reliable uniform of shiny black PVC pants and a black chemise under my Formula X jacket I started going to Divas because I could and because *because i could* continued to be the best reason to do anything. I had hung out at the Lexington during the Arrangements, and I still often went there when I had time to kill before something at the Dark Room, but I never felt at home at the Lex the way I did at Divas. The first floor of Divas got packed on weekend nights, a touristy crowd full of curious straight cis people who seldom traveled upstairs, while the third-floor dancefloor tended to be occupied by the more dedicated crowd, trans women and weekend crossdressers and all possible derivations thereof. My people! The DJ's steady stream of bangers also helped to make the third floor of Divas one of the better-kept club secrets in town, our own Revolution Ballroom where we shone like rainbows in the dark. The walls were mirrored, and some of the regulars at Divas lived for gazing across the dimly-lit room as they danced with the disco ball and laser lights above them and the fog machine occasionally obscuring their ankles. That had been me at the Stud back in the day, and I was glad Divas could serve that purpose for others now because we deserved at least that much, but I was no longer as much of a mirror-gazer. I had enough faith in the persistence of my hotness to know that even when I wasn't looking, my beautiful ghost was always there.

Sometimes I would hang out in front near the Motherlode Girls, and I also walked the Circuit just to see the cars slowing down and checking me out: Post to Larkin, Larkin to Sutter, Sutter to Polk, and Polk back to Post. Motorcycles gathered outside the R Bar on Sutter near Polk, and though I never went inside the R Bar, I always enjoyed hearing the motorcycle engines roar like the Bombers outside Torchie's in *Streets of Fire*. I had recently re-watched Walter Hill's clusterfuck, and if anything, *Enterprise Incidents* undersold the film to 11-year-old Sherilyn. That magazine's coverage of *Streets of Fire* did not hint at the matter-of-fact androgyny of French dancer Marine Jahan, who got a lot of press in 1983 when she announced to the world that she had been Jennifer Beals' body double for much of Adrian Lyne's *Flashdance*. It's Jahan in a bad wig doing most of the work, and the film makes little effort to hide her. (The scene with the dancing traffic cop? That's Jahan, not Beals.) The waifish, accented Jahan had requested screen credit in *Flashdance* in the form of the unassuming *special thanks to marine jahan* but did not receive any credit at all—though the dog in the film received credit because dogs were more respected in 1980s Hollywood than immigrant women with funny accents who violated the gender binary. Director Lyne and the movie studio Paramount asked Jahan to please keep it to herself that she was the one making Beals look so good, and while neither *Flashdance* nor *Streets of Fire* are good, *Fire* is bad in a much better way. Lyne directs *Flashdance* as pure male gaze, and its script by future *Showgirls* scribe Joe Eszterhas wants you to know that the men behind *Flashdance* fuck women and women only, while *Streets of Fire* is far more fluid.

Fire was supposed to be Jahan's big breakthrough since she was going to have a speaking role—just two words, *back up!*, but an improvement over no words—and her name was going to be in the credits. While she did get screen credit, *Fire* did nothing for her career. If her words were filmed they were cut, and what's left is her dancing to a couple of Blasters tunes at the biker bar Torchie's—not to be confused with the country bar Torchy's from Hill's previous film *48 Hrs.*, though neither scene was shot at 2263 Mission. (Also, *Flashdance* is full of glass blocks and neon though it was not production-designed by John Vallone, because it was the early 1980s and that was how we liked it.) *Fire's* costume designer Marilyn Vance put Jahan in a fishnet bodystocking with backseams and a short black skirt and a short black top and Jahan's natural hair is short and boyish and let's shame the devil: the 25-year-old cis woman is made up to look like a 14-year-old of indeterminate gender. That is not a criticism and I am not saying her genderqueerness isn't hot, because I will swear on a stack of Bibles that the whisper-thin Marine Jahan is super-hot in *Streets of Fire*, and then swear on a different stack of Bibles that for as much as I imprinted on Diane Lane's look and energy as Ellen Aim, if we're trying to get a sense of how I envisioned myself deep down, of the soul operating this body which got cramped and misshapen in the womb in spite of being the last of four, count 'em, four fetuses gestated to term within said womb, which is to say that if you plugged me into the Matrix the residual self-image which materialized would be a scruffy gamine indistinguishable from Marine Jahan in *Streets of Fire*.

Because the universe is a closed system where lines always converge, when reading up on *Fire* in 2005 I discovered that Snoopy's dancing in *It's Flashbeagle, Charlie Brown* was rotoscoped footage of Jahan. It made perfect sense to me that nobody saw Jahan, only the grotesquerie projected over her, because I was only now beginning to understand how much scarier and unsettling my simplest emotions were to humans after those emotions were distorted and amplified on their way out of this ridiculous, misshapen meat puppet. This disconnect made me difficult to relate to, which was why Operation Archangel was so effective. My own mother casually dehumanized me in 1999 because of the two very bad and wrong things I did, so it was dead simple for friends and acquaintances to write me off with no follow-up questions after being told *ad nauseum* in 2005 that I was a bad person who had hurt a good person. My sins were almost as unforgivable as telling the world that you were Jennifer Beals' body double after being told to keep it to yourself, Frenchie, and that Marine Jahan had gotten in trouble for just talking about her experiences in front of the camera made me empathize with her all the more. It sucked for both of us, but it was nice to know I wasn't the only alien woman who got a raw deal for telling her story.

Marine Jahan is onscreen for a little under 90 non-consecutive seconds in *Streets of Fire*, while the second-billed Diane Lane gets far more time. For the opening number "Nowhere Fast," in which Lane lip-syncs to Laurie Sargent's voice over a deliciously overcooked track from "Total Eclipse of the Heart" producer Jim Steinman, Marilyn Vance put Lane into a red-and-black one-shouldered number which may be the sexiest outfit ever committed to celluloid as of 1984. To get the one negative out of the way, I don't care for the cleavage because I've never found breasts attractive. (They were such a non-issue to me as a teenager that I didn't realize Tira was considered buxom for her age until someone pointed it out to me after she and I became a couple.) But I do love how the harsh colors and sharp angles of Vance's outfit for Lane suggest not sex but violence, and for the sake of this argument we will pretend that sex and violence are two different things, what with the red leggings going down to Lane's ankles behind a black skirt panel which is practically a butcher's apron, and then there's the full black sleeve on her left arm and the bare right shoulder and the long leather glove on that right arm with shorter black Lux Interior–type PVC fingerless gloves on both hands, not to mention the thick black choker, and the whole thing is like Vance saw the Black Ghoul's dress in A.C. Stephen's 1965 no-budget *Orgy of the Dead* and said **challenge accepted!**

Vance's red-and-black outfit is also designed to be practical because Lane wears it for the first hour, and she spends a fair amount of that time running while also wearing a high-collared jacket which protects her against the elements and hides the cleavage and other skin which was revealed during "Nowhere Fast." Walter Hill passes up many opportunities to ogle the 18-year-old Lane, who wears that high-collared jacket during a scene in which a struggling songwriter played by Elizabeth Daily is asking Ellen about her creative process, and to confirm, it is a scene in which two women are talking to each other and they are not talking about a man, and thus *Streets of Fire* passes the Bechdel Test almost despite itself. Ellen is a hateful jerk in the scene because almost every character in *Fire*'s baffling script is written to be a hateful jerk, and Diane Lane herself seems to hate being in this stupid movie. This makes Ellen seem like a real person and an evolution of Lane's role as the cranky 15-year-old rocker Corrinne Burns in one of Ivy's favorite movies, Lou Adler's low-budget, R-rated 1982

Ladies and Gentlemen, the Fabulous Stains. Lane's youthful *Stains* and *Fire* abrasiveness would be sanded away in 1987 for Ben Bolt's medium-budget, R-rated *The Big Town*, a boys' power fantasy in which Lane plays an under-written and often underdressed plot device designed fill the spank-bank of straight male viewers between the ages of 18 and 34, and ugh, I hate *The Big Town* so much.

The big-budget, PG-rated *Streets of Fire* is subtitled *A Rock and Roll Fable,* and director Walter Hill and cinematographer Andrew Laszlo shoot the opening number as an Ellen Aim and the Attackers rock concert. Though Ellen tends to be in the frame because she's the singer, she is only one of many shiny objects, and Hill and Laszlo are less interested in glam-orizing her and more interested in glamorizing the glass blocks and neon squiggles of John Vallone's production design as well as Marc Brickman's excellent stage lighting. They succeed, and with "Nowhere Fast" the fiction film *Streets of Fire* picks up where the Band performing "The Weight" with the Staple Singers in the nonfiction film *The Last Waltz* left off in terms of storyboarding, lighting, and shooting rock performances with the same care as feature films. For the myriad ways *Streets of Fire* trips over its own feet, the lighting and cinematography in those first six minutes are so effec-tive it almost compensates for how the film spends the rest of its running time bloodying its nose.

Lane is never standing still during "Nowhere Fast" but also never come-hitherish or sex-kitteny, never smiling or otherwise signaling to the boys that she wants them to fuck her, and a film not pandering to the straight male gaze is borderline queer for 1984. *Flashdance* became the third highest-grossing film of 1983 because Adrian Lyne filmed Jennifer Beals and/or Marine Jahan in ways designed to give Lyne and his screen-writer Eszterhas boners, after all, while the far queerer field which the box-office bomb *Streets of Fire* is playing on becomes clearer in the moment when Willem Dafoe's Bombers leader Raven decides to kidnap Ellen. She is dancing in a frenetically-edited manner during the song's outro which appears neither choreographed nor intended to be teasing or seductive but instead looks like Diane Lane letting herself go and it is awesome, make no mistake, and it's more awesome when she starts to pump her fist in a man-ner which is as aggressive as Mavis Staples' clapping during "The Weight" is joyful and Lane's pumping fist is intercut with a light shining on Dafoe's face for the first time as his eyes start to widen, and once again let's shame the devil: Ellen is making a gesture which suggests the act of fisting, which is why Raven decides to kidnap her and sets the film's Jahan-thin story into motion. Ellen's gesture is not how fisting works in real life, but we're talking about super-basic symbolism, real Kuleshov Effect 101 stuff. But for all its crudity it is still too mindful for the film's mindless script, and it feels instead like it was discovered in post-production by one of the four, count 'em, four credited editors.

Ah, good ol' *Streets of Fire*. Ever since I was 11, it was the gift that kept on giving.

Some nights when I was walking the Post-Larkin-Sutter-Polk Circuit, I would stop and lean against the Larkin-facing wall next to the window of the old Motherlode location that I used to be too afraid to enter, full-on posing with one foot on the wall and feeling like it was Possum Day and I was the only market girl left standing. Beyond my literal posing, I knew I was a *poseur* to an extent with my comfort and privilege as an employed taxpayer with a massive student loan debt and a 401K and a flawless voting record, and I knew the more respectable trans women in town tended to consider Divas and this neighborhood and everything it represented as a ghetto to be risen above. In her 2004 *Chronicle* interview, the San Francisco-born Courtney Love had referred to rocking the Fillmore as her **birthright**, and being here now in this trans ghetto while this *here* still existed to be in, this was the Fresno-born Sherilyn Connelly's birthright as much as rocking the Fillmore had been Courtney's. Use it or lose it!

Using it lest I lose it was also how I felt about my showbiz career, which continued to zag in unexpected but wonderful directions, like when Mikl-Em and I were among the celebrity judges for *The Gong Show Live* at the Dark Room. Thanks to Phred I was a proud owner of a bootleg of Chuck Barris' 1980 *The Gong Show Movie*, and I was thrilled to get to be a judge on multiple nights and to get to bang the gong. Though I was a little bummed that nobody got it on by doing a Rip Taylor, my friends and fellow Dark Room staffers Rhiannon and Alexia stepped up as the Popsicle Twins, and getting roasted by Denzil Meyers as the Unknown Comic may well have been the greatest moment of my showbiz life.

Elsewhere in showbiz, Madonna released a fine, ABBA-sampling single in late 2005 called "Hung Up." The first version I heard was the remix "Hung Up (SDP Extended Dub)," and it floored me. After about two minutes the percussion and most of the treble disappears and the main riff is buried deep in the mix, then re-emerges over the next 30 seconds before the percussion returns. I would later learn it was a common techno technique called **pass filtering**, but the first time I heard it through headphones while sitting at my desk at NakedSword, my amygdala sparked to life and I was walking down the Maritime stairs to Shrine of Lilith, the music muffled at street level, but becoming louder and clearer as I descended. Listening to "Hung Up (SDP Extended Dub)" in 2005 and 2006 never failed to bring back that sense of adventure and excitement which poor awkward Babygoth Sherilyn had discovered back in 1999. But now, I felt ready for it.

It helped that I was already in a state of euphoria when "Hung Up

(SDP Extended Dub)" dropped because of a cis woman named Anais. She had seen me at a few shows, I had seen her, and we both liked what we saw. Our first date was Jeremy Blake's *Winchester Trilogy* at the San Francisco Museum of Modern Art the Thursday before the 2005 Folsom Street Fair, and our second date was a more impromptu affair when we ran into each other the following evening at a Folsom Friday event. After making a public spectacle at Studio Z, Anais suggested we return to the Black Light District, where we spent the night fucking and biting and laughing and scratching and clawing like a feral pair of sexual endorphin addicts who had met their match, and if I wasn't a pheromone junkie before I sure was now, and I fell deeply and madly in love in a way I never had before.

I was supposed to speak on a panel at a convention on Saturday afternoon, something having to do with censorship as it related to my job at NakedSword, but I played hooky. If it had been a workday, I would have called in sick. There were a lot of interesting things happening in San Francisco, including the second annual Love Parade down Market, which was coincidental to the dozens of Folsom-related kink events (and it also guaranteed that since the major traffic arteries Folsom and Market were both closed off, driving anywhere east of Twin Peaks would be a nightmare). But nothing was as important as the time Anais and I were spending together, this extended moment of tenderness and affection. I didn't want to be apart from her, not ever, and my heart broke a little when she left early in the afternoon.

As planned, Ivy and I went to the Folsom Street Fair together on Sunday, and I felt uncomfortable the entire time. Though I'd done well for myself that weekend, being *with* someone at the Fair didn't feel right. I wanted to be a free agent, to take things as they came, be open to any possibilities. To be, in a word, a slut. I hated feeling so … *committed* to somebody else, even somebody like Ivy who cared for me so much, and so gently. Ivy and I didn't say much of anything on the Muni ride back to the Black Light District, and when we arrived, I broke the silence by breaking Ivy's heart. She had such grand hopes and ambitions for us, and she was certain she was meant to be with me and to show me so much—and she may have been right, but all I knew in that moment was that I couldn't continue to be with her, that as the Diane Lane oeuvre went Ivy was *Ladies and Gentlemen, the Fabulous Stains* and I was *Streets of Fire* and though I was grateful neither of us were *The Big Town* because I hate that movie so much I still had to call the whole thing off. Like all my breakups it got messier than it needed to be because I always did these things in the worst way possible, and as the pure mother-of-pearl bone tumbled out of my mouth and into the water, many people who had remained sympathetic during Operation Archangel stopped talking to me. But I didn't care that I was offending in every way because I was falling for Anais more than I'd thought possible, becoming delirious with happiness in those last few months of the year, as if Maxwell's Demon were at the door and keeping me awash in low entropy. I knew this energy which Anais and I created, this *us,* could end tomorrow. I cherished every minute, and the final night of 2005 was as loving and warm as the final night of 2004 had been resentful and alienating.

6

The Lightning
of Early May

A Walking Study in Demonology

As 2006 progressed, Anais and I had our first fights, spats, and vehement disagreements. We were still in love, I was sure of that, but our entropy was increasing. She wanted to spend more time away from me, and my own restlessness was returning. We had known from the start just how this would end, we were always clear that we were not going to be monogamous and that we would keep things open to new possibilities, but my old fear became overwhelming, and on the first Tuesday of May I went to Divas with intention. I arrived at a quarter to midnight, and the pickings were slim: many cis men and a few Motherlode Girls. Nothing for me, and that was okay. It was all about patience, and I found the glow of the purple neon **The Motherlode** sign behind the bar to be comforting, a homefire that was always burning.

A cis woman walked in at half past midnight and ordered two drinks, though she didn't seem to be meeting anyone. She flirted with a Motherlode Girl to no avail, and when she was alone a few minutes later, I approached and told her the only reason I wasn't offering to buy her a drink was that she already had two. (Math is power!) With a broad smile, she patted the stool next to her. She told me her name was Ryder and that she was looking to pick up a trans woman, I told her my name was Sherilyn and that I was looking to pick up a cis woman, and we established that we were both in open relationships, our semantics going from general to specific for both her (**partner, wife, rusty**) and me (*partner, girlfriend, anais*). Ryder said Rusty knew she was out cruising, and I was vague about what Anais knew. We told each other about ourselves, occasionally interrupting to gush about how hot we found the other, one hand always on the other's leg or waist. Ryder was in her late twenties, she was currently appearing in

133

the second-most-rented porn movie at Good Vibrations after *Pirates*, and she finally asked the question which had been implied from the start but needed to be spoken aloud: ***will you spend the night with me?***

I wasn't sure if waking up next to a porn star in a Tenderloin-adjacent hotel was worthy of getting beaned with a measuring cup and slut-shamed, but as I awoke next to Ryder the following morning, I figured it had to be, right? This was my first one-night stand, and I wondered if the right thing to do would be to leave before she woke up and realized what a terrible mistake she'd made. Instead, when Ryder opened her eyes a few minutes later, she smiled and pulled me close. So, this was not a one-night stand, but for sure it was my first real Walk of Shame! Just out of the Monarch Hotel at Geary and Polk and around the corner to the 24-hour garage where I'd parked my Neon, but still, it was happening! It was a genuine Walk of Shame, and I could not have been prouder. I had woken up in my makeup many times over the years, but I had never felt so used up as I did now after my night with Ryder, who had been eager to delve into her bag of toys straight from the Mantle Clinic. Ryder was not a selfish partner, however, and she showed me how to trigger the best toy of all, her gushing orgasm which was the money shot of the porn movie which I hadn't known existed 12 hours earlier.

We went out for sushi the following Saturday, then returned to the Black Light District and watched a few episodes of *Twin Peaks* before continuing what we'd started at the Monarch. Ryder left at 11:00 a.m. on Sunday, and at half past noon I was picked up by my friend Karla LaVey. I got to know her because her show *Satanic Church Radio* used to follow *Rush Hour on the Event Horizon,* and though *Rush Hour*

Flyer for Karla LaVey's Devil's Valentine Ball at the Edinburgh Castle, February 2006. Just like all dress codes should include "vampiric," all tickets should be $6.66.

ended in January 2006 when Pirate Cat Radio moved out of the Dark Room, we kept in touch. I read at her annual Devil's Valentine Ball at the Edinburgh Castle, and more recently at her Walpurgisnacht event, which turned into an unexpected career highlight when I shared the stage with the world's most famous necrophile, Karen Greenlee. And now on this fine May Sunday, Karla and I went to the Yerba Buena Center for the Arts to see the Inbal Pinto Dance Company's production of *Oyster.*

Something I loved about working at NakedSword was that since our business was gay porn and our philosophy was to enjoy the things you enjoy without judgment, most anything went in terms of individual workspace. So, as you do when you're an employed taxpayer with a massive student loan debt and a 401K and a flawless voting record, I put up posters for Cronenberg's *Crash,* Hole's *Celebrity Skin*, and David Lynch's *Twin Peaks Fire Walk with Me* as well as various club flyers and posters for a few Manson records. It was also a vision board for aspirational images such as Kelly Clarkson on the cover of the January/February 2006 *Blender* and Courtney on the February 1997 *Film Threat.* But the most perfectly perverse perk of my position was that our public-facing parent company Cubik Media had many non-porn clients, and since one of the non-porn clients I worked with was the fancy-pants organization San Francisco Performances, I got free tickets to many of their fancy-pants and thus hella-expensive events.

The author's workspace at NakedSword, July 2006. That's a black light bulb in the foreground, and there's a *Velvet Goldmine* ad if you know where to look.

This was how during what we came to think of as our Week of Artfaggery in February 2006, Anais and I were able to see Meredith Monk performing *Impermanence* at the Yerba Buena and the best two-thirds of Godfrey Reggio's *Qatsi* trilogy with Philip Glass playing the score live at Davies Symphony Hall. *Koyaanisqatsi* was on Friday, my personal favorite *Naqoyqatsi* was on Sunday, and we gave Saturday a miss for obvious reasons. (Ya burnt, *Powaqqatsi*!) After *Naqoyqatsi*, Anais and I went to the Dark Room to catch the tail end of Bad Movie Night, where the feature was Bud Townsend's 1976 porn-musical *Alice in Wonderland*. One of the *Alice* hosts was my friend Anomaly, a proud sex worker and Annie Sprinkle–style slut and activist. She and I would act together in the Dark Room's annual *Twilight Zone Live* series a few months later, and I was also honored to read at the afterparty for Anomaly's fourth annual Paul Reubens Day. Like SantaCon without all the bros, on Paul Reubens Day people dressed up as Pee-Wee Herman or Herman-universe characters and rampaged through San Francisco to commemorate what by 2006 was the 15th anniversary of Reubens' unfair arrest for masturbating in the South Trail Cinema (formerly a Jerry Lewis Cinema!) in Florida during a triple feature of *Nancy Nurse*, *Catalina Five-O Tiger Shark*, and *Turn Up the Heat*. According to *Koyaanisqatsi*'s opening titles the k-word meant **life out of balance**, but I rather thought that experiencing the high art of Philip Glass and the low filth of a porn desecration of classic literature getting heckled on the same night—not to mention getting to **scream real loud** in public with a group of Wees because someone said the secret word on Paul Reubens Day—was evidence of a life that was *in* balance.

Oyster at the Yerba Buena in May was as dark and surreal and unsettling as I had hoped it would be, and the lead dancer reminded me of Daryl Hannah as Pris in her death scene in *Blade Runner*: ratty blonde hair with pale makeup heavy on the rouge, though without the signature black band across her eyes. Karla and I parted company afterward, and I walked from the Yerba Buena to a NakedSword colleague's rooftop party on Howard Street, overlooking the How Weird Street Faire. Ryder was at the party because San Francisco is a closed system where lines always converge, and we determined that we had been in the same room at the same time for past events as far back as Pink Saturday in 2002. A few of my NakedSword colleagues now pulled me aside at the 2006 How Weird party because they knew and liked Anais, and they were concerned that this woman I was getting gooey with was not Anais. Understandable, since I also knew and liked Anais. I loved her, in fact! But Anais was elsewhere doing her own thing, and she would have been elsewhere doing her own thing even if I had not been here with Ryder doing my own thing.

Ryder's wife Rusty was at the party, and she regaled me with their

Flyer for Paul Reubens Day IV and the afterparty at the Dark Room, July 2006. As career highlights go, being listed along with "pornography" is one of them.

origin story: Ryder was stripping in a sex show in 2000 while Rusty was fucking somebody on stage, their eyes met from across the room, and the rest was romantic history. They were proud of their ability to communicate with each other, to be open about who they were and what they wanted, and Rusty was happy to meet me, this person that Ryder was currently wanting. After Rusty relocated to a party at the SF Eagle on Harrison, Ryder and

I took a cab back to her house. She conveniently lived within stumbling distance of the Dark Room, and Ryder and I fucked until it was time for me to stumble to the Dark Room and be on mic for Roger Christian's *Battlefield Earth*. Bad Movie Night had been developing a not-good reputation among cinephiles, one of whom lamented to me that it *just makes us all that much more stupid*. He meant it as an insult, but I will always be flattered if you ask if I'm supposed to be a vampire, so *Making Us All That Much More Stupid* became Bad Movie Night's new ... um ... slogan? Motto? Tagline? Synecdoche? Epitaph? (One of those big words that means, like, another thing? I dunno, math is hard!) So this was my second Walk of Shame in a week, and my destination was a public performance in a show which lowered our collective I.Q. while I reeked of daytime sex! Yeah yeah yeah, now I'd really made it.

One of the most common themes in the queer lit scene in those days was how much cooler San Francisco used to be, that in spite of the AIDS epidemic the City peaked as a queer fuckorama in the early to mid–1990s, and Michelle Tea's *Valencia* was considered the defining memoir of those last days of true hedonism. That may well have been the case, but San Francisco in the mid–2000s was doing all right by me—even when, three and a half weeks and a half-dozen dates after we met, I got an email from Ryder saying she had to go away, so sorry, thanks for everything, goodbye.

Incept Date: 22 Sept. 2006

Anais and I observed our one-year anniversary on Thursday, September 21. Our first date had been on September 22, but we invoked the queer right to floating holidays and decided to celebrate our anniversary on the Thursday before the Folsom Street Fair, no matter what day it was calendarwise. We had been so focused on Thursday, we didn't make plans for Folsom Friday. I was still co-hosting QOM at the Legbutt with Cindy; sometimes Anais attended and sometimes she didn't, and she never decided until that afternoon. Around three on Folsom Friday, Anais told me she had something better to do that night.

After QOM, I decided to go to the Power Exchange. I needed to be somewhere which would provide enough external stimuli that I would be less inclined to ruminate about what might be happening elsewhere, and what's more, I still wanted to be Annie Sprinkle at the Hellfire Club. Being with Anais had diverted me from that mission, and it was the most wonderful way to be diverted. Those first few months with her had been the happiest time of my life by an order of magnitude, but Anais now had better things to do, and it was my responsibility to find my own better things.

Studying myself in the mirror of the well-lit, gender-neutral restroom on the ground floor of the Power Exchange that night, I took out my eye shadow and made a dark band across my eyes from temple to temple. With my blonde bangs edging close to my eyebrows, the makeup job resembled Daryl Hannah's most iconic look as Pris in *Blade Runner*. That was the intention, anyway. I topped it off with a pair of black kitty ears which I'd often worn in the past while clubbing or at readings. I liked the way they looked, and now more than ever the secret of becoming a star was knowing how to behave like one, and if stardom doesn't involve kitty ears, then what was even the point of this whole exercise?

I walked downstairs to the Dungeon, where I promptly was invited into the Cage by a transvestite named Robin. The consensus among the regulars was that I belonged, that I was a Local and not a Tourist, and Robin enjoyed pimping me out: ***isn't she fuckable? look at those legs, and that face.*** Some people meowed at me, which is to be expected when wearing kitty ears, and a few people said I looked like ***that one girl in blade runner.*** Mission accomplished! Robin introduced me to a cis man named Al, warning me that he ***wasn't much to look at*** but knew his way around a flogger. Robin and Al were old friends who were constantly dissing each other about their looks, and I felt at ease with both of them. Al had a terrific sense of humor, and as Robin had promised, a way with all manner of flogging and slamming and slapping and stinging equipment, the majority of which he brought along in his seemingly bottomless toybag. Any BDSM enthusiast worth their salt knew the average hardware store contained the required equipment, and Al demonstrated that one didn't have to bother with a higher-end store such as Good Vibrations for all of one's vibratory needs. He was always showing off the latest humming or paddling device he'd found at a dollar store or Walgreens, and being a generous sort, he happily gave permission to use his toys to anyone who asked.

I wrote in my notebook a lot, and people often interrupted me to ask if I was writing a book about the Power Exchange. I wasn't, not yet. Nor was I quite ready to start with the sluttery. I was processing my feelings about how Anais and I were slingshotting away from each other like rogue planets, and as I sat writing, a man watched me from outside the Cage. Though I wasn't doing anything exciting, there was always the possibility that I might set the notebook aside and start playing with myself, or someone would come over and we'd fuck, or maybe I'd find the spectator irresistible and drop everything to suck his dick. He'd paid a fair chunk of change to get in, and he was going to keep a positive attitude.

The important thing to me was that he paid, and I did not. I was struck by the power, the utter brilliance of playing in such an environment and having it funded by someone else. Considering the tradeoff was the presence of the men, it wasn't so bad. The sometimes-exorbitant cover charge they paid allowed this place to exist, this place where the elderly bearded crossdresser wearing a teddy, fishnets, and a rose choker walking around that evening could do so safely. Some of the Tourists looked as though they would beat the shit out of someone like that beyond this block of Otis, but if the Tourists had anything to say they kept it to themselves. Their self-conscious machismo was neutered on the off chance of seeing some live fucking or getting their dick sucked, and I loved it. But aside from experimenting a bit with a handheld massager, I didn't play on that first Folsom Friday night. I flirted a little with one of the few other trans women—it was mostly transvestites or crossdressers, and trans women like me were rare—but I didn't expect or even want anything to come of it. The evening was about being *elsewhere*, and the Power Exchange was the best possible elsewhere.

I returned the following Thursday, since it continued to be a welcome distraction from the painful places my brain was taking me, especially after Anais and I had walked around the Folsom Street Fair watching other people enjoy themselves. I played with Al on the St. Andrew's Cross, my hands lightly bound in leopard-print cuffs, him flogging me slightly and not so slightly with his array of devices. This lead indirectly to me sitting on the red couch, Al's vibrating massage chair underneath me and a neck massager thingy on my shoulders. Robin came and went, returning with stories both of sucking dick and of the ones that got away. I'd been in a dry spell since Ryder went away, and what I wanted was an anonymous hookup with a cis woman. Robin told me such things were rare but not unheard of; most of the cis women who visited were part of a couple, and they kept close to their companion. A major component of the Power Exchange's reputation was as A Place Where Women Should Not Tread Alone, Or Ever. A respectable sex columnist for the *San Francisco Chronicle* implied that an unescorted cis female would get descended upon the moment she walked through the front door, provided she made it past the roving rape-gangs which prowled around outside—and if the woman *did* make it inside, she would be that much easier to catch, since the floors were allegedly stickier than a movie theater after an all-syrup showing of *The Rocky Horror Picture Show*. The danger of the Power Exchange was considered unquestionable truth by many people who never set foot inside, and while I had no patience for online discussions, Robin was active in forums such as the trendy Tribe. net. She told me that whenever she said anything positive about the Power Exchange, or just suggested that maybe it wasn't the dirtiest, most dangerous place ever, she got flamed to a crisp by the guardians of San Francisco's sexual hierarchy.

The place was hopping after midnight, with wankers and Towelboys and Tourists on the outside of the Cage and us on the inside. Robin flirted with passersby, and Al waited more patiently for them to come to him. I hovered at the entrance of the Cage near Robin, my fingers interlaced through the links of fence, posing in kitty ears and full Pris makeup, flirting with the occasional passing cis woman, soaking it all in. This was neat! I felt safe and comfortable and desired, and this was surely where my sluthood would blossom, my own Hellfire Club.

After hanging out for a while in the Cage with Al and Robin, I ventured beyond the Porn Room into the far end of the Dungeon. To the left were actual room-rooms, with walls and doors and everything, unlike the Red, Blue, and Frankenstein Rooms-In-Name-Only. The Cow Room was so called for the cow patterns on the wall, and the door had a large window where there was usually a crowd of men watching whatever action was transpiring. Judging from how often there was a crowd, there was either a lot of action or the men liked bovine patterns. To the right of the Cow Room was the Undersea Room, its brick walls painted light blue with fish and seashell decorations, the black lights adding an extra glow to the oceanic theme which was only slightly undercut by the presence of a medical table. Beyond the Cow and Undersea Rooms was the women's restroom, where at any given time there would be a few T-girls preening in the mirror, and sometimes I was one of them. (There wasn't a men's room in the Dungeon, because they could bloody well go back upstairs.) The restroom door faced the Alley, with couches and stools often occupied by Motherlode Girls looking to pick up Tourists. I sat there occasionally, both to be on display and to keep an eye out for a man with whom I could ... well, I wasn't sure what, exactly. Blow him, right? That seemed to be the thing to do, and if I were going to do it I ought to go ahead and do it so it would be done and I could say I did the thing, but it had to be the right guy. If I didn't find him aesthetically appealing on some level it would be like trying to put the north poles of two magnets together, and I'd been to enough NakedSword parties full of sweaty, underclothed men to know that their least offensive smells were a major turnoff. I was a pheromone junkie, but only with women, be they cis or trans. Cis male funk was intolerable across the board.

There were many good reasons for me to have stayed home the following Thursday, but as I finished my Pris makeup and put on my kitty ears in the Power Exchange's ground-floor restroom, I did what countless peroxide-*shiksas* had done before me and quoted Rabbi Hillel to myself: *if i am not for myself, who will be for me? if i am only for myself, what am i? and if not now, when?* After I was in the Cage for a while a couple went into the Blue Room, and within two minutes a crowd of men formed. It reminded me of how a fight at my high school changed the center of gravity of the campus, drawing all the kids to the scuffle. An occasional group of hipsters walked past the Cage, giggling among themselves, and I could tell they were slumming, that their curiosity about the Power Exchange got the better of them. Al arrived, and soon I was leaning against the St. Andrew's Cross, *flog-flog-spank-flog-spank* and combinations thereof, getting familiar. As I later sat and wrote in my notebook, one of the hipsters motioned me over. Unsure why I was indulging him, I walked to the fence, and he asked if I didn't think it **was a little weird to have everyone watching.** I had just been sitting and writing, but I figured he meant the whole public sex 'n' play thing, so I replied that there wasn't much point to being here if you weren't okay with being watched. Undeterred, he said that it might be fine in one of the smaller rooms with one of the little windows, but here where a crowd can see you—**isn't that weird?** He was repeating himself, so I repeated myself and said that you knew what you were getting yourself into when you came to the Power Exchange in terms of being watched. I knew that what he wanted was for me to agree that, yes, it was all so weird! Anyone who would come here to **do things** while people are watching must be weird indeed. That he came here to **watch other people do things** wasn't weird at all, since he kept his ironic detachment and moral superiority over the weirdos. Good for him.

Meanwhile, I was embracing my weirdo status. Being at the Power Exchange may have made me a bottom feeder, but at least I was eating.

Visions of Dazzling Rooms

Diamanda Galás performed *Defixiones: Orders from the Dead* at the Yerba Buena Center for the Arts on October 19, and while I did not get to meet Diamanda and thus I did not get to tell her about using *The Divine Punishment* on *kittypr0n*, I did feel like I was getting back in touch with my goth roots. Everyone in San Francisco with black in their wardrobe and an affinity for eyeliner showed up, and there were many familiar faces from Shrine of Lilith and elsewhere. We made a fine-looking audience! Sadly, when I returned to the Yerba Buena the following evening for a screening of a new 35mm print of Dennis Hopper's 1971 *The Last Movie,* the audience was dominated by unsightly cinephiles in denim and plaid. I had read a lot about Hopper's shaggy, little-seen follow-up to *Easy Rider* over the years, and the film itself did not disappoint. Setting aside the picture's racism and misogyny as one so often must with film history—and make no mistake, there is a metric fucktonne of racism and misogyny to set aside when talking about *The Last Movie*—I loved how it chomped the hand of the studio system which fed it, and the dinner party sequence alone captured the vibe of a bad drug trip far better than *Easy Rider*'s pedestrian Mardi Gras scene. I also respected how *The Last Movie* blew itself up in its last 15 minutes, like no other movie I could think of this side of Zebedy Colt's *The Farmer's Daughters.*

When the lights came up at the end of *The Last Movie,* one of the unsightly cinephiles sitting behind me said ***now i know why it's one of the fifty worst movies ever made!*** Ugh, gross. They were referring to Harry and Michael Medved, who tore into *The Last Movie* in their 1978 book *The Fifty Worst Films of All Time.* I owned both that and their 1980 *The Golden Turkey Awards* because I collected film books, but I never liked the Medveds' style. Danny Peary's *Cult Movies* and *Guide for the Film Fanatic* were my jam as a teenager, I of course followed Roger Ebert's every word, and I read reference books like *VideoHound's Golden Movie Retriever* from cover to cover. Heck, on the night of *The Last Movie* I had a half-dozen film books checked out from the newly-opened Mission Bay Branch library, which was conveniently located a few blocks from NakedSword. It also pleased me to no end that Mission Bay carried the *How Loathsome* hardcover, because it was one step closer to my dream of walking into a library and seeing one of my own books on the shelf. (Someday!)

The freakin' Medveds, though. Their *Golden Turkey Awards* was responsible for making Ed Wood and *Plan 9 from Outer Space* infamous as **the worst director of all time** and **the worst film of all time**, respectively. Though Scott Alexander and Larry Karaszewski's Tim Burton-helmed 1994 biopic *Ed Wood* rehabilitated Wood and his charmingly ramshackle films to an extent, the Medveds were open in their contempt toward Wood for

061020SEF

11

Patron#

102

766249

$8.00

213312

Reg

YBCA Screening Room
701 Mission St. at Third
YBCA Presents
The Last Movie
by Dennis Hopper
(1971, 108 min, new 35mm prnt)
Fri Oct 20 2006 7:30 PM
General Admission $8.00
SEATING SECTION   ROW/SEAT   PRICE

Ticket stub for *The Last Movie* at the Yerba Buena Center for the Arts' Screening Room, October 2006. Speaking of events for which the dress code should have included "vampiric."

being a transvestite. Nothing was more hilarious to straight cis people in the 20th century than men in dresses! It was something Quentin Crisp (the best person named Quentin) summed up in Rob Epstein and Jeffrey Friedman's 1995 documentary *The Celluloid Closet*:

> There's no sin like being a woman. When a man dresses as a woman, the audience laughs. When a woman dresses as a man, nobody laughs. They just thought she looked wonderful.

As if to prove the Best Quentin's point, on the week of my 27th birthday in June 2000 while Raja Gosnell's crossdressing comedy *Big Momma's House* was doing boffo business at the box office, the straight cis cinephiles at the American Film Institute released their list of the 100 funniest domestic films. It was bad enough that Leo McCarey's 1933 Marx Brothers masterpiece *Duck Soup* and Buster Keaton & Clyde Bruckman's 1926 *The General* were not in the top two spots where they belonged, seeing as how they are the two funniest American films ever made. What made it worse was that those top two spots were occupied by Billy Wilder's 1959 *Some Like It Hot* and Sydney Pollack's 1982 *Tootsie,* despite those not being Wilder or Pollack's funniest films.

Okay, *Tootsie* is probably Pollack's funniest film, which isn't saying much because Pollack was shit at comedy and I hate mentioning that movie—but as long as we're on the subject of 1982 films, Roberta Muldoon in George Roy Hill's *The World According to Garp* is the decade's best portrayal of a trans woman, which is all the more remarkable considering *Garp*'s main themes are gender roles and castration anxiety. Roberta is a sane, three-dimensional, non-homicidal character with hopes and dreams who is good at her job, is loved and accepted by the people around her, and does not hate herself for being trans. She is just a person. (One step forward!) The cis male actor John Lithgow was nominated for an Academy Award and won three critics guild awards for playing Roberta as just a person, which meant that while trans women were still available to be feared in horror movies and laughed at in comedies—or maybe treated with a modicum of respect, but only if the movie was trying to push its R rating to the limits of taste and decorum—we could not be sane, three-dimensional, non-homicidal characters in the foreseeable future because Lithgow got showered with awards for doing it that one time, and thus we were damned by the faint praise of being Oscar Bait. (Two steps back!)

Billy Wilder's 1959 *Some Like It Hot* would remain witty if you removed the crossdressing because Wilder and his co-scenarist I.A.L. Diamond wouldn't start writing witless scripts until the 1970s, but there is no universe in which *Hot* is a funnier film than Wilder and Diamond's 1961 *One, Two, Three.* That unsung Cold War classic didn't make the AFI's comedy list, while Wilder's 1955 work-for-hire *The Seven-Year Itch* charted for the same reason that in 2002, the British Film Institute's every-decade critics poll of the greatest films ever made put Alfred Hitchcock's 1958 *Vertigo* in the #2 position after Orson Welles' 1941 *Citizen Kane.* The reason is simple: cinephiles are pervy in the most banal ways possible. Up your pervy game, cinephiles! I know you get off on a sexy woman-child, so may I humbly recommend Billy Wilder's 1942 *The Major and the Minor,* which features the 31-year-old Ginger Rogers pretending to be a 12-year-old? The tricky part is that Rogers' character Sue Applegate is a strong, intelligent career woman who pretends to be a child for practical reasons, so she won't give you a boner like Marilyn Monroe's ditzy, nameless child-woman. But *The Major and the Minor* is a funnier film than *The Seven-Year Itch,* and pervy in a more interesting way.

Tira and I bonded over *Citizen Kane* as teenagers, and we once drove from Fresno to Santa Cruz to see it in 35mm at the Old Sash Mill Theater. Any excuse to visit Santa Cruz was a good one in those days, and other films we made the Sash Mill pilgrimage for included David Lynch's *Eraserhead,* Wim Wenders' *Wings of Desire,* and Nick Broomfield's film of my favorite Spalding Gray monologue, *Monster in a Box.* (We also saw Spalding in person twice: performing *Gray's Anatomy* at UC Santa Cruz in 1993 and *It's a Slippery Slope* at the American Conservatory Theater in 1997. To say he was a major influence on my writing would be an understatement.) I saw the 1996 restoration of *Vertigo* in 70mm at the Castro twice, so I have eaten my vegetables when I say that *Citizen Kane* and *Vertigo* are both about damaged men who take out their anger on blonde or potentially-blonde women by abusing and abbreviating them into becoming what the men want them to be. *Kane* is also about other things including but not limited to the way power can twist good intentions and lead to such abusive behavior, while *Vertigo* is a straightforward **bitches, right?** narrative about Hitchcock's issues with women. We're expected to sympathize with *Vertigo*'s abuser because he's played by the cornfed Jimmy Stewart instead of a more accurate Hitchcock analog like Joe E. Ross or Broderick Crawford, and that's setting aside Hitchcock's lazy visual style. Everyone talks about those dolly zooms and the Saul Bass animation and Kim Novak at Fort Point under the Golden Gate Bridge, and I don't deny that I always feel connected to film history when I visit Fort Point, just like I feel a sense of religious awe when I step into Grace Cathedral. But the zooms and animation and Golden Gate Bridge stuff is about five of *Vertigo*'s interminable 128 minutes, and much of the rest is either men in suits having boring conversations in uninteresting locations or bad process shots. Way to use VistaVision to its fullest, Hitch!

Citizen Kane's Bernstein saying he called Susan Alexander Kane after Charles' death because *i thought maybe somebody ought to* as Gregg

Toland's deep-focus camera slowly dollies in is a more interesting and emotional composition than anything in *Vertigo* and more compassion for a female character than you'll find in most any Hitchcock film after *Shadow of a Doubt* in 1943. *Kane's* natural blonde survives to the final reel with her freedom and dignity intact, while *Vertigo's* peroxide-blonde dies a Disney-villain death which keeps her abuser's hands clean. Was Susan Alexander Kane a character assassination of the real-life Marion Davies? Yes, and the way Emily Monroe Norton Kane gets killed offscreen for the sake of plot convenience is downright Hitchcockian—and probably Welles' co-writer Herman J. Mankiewicz's idea. Also, there are racist jokes in *Duck Soup*, and the hero of *The General* is a Confederate soldier. We can have film history or we can have nice things, but we can't have both.

My 2006 *Kane* rewatch gave me a new respect for Dorothy Comingore. Many cinephiles consider her the film's weakest element, both because of scenes in which Welles directed her to speak in a manner cinephiles call **shrill** and because they don't want to fuck Dorothy Comingore the way they want to fuck Kim Novak in *Vertigo*. Her comparative unfuckability has the effect of dehumanizing Susan in their eyes, but Comingore does the heaviest emotional lifting of anyone in the cast—particularly during scenes in which Susan's fate is being decided for her by Charles, who has less than no interest in who she is as a person. Susan complains a lot, sometimes softly and sometimes less so, but her tone does not change the fact that she is correct. She *should* be able to go out and have fun when it's 11:30 p.m. in New York and the people are going to nightclubs and restaurants, and not be stuck in a tomb on the Florida coast. Susan never wanted this life Charles forced her into.

Dorothy Comingore's penultimate scene is Susan's flashback to leaving Charles in the early 1930s. She's about to walk out of her expressionistic Xanadu room forever, and Charles tries to shame her by invoking the opinion of others. When she says she's aware that people will find out, Charles then tells her that *from now on, everything will be exactly the way you want it to be—not the way i think you want it, but your way.* Susan does not respond to this most empty of an abuser's promises, so Charles stops pretending to care about her: *you mustn't go. you can't do this to me.* Comingore's reaction is one of the best in a film that does not lack for great performances: Susan's face drops for a frozen moment as she sees what has always been at the end of Charles' fork, and her smile returns as she says *i see. it's you that this is being done to. it's not me at all. not what it means to me.* Comingore's smile grows to near-giddy proportions as Susan realizes she is calling Charles' greatest bluff. *i can't do this to you? oh, yes i can!*

Susan Alexander Kane has one power move, and she uses it: she walks the hell away and does not look back.

That's already a great mic-drop, but it gets better when the flash-back ends, and we're back in Susan's nightclub in present-day 1941. (The script's stage directions describe her as *fifty, trying to look much younger, cheaply blonded*, to which I say *fuck you, mank*.) Having had the catharsis of both a weeklong bender and a night of telling her life story to *News on the March*'s Thompson, Susan is chill about the past decade, both her regular depression and the Great Depression be damned: she lost her money, but she gained her freedom. Susan's mood drops a little when Thompson says he still feels sorry for Mr. Kane in spite of everything, but she finishes her drink and pulls herself back together, and as Susan looks up at the sun streaming in through the skylight—the stage directions say the light is *revealing mercilessly every year of susie's age*, to which I say *fuck you, mank*—she clutches her coat to her body and says with a smile, *whattayak-now, it's morning already!*

I've always considered that to be the film's emotional climax, and the remaining 10 minutes are a coda. It's a great coda, what with the Rosebud reveal and Charles throwing a tantrum because his needs are always always always more important than Susan's at all times and in all situations, and those last 10 minutes of *Citizen Kane* are better than any 10 minutes of *Vertigo*. But Dorothy Comingore emerging from a terrible emotional and physical ordeal with her dignity intact doesn't give cinephiles a boner like Kim Novak falling to her death after being abused and abbreviated by Jimmy Stewart. I'll say it again: up your pervy game, cinephiles! May I humbly recommend Charles Laughton's 1955 *The Night of the Hunter*, which is a better film than *Vertigo* and also features a blonde woman being abused and killed by an alpha male? The blonde in question is Shelley Winters, and I know that's a problem because you want to fuck her even less than you want to fuck Dorothy Comingore, but trust me, *The Night of the Hunter* is worth it. And for the record, Hitchcock's best film was *Rear Window*; watch it back to back with *Vertigo*, and you will see there is no comparison.

When I arrived at the Power Exchange on the night of *The Last Movie*, there was a more sinister vibe than usual. I paused for a while in the strobe-lit Electric Zebra, watching the way men were milling about, sometimes bumping into each other with nary a thought in their brain like the ghouls in Romero's *Night of the Living Dead*. (It had been three years ago this month that I played Barbara at Spanganga, but it felt like another lifetime.) When I walked downstairs and into the Dungeon, the sense of *cinema vu* shifted to Romero's 1985 *Day of the Dead*: many of the ghouls hung onto the Cage from the outside, fingers curled over the links, rattling the fence. Their numbers were disconcerting, though I knew if they entered the Cage and didn't take *get the fuck out!* as an answer, the bouncers would have been on the job. But not only did I keep imagining I was seeing people sneaking into the Cage, a Tourist wearing a long white shirt under the black light in my peripheral vision was indistinguishable from a specter. I didn't believe in the supernatural, but this was where I'd expect to see such a thing, and that was part of the Power Exchange's appeal. It never felt unsafe, but sometimes it was unsettling in a fun way.

I was a little bummed that Al and Robin didn't make it that night, but there were other regulars such as the Naked Guy Masturbating in the Sling, as well as Blemish. I had seen the latter working the coat check and the door, but he spent most of his time in the Dungeon, and I found his routine comforting. Sometime before midnight, Blemish would take off his clothes, put on a leather mask with a thick metal collar, and shackle his hands about twelve inches apart. After chugging a few bottles of generic NyQuil, he would shuffle and clank away to find a place to spread his towel, usually outside the Cage. Having found his spot, he would masturbate for well over an hour. It wasn't the slow, deliberate stroke of the Naked Guy Masturbating in the Sling, either. This was a full-tilt wank, and when he finished, he put his clothes back on and slept on the couch for much of the rest of the night. Sleeping in the club was against the rules, but the staff never objected to one of the regulars taking a snooze. Sometimes it was necessary after an intense scene, or if it was two in the morning and you had several pints of cold medicine in your system. I admired Blemish for knowing what he liked to do and for having a safe place to do it. Everyone should be so lucky.

On this specter-filled night I was soon visited by Chana, a Mother-lode Girl with a flawless body and a Cajun accent as thick and impenetrable as a Splosh Burrito. Through no fault of her own she made me feel not great about my own ridiculous, misshapen meat puppet, but Chana made up for it by always being happy to see me and insisting that I join her for a walk through the rest of the Power Exchange. She had lots to tell me on our walks, though I couldn't make heads or tails out of most of it: *girl,* _____ _____ _____, *big dicks* _____ _____ *big dicks* _____, _____ _____. I gathered that Chana had a thing for big dicks, but otherwise I just nodded and smiled a lot, feeling like a world traveler who was unable to grasp the pidgin but was grateful for the fellowship.

Perilous Night, Their Voices Calling

I parked across from the Power Exchange around six on the Saturday before Halloween, then walked to the Dark Room for the second-to-last performance of Jim's adaptation of Mel Brooks' *Young Frankenstein,* which featured Mikl-Em as the Monster and Anomaly as Frau Blücher. Though I directed the *Twilight Zone Live* episode "The Midnight Sun" and acted in

David Stein's episode "The Silence" earlier that year, and I had more fun than humans should be allowed to have in *The Gong Show Live*, I hadn't been in any feature plays since *Zippy the Pinhead in Fun: The Concept* in 2004. Jim and Erin had briefly considered doing a stage version of Bryan Forbes' 1975 *The Stepford Wives* with me in the Katharine Ross role, an idea they dropped when the news of Frank Oz's remake hit, and I understood why they passed me over for roles in *Clue* and *Batman: The TV Show: The Play* and *The Princess Bride*, productions which I saw many times and always enjoyed. I knew Jim and Erin loved me and that I would always be a foundational member of our scrappy little Dark Room family, but it still hurt to no longer feel like their golden girl, insofar as I ever had been, which I had not. They were currently in pre-production on an adaptation of the funniest American comedy ever, *Duck Soup*, and I offered to take on the Zeppo role since there was no reason that non-character couldn't be female. They gently declined my offer. Always a Gummo, never a Zeppo, community theater is not for the meek, y'all!

After *Young Frankenstein*, I took BART to the Porn Palace, the aptly-named studio of Kink.com. Ryder had given me a DVD of water-bondage videos she made for Kink, and they were difficult to watch, but now I knew seeing someone almost drown was not my thing. (Knowledge is power!) The Porn Palace itself was hidden in one of the alleys between Market and Mission and 5th and 6th, and the event was a dance party called the Feast of Souls. It felt like the goth clubs I'd gone to in early 1999—Bound, maybe? Or Sanctuary? Despite the Porn Palace's BDSM element, it felt more like Sanctuary, and the DJ was kind enough to spin a few Marilyn Manson tunes without me asking. I remembered what it felt like going to both Sanctuary and Bound for the first time, and I missed that sense of wonder and discovery. Could I ever get that feeling back? I had seven years to make up for. Okay, that wasn't fair; more like six years. Whatever I had or had not done since the first Bad Movie Night was my own responsibility, but the more distance I got from those six years, the less real it all felt. How did I bungle my first true shot at adult freedom, to allow myself to be diminished in my own home, to have to negotiate my every freakin' movement Freyja called it ***abbreviation*** during those bad early months, and it was that, but after a while it became the worst possible combination of weakness and pride. I was too proud to acknowledge that after my mother flayed my self-esteem as a punishment for doing those two very bad and wrong things, my opinion of myself was so low that I allowed an angry biped to step on my tail and punish me for the sins of strangers thousands of miles away. *no, no, her moving out here was a great idea and it's working out like we'd hoped! everything's going swell! i slash we are happy!* It had all been lies, goddamn lies, and false statistics.

I could feel a callus developing on my left big toe by 1:00 a.m., so I took my leave of the Feast and caught a cab back into the Mission. Needing a feast of my own, I went to Taqueria Cancun, which was my favorite taqueria by virtue of being across the street from the Dark Room. Cancun was always a spectacle at this time of the night when I was the only sober person around—as I was tonight, and on most nights—but it was more of a carnival on this pre–Halloween Saturday, full of drunkards whose costumes were in various states of disrepair as the line stretched down the hallway to the restrooms and back again. Though vegetarian by disposition I had been eating meat for the past year as part of my decadent spiral, and I decided that if I was gonna eat meat, I was gonna eat all the goddamn meat. I'd already had Cancun's *lengua* (beef tongue) and *cabeza* (beef head) burritos, but tonight was the night for the *sesos* (beef brain).

I enjoyed my brain burrito across the street at the Dark Room. Jim and Erin invited me to stay overnight in the green room, and I was grateful for the offer, but the night's adventures weren't over. Walking back to the Power Exchange wasn't an option since it would have involved hoofing it through some neighborhoods which were unpleasant enough in broad daylight, let alone as the bars were letting out on the most drunken night of the year. Being trans in public was always dangerous, but I also knew my accursed build granted me the privilege of being safer than I would be otherwise. I still tried to avoid sketchy areas after the sun went down, so I took the always-squalid 49 Mission bus, which like Taqueria Cancun was filled with increasingly disheveled revelers, making its squalor more colorful than usual. After I disembarked from the 49, I stood at the tangled corner where Otis, 12th, South Van Ness, and Mission all converged. The Power Exchange was a block away to the southeast on Otis and the Mel's Drive-In seen in George Lucas' 1973 *American Graffiti* had once stood about a block south of it on Mission. Mel's was demolished before I moved to San Francisco, but I reckoned that if you removed the buildings between the two spots, you could hit the old Mel's location from the door of the Power Exchange with a decent potato cannon.

It also made me think of Fritz Leiber's 1977 San Francisco horror novel *Our Lady of Darkness*. That book's protagonist discovers that their apartment at the corner of Geary and Hyde is the third point in a triangle formed by Sutro Tower and the rock outcropping at the top of Corona Heights, and the dark urban magic of that triangle—***megapolisomancy***, to be precise—allows nasty creatures called paramentals to enter our world. Setting aside that it was all made up, who was to say that this much smaller triangle formed by the Power Exchange, this tangled corner, and the specter of Mel's Drive-In didn't also have some of its own dark urban magic? As if to prove my point, I heard a man in the shadows say, ***hey cutie, wanna suck my dick?***

They may not have been the pale brown things waving in distant windows which Leiber described, but there were paramentals out here after all.

This perilous night was the end of Daylight Saving Time, and I arrived at the Power Exchange as the clocks fell back. A free hour! It was also the night of the monthly fetish ball, in October called the Swalloween Ball. $20 to get in! Having to pay offended my sense of entitlement, but I did it anyway because I was feeling lonely and I wanted to see my friends Al and Robin. The Dungeon was busier than ever, packed with new faces enthused by the Halloween spirit. Robin was her usual sex-carny self, trying to lure new fish into the Cage to play, and there were a lot more people to try tonight. A cis woman who looked like the actress Geneviève Bujold had been circling the Cage like so many others, alternately shocked and fascinated. She had never seen such goings-on, and she decided to take the leap, agreeing to a mild spanking and flogging by Al on the St. Andrew's Cross.

An advocate of both consent and sharing, Al asked the woman if it was all right if his friend Sherilyn (*hey, that's me!*) spanked her. The woman said yes, so I spanked her a few times. It was okay, but I was also partying like it was Q3 2003: my deepest, most unspeakable fantasy in Q4 2006 was to share simple, fully-clothed warmth and affection with a woman who wanted to be warm and affectionate with me. If faux–Bujold had wanted to go the full *Dead Ringers* with surgical tubing and clamps I would have been game, but all I wanted was a little human connection. Did I suggest any of this? No. It still felt like too much to ask a stranger, and what's more, that sort of thing was not why anyone came to the Power Exchange. It just wasn't done.

A Flicker of Light Before the Dawning

I parked at the Power Exchange early in the evening of the first Friday in November and then walked to the Lexington to nurse a margarita and write in my notebook. The Lex's CD jukebox included *The Best of the Velvet Underground*, so I put on "Sister Ray," resulting in the jukebox being unplugged before the song ended. (I counted that as a victory.) I next hit the Dark Room for a 10 p.m. show by the sketch comedy group Uphill Both Ways. It was an anniversary show with material I'd first seen at Spanganga in 2003, but I still laughed so much it hurt when some sketches went so far off the rails that the errors took on a life of their own, which seemed like it was probably a metaphor for something. After getting a *lengua* burrito from Taqueria Cancun and choking down a Red Bull just to be on the safe side, I walked back to the Power Exchange, again thinking of *Our Lady of Darkness* and **megapolisomancy** and all that. Also, weren't ley lines a thing?

Lines of power from under the Earth or some such? Since all supernatural stuff was make-believe, I could make it be whatever I wanted, so I decided that the triangle whose three points were the Power Exchange and the old location of Mel's Drive-In and the tangled corner where Otis, 12th, South Van Ness, and Mission all converged did generate a magic I could use. It would bring me the miracle I needed.

But miracles always required hard work, so as I thanked the bouncer for holding the door open for me, I decided I was going to introduce myself to people I'd been meaning to introduce myself to, to throw my hat into more rings than usual, and stop being so damn timid. A lesson I couldn't have drilled into my *sesos* enough was that good things wouldn't happen unless I took steps to make them happen, and that included proving that I was capable of being a slut, that I was worthy of getting beaned with a measuring cup just for having a hickey. Things would go the way they were supposed to go, but I had to state my intention to the universe somehow, so I introduced myself to the Alpha Twin. Known to be a consummate sucker of dick whose breath smelled more and more like semen as the night progressed, the Alpha Twin was a gorgeous transvestite whose long, straight blonde wig couldn't have looked less like it grew out of her own scalp, and yet it worked. She was often accompanied by the Beta Twin, whom Robin informed me was the Alpha's cousin. Compared to the Alpha Twin's smiling gregariousness, the Beta Twin was introverted, often trailing a few paces behind. I found them both sexy and their pheromones were delicious, but I got no sense that they had any interest in me. For as much as I would have enjoyed making out with either of them on the red couch, the Twins were all about the dicks attached to cis men, and snogging a trans woman was beyond their experience.

There were a handful of mixes in rotation in the Power Exchange's sound system, and I often danced in the Cage. I got to know Eminem's "Cleanin' Out My Closet" well, the song's anger feeling equal parts cathartic and cautionary, and heaven knew I could have used more snare in my headphones. I had recently given Robin a disc of goth-y club music which she was going to give to the people in charge of these things, though it wasn't in rotation yet. After dancing to "Purple Rain" on this night, I jotted something down in my notebook. Observing this, Al said, **chapter 87: dancing to prince**. (Maybe!)

Al and I were playing on the cross later that night when I saw a redheaded trans woman walk past the Cage. Though my natural inclination when being flogged, spanked, or otherwise roughly stimulated was to close my eyes and zone out—a valuable skill I'd developed when I began electrolysis the previous decade, because overdosing on the Green Death was only half the battle—I kept my eyes open now. The scene itself was almost incidental. I was enjoying myself, hooray for endorphins and all, but I was determined to not lose track of this most toothsome redhead. Everything was consensual with Al and I could have been decuffed and out of the Cage in fifteen seconds flat, but I was enjoying myself and not quite ready to stop. I was sure she would come back this way...

...and she did. The redhead glanced in my direction as she walked by, and good heavens, how had I not noticed she was wearing glasses the first time around? I made four-eyed contact and smiled. She smiled back, which was a start, and she stopped to talk to someone before moving beyond my neck's turn radius. We made eye/smile contact again, and I gestured for her to come inside the Cage. She nodded and walked in. So far, so good. I hoped she'd come up to me at the cross, because like a new convert wanting to spread the good news, I needed to tell her she was the hottest thing on two legs ever seen in this room.

Instead, she stood behind the long table and watched. I motioned for her to come closer, but she shook her head. Fair enough, and I glanced back often to re-establish eye contact. Again, I could have ended the scene at any time, but I was existing in a moment: I was feeling a strong attraction to a stranger as I was being flogged and spanked and rushing on endorphins and adrenaline. An alchemy was at work, elements combining and altering, a rare moment of *feeling* after a long period of post–Ryder numbness, and I wanted to experience it. Besides, the redhead had made it this far, right? Then she wasn't at the table anymore because she was at the gate talking to a Tourist, and oh, no no *no*. Picking up on my *kitty needs to go outside right NOW* vibe, Al leaned in and asked if I wanted to pursue the young lady. As I started to undo the cuffs, I answered in the affirmative. Yes. Yes, I wanted to pursue the young lady. I wanted to pursue her, and I wanted to ... well, the only word for it was *court*. I wanted to court her. I walked over to the young lady, and taking great pleasure in ignoring the Tourist, I extended my hand and said *hello. my name is sherilyn.*

Her name was Soma Red and we got right into getting to know each other, figuring out to what extent we were on the same page, and never skimping on the mutual you're-so-cute gushiness. The 23-year-old Soma was born a few days shy of my own tenth birthday in 1983, and Soma guessed my age as 27. When I was growing up, people always thought I was older than I was; my abnormal height had a lot to do with it, but I also didn't like being a child, so I tried not to behave like one. But my apparent age had dropped by an average of five years since I began transitioning, which goes to show what a difference it makes to have a body that isn't completely at odds with your soul.

Since Soma and I were a pair of women engaged in a conversation about ourselves and thus were passing the Bechdel Test, a cis man took that as his cue to enter the Cage and insert himself into the scene. He wanted to know how to get a woman to fuck him with a dildo, and though he would have been thrilled if Soma or I strapped one on and had at him right then and there, he was not propositioning us. Instead, he seemed desperate for advice. Where should he go? Who should he ask? How can he tell? What should he say? As we talked to him, I put a hand on Soma's thigh and another around the waist which she'd informed me had been surgically feminized. Soma returned the gesture, and I moved in a little closer. Perhaps seeing us cuddling lead to a moment of clarity, since the man asked if he was interrupting. Soma thanked him for asking and confirmed that he was indeed interrupting: by Soma's math, we had about another hour of talking to do before we slept together.

Oh, shoot. The time. What time was it now? I pulled my phone out of my boot. Almost half past three! I'd have to leave soon, so Soma and I turned our attention to each other and made do with what little time we had left. Kissing her felt like a revelation, an undiscovered country, and when we came up for air after a few minutes she said **sherilyn, do you realize you're hotter than, like, nine-tenths of the other women here?** I replied *i was thinking the same thing about you* and I stopped myself before I could add *the difference is that it's true in your case* because this was no time to be self-deprecating. Soma and I each felt like we'd hit the jackpot, the equivalence principle meant we were both right, and as I nuzzled Soma's cheek I thought to myself *you are real, you are happening* and dove back in.

I gave Soma a ride back to her apartment, the Indus River Valley. She invited me inside, but the realities of City life got in the way: I couldn't find a parking spot. So, we promised each other we would pick up where we left off as soon as we could.

Welcome to Annexia

Partners in a Benevolent Psychopathology

I brought Soma home on Sunday night to pick up where we left off. The sex was hot and rough and delicious, and beyond having to go easy on her hips, no holds were barred. Afterward we went to see the ocean because everybody wants to see the ocean when they first visit the Black Light District, and the Pacific was especially lovely at 2:00 a.m. under a low full moon.

We made our street-level public debut that Wednesday at the 12 Galaxies for Ask Dr. Hal. Hosted by impresario and former GG Allin bandmate Chicken John, Ask Dr. Hal involved the audience asking questions to be answered by Church of the SubGenius co-founder Dr. Hal, the more arcane or silly the question the better. Amateur astronomer Pete Goldie opened the show with a Space Science Report relating NASA's latest discoveries, famed yo-yo expert Cappy projected visuals throughout while my now-former fellow Pirate Cat Radio DJ KrOB provided soundscapes, and local eccentric Frank Chu spoke for a few minutes. Frank could be seen at most public gatherings carrying a sign full of ~~nonsense~~ cryptic words, and the 12 Galaxies itself was named after the most prominent phrase on his sign from over the years, which as of April 2006 read:

ELMSFORD
12 GALAXIES
CESJROGRENICAL ERGONOMICS
NBC: XOXPHROZENIGUL COVERAGE
WASPROVRENIKIL
ADMONISHMENTS MINISCULE
STRATOSPHERICAL

Chicken John and I tended to keep a polite distance, but I had been getting to know Dr. Hal, Pete, and KrOB over the past year because we all did stuff at the Dark Room, including but not limited to Bad Movie

The front and back of the flyer for Ask Dr. Hal at the 12 Galaxies, November 2006. Not pictured are the show's biggest stars, Fernet-Branca and nitrous oxide.

Night. (I'd also once seen Frank Chu hock a loogie into the gutter, so I had that going for me.) Because San Francisco is a closed system where lines always converge, Soma was able to get us on the guestlist because she was friends with Cappy, and Soma reported back that when she mentioned my name, Cappy told her how funny I was at Bad Movie Night. Soma and I had already locked into each other by that point, but outside validation about my sense of humor was always welcome. For as much we meshed into each other sexually, the best part of being with Soma was how much we made each other laugh—and to whatever extent Soma was turned on by the bargain-basement starfuckery of being with me, I was there for that, too. We bounced our questions for Dr. Hal off each other before the show, mine being the highly-scientific *what would be the impact on human affairs if mercury went into transit and retrograde at the same time?* Soma's question was no less practical: **new york's seething, bitter enmity manifested as a giant pink protoplasmic mass underground. what form does san francisco's psychic sewer entity take?** Sadly, Dr. Hal's answers to our pertinent queries have been lost to the sands of time.

Being with Soma Red felt like the first time I had ever been well and truly *queer*, and now I got it, felt that rush. Though ten years younger she had been on estrogen for as long as I had, and while her body was surgically augmented with aftermarket breasts and hips, it still allowed me to understand things about my unaugmented body which had always been just out of reach. It also meant that I had someone I felt close to who could hear and understand me about being trans in a way that not even the most empathetic of my cis partners could. One night as we were cuddling in my bed, Soma said *i find being trans irritating in two ways*. I was studying her face under the black light. So many freckles! I was no less freckly myself, but I tended to hide them with many layers of pale makeup. Soma continued, *first, i have to tuck, and second, i can't get triple-penetrated*. For as ridiculous and misshapen as my meat puppet was, I got lucky in terms of certain extremities: my hands were not large, I didn't have a noticeable adam's apple, I didn't need to tuck since *le petit sherilyn* was never more than a glorified clitoris with a urethra, and my face wasn't all that masculine before the estrogen and spironolactone went to work. I was conscious that at 33 I was now the age my mother had been when I was born, and while I never suspected I was adopted, the degree to which I now resembled her confirmed that I was my mother's biological daughter. As for the second irritating thing, Soma said, *it's every girl's god-given right to be triple-penetrated by the time she's nineteen, and, goddammit, that's been stolen from me*. It was true, we walked a difficult road—and that I was able to have this discussion with Soma while we cuddled in my bed made me all the more grateful that the road I was walking couldn't have been more different than my mother's road at this age.

It felt significant that the 23-year-old Soma had guessed I was 27. Not just because it's the age when all the cool kids used to die, but because I should have been coming into my own the year I turned 27. I should have been out exploring the world and further discovering myself in the process, but I didn't because I let someone else's fear and self-hatred hold me back, so much so that I got cursed and screamed at just for going to a movie. I was almost beginning to forgive my younger self for allowing the mistreatment and abbreviation to happen, and I was learning to feel compassion for her, for the damage that was visited upon her tail and her soul. Twenty-six-going-on-twenty-seven-year-old Sherilyn was not an angel or all that good a person, and she tended to do everything in the worst way possible, but she did not deserve what happened to her. I decided that being with Soma would be a do-over on that painful, misbegotten year.

But not without some new pain. One of the first things Soma had said to me was that she was sure my eye makeup would look exquisite with tears of pain running through it, and I discovered a new baseline for searing physical pain at the Power Exchange that Saturday as she went at the backs of my thighs with the non-scratchy end of a backscratcher. Always in the same damn spot, for it was a method called Same Damn Spot. Anomaly came along for moral support, and while I had no idea how long Soma went at my right thigh, she only went at my left thigh for a few minutes before Anomaly decided I'd had enough. Nobody was keeping track of the time, but the best estimate was that the entire scene took twenty minutes. Not long, and a freakin' eternity, like the lingering afterimage of an astronaut as she crosses the event horizon. Soma had warned me beforehand that she had no interest in providing aftercare, and true to her word, when she was done she exited the Cage to resume her usual mission at the Power Exchange: sucking as many dicks as possible. I remained on the couch with Anomaly, rushing and floating, and as Soma walked away, I thought to myself, *i think i'm all right.*

Which meant that Annie Sprinkle at the Hellfire Club was the wrong goal for me. It had always been the wrong goal, though Annie's grapes were not sour. I had no doubt that they were delicious grapes, and I wished I could taste those grapes, but they were beyond my personal horizon. Maybe I could have reached those grapes if I were wired to be sexually attracted to men. Maybe if I was petite. Maybe if I looked like Soma. Maybe if I'd been born cis rather than trans. Maybe if I wasn't myself … but I didn't *want* to be anyone else. For as much as strangers and loved ones and the whole culture had drilled into me how wrong and aberrant I was, that I was unworthy of compassion and nobody was going to take my side and I deserved whatever bad things happened to me, I was still happy to be myself, to be the one to live this uncharted life. And part of being myself was recognizing that I was not Annie Sprinkle at the Hellfire Club.

I was Catherine Ballard in *Crash*, and Soma Red was my James.

Two Semi-Metallic Human Beings

I developed a spectacular bruise on each thigh by the next time I saw Soma Red, two dark purple SDS nebulae. I brought her to the Black Light District to watch Cronenberg's *Videodrome*, after which we had sex as one must after watching *Videodrome*, and I gave Soma a Messier Object to match my own nebulae, a galactic cluster which would have fascinated Fritz Zwicky no less than the one in Coma Berenices. As we lay in my bed at 1:15 a.m., Soma coming down from the mini-torture, I told her that one of these times at the Power Exchange I was going to follow her, do what she did, see what happens, dive in. Soma laughed, then leaned in and whispered, **sherilyn, you don't like dick.** I reached down between her legs and said *that's not entirely true.* As Soma gasped and squirmed, I clarified that the cis men most dicks were attached to were the problem, and if I could get past that ickiness, maybe I could be like her. Climbing on top of me, Soma's large aftermarket breasts eclipsing my own shy but proudly homegrown pair, she said **maybe, but what you need right now are cookies and donuts, and i** *need to make them for you.* So we got out of bed, much to the annoyance of Perdita, who had just concluded it was safe to join us. Soma and I made it to the Safeway on Noriega before it closed at 2:00 a.m. and acquired the appropriate ingredients for cookies and donuts. They were delicious, as was the fried-toast-and-egg concoction Soma made us for breakfast after we managed to sleep for a few hours. (Dogs love sleeping. It's a fact.)

Bad Movie Night was still finding its identity after a year and a half, and we began a mid-week spinoff called Bad Porn Night. I was on mic that Wednesday to heckle the Mitchell Brothers' 1972 *Behind the Green Door* starring *Rabid*'s Marilyn Chambers, feeling proud to have seen the Green Door in real life. I'd also just had my roots bleached for the first time since July, and after *Behind the Green Door* was over someone complimented me on my blonde wig. I yanked at my hair to assure them that it was all mine, *plzkthxbai*, but this sort of thing was why I'd gotten into the habit of waiting four months to get my hair reblondified. Strangers tended to assume I was wearing a wig if I didn't have visible roots, and they felt free to inform me that they knew I was wearing a wig, **nudge nudge wink wink**.

Soma ventured out to NakedSword to have lunch with me a few times that week, and I was pleasantly surprised the first time she took my hand

in hers as we walked down the street. We were already in the habit of kissing hello and goodbye and for whatever reason whether we were in public or private, but this most basic gesture of affection made me realize I was getting through to something in her. Maybe it was because I had sat still for the SDS torture? And everything else before and after that, but that act felt significant.

Since Soma was newish in town and in between jobs, I did what I could to help her find employment. She was open to exploring sex work as a short-term solution, but she had never been to Divas, wasn't

The author's own freshly-reblondified hair, and not a fucking wig, thank you very much, July 2006. Also, the seldom-seen Sherilyn freckles (author photograph).

familiar with the Tenderloin, and was nervous about getting arrested. I did what networking I could for her, and while Soma was all about sucking anonymous dicks, she found the idea of kissing the men attached to them to be gross, making what was known as the Girlfriend Experience something she would charge way extra for. She seemed genuinely touched when I told her she would be great at the Girlfriend Experience, because I was experiencing it with her, and it was great. We were falling for each other, and it was improbable for many reasons, not the least of which being that I was a cat and Soma was a dog. Soma was as proud of being a dog as I was proud of being a cat, and I often called her *puppy* while she called me **mommy** or **lover**.

One night we were cuddling in Soma's bed at the Indus River Valley, and I was telling her about a recent date I went on with Storm, a professional dominatrix who was a regular at the Power Exchange. Storm had insisted at first that I pay for everything since she was the lady I was taking out, and I told Storm that as far as I was concerned, *I* was not taking *her* out. We were two women going out together, and I rejected the premise that it was my obligation to pay for her. Storm shrugged and dropped the issue.

Soma sat up a little. **you know one of the things i really like about you, lover?**

oooh, i know this one: you like my peroxide-blonde hair!

She grabbed a handful of that hair and said, **i like that you don't put up with shit**.

Soma had complimented me many times before, usually about my hotness or how good I was getting at sucking her off, but this one cut me to my core. I didn't feel like I deserved it, at all. I just said *i'm getting better at it, i think.*

i mean it, mommy. so many girls, especially t-girls like us, will tolerate anything. but you're so confident and capable. it's hot.

thanks, pup. my role models have always been tough women, like my first girlfriend tira. and i try, but sometimes i've failed, and i've been trying lately to figure out why i let what happened, happened.

Soma hugged me. **you mean with...**

yeah. her. all that. all those years.

look at you now, though! people grow up! it's rad.

thank you, my little skankburger.

Soma laughed at *my little skankburger*, and as I wrote down our conversation in my notebook, we discussed our favorite filthy phrases. Though I hated the word *cock* and swore to never use it in a book outside of a linguistic discussion, I liked *cock-socket* because of the hard consonants and the internal rhyme, while Soma had quite enjoyed it when porn star Taryn Thomas referred to another woman in a snowballing movie as a *cum-reservoir*. Soma had been called a ***cum-dumpster*** a few times—indeed, Soma was proud of having been called every disparaging term there was—but that one didn't work at all. We both knew from experience that it was sexy as hell to go the full *Sid & Nancy* and make out against a dumpster, but there was nothing sexy about dumpsters themselves.

I thought to myself, *soma's right! it's rad to be a grownup*.

* * *

Soma and I went to the Power Exchange the day after Thanksgiving, and we chatted for a while with Artwhore at Checkpoint Charlie. I was embarrassed that I had always breezed past him before, which was bougie of me, and I discovered that he was a sweet guy. He said to Soma and me, ***i'm an asshole, but i like the two of you***. Awww! I already knew Robin and Al liked me, and they thought Soma and I made a great couple, though they were aghast at the visible damage on my arm from our play. Maybe that meant Soma and I were going too far? I had no idea, and we spent the first few hours inside the Cage having at each other, me over Soma on the red couch, the Johnny to her Sophie as my fingers *tink-tink-tinked* against her nipple piercings for a trancelike hour, first the left then the right, back and forth, then my mouth covering hers, my hand over her nose, pinching it closed, my inhalations taking her breath away and replacing it with nothing in particular because nothing else was getting in or out and I couldn't breathe either but I at least had a lungful's worth of a head start, *power*, looking into but not seeing her eyes, gauging her body language and increasingly urgent muffled sounds, her body starting to buck, my own vision starting to get blurry as my brain got cranky about the lack of oxygen, and—

—Soma's gasp for air would have been heard on the Power Exchange's shuttered fourth floor, had there been anyone up there to hear it.

Later that night, Soma excused herself and headed to the Blue Room to watch an odd event which Al told me happened every few months. A small, loud gentleman recruited a group of willing men and one willing woman. The fellow barked orders to the men (***you! turn her over! you! put more oil on her!***) as the woman lay on the circular bed, getting prodded in assorted ways, the men occasionally being shifted around by the ringleader. It was a musical gangbang, an orgiastic unbirthday, albeit one with no penetration, not so much as a finger. A man walked up to Soma and started groping and propositioning her, but she didn't take him up on whatever he was offering. Dammit, she was trying to enjoy the show. As I was willing the man to leave Soma alone, a Motherlode Girl walked up to me and said, ***hi! i'm violet. you look like courtney love***. Well, there it was: a woman named Violet (!) told me without any prompting that I looked like my spiritual big sister. I had reached the top of the mountain, and the sky was indeed made of amethyst. We hung out for the next hour, talking and flirting, though I wasn't sure if Violet was reciprocating, since a T-girl flirting with another T-girl was still a lowercase-a anomaly at the Power Exchange. Violet mentioned that she could draw Ursula from Disney's *The Little Mermaid*, so I handed her my notebook and pen, and she drew Ursula as promised. A decent party trick, especially for the rare times Violet encountered someone with a notebook and pen.

Violet left a while later, and I walked deep into the Dungeon through the back alley, past the Motherlode Girls perched in wait, and into the Barracks. Its walls were painted in camouflage patterns with a large USMC logo, though these design elements were often difficult to see because of the dim light, the thick mosquito netting, and sheer number of men present at any given time. Pound for pound, the Barracks were where the most dick got sucked, and at the moment, most of it was being done by Soma. I generally only went into the Barracks when I was bored and decided to wander, and I'd ended up in there with Chana a few times, but I could tell the tenor was more hostile than usual. Not the guys getting sucked or waiting to get sucked, but the spectators along the walls. Amidst the hoots and hollers there were also things like *suck it, bitch!* and *we paid forty bucks for this!* As one spectator left, he complained that Soma's angle and technique were all wrong. Soma called after him: *if you think i'm doing it so badly, why don't you come over and show me how it's done?* He chose not to.

Despite the menacing vibe, I felt safe. Thanks to my Girl Army training I could defend myself, and if shit got too real, I knew security would be there in a flash. I was one of the only other women in the room, and a highly visible one at that, but I managed to stay off the hecklers' radar. That was fine, because I didn't want Soma to know I was there, lest she feel self-conscious. She did gasp for air at one point and said *i have to get back to my girlfr—*. The dick was shoved back in her mouth before she got to the final phonemes, but, awww! Even when she was surrounded by men shoving their dicks in her face as a hostile crowd heckled her, Soma still referred to me as her girlfriend, and not long after someone else had told me I looked like Courtney. This surely was the top of the mountain, and the stars were just like little fish.

That didn't make the running commentary from the crowd any less chilling: *check her for an adam's apple!* and *make sure it ain't a man! you never can tell at this place!* Well, there it was. I'd always wondered how certain hypermasculine Tourists reconciled their macho heterosexuality with the anti-macho polysexuality of the Power Exchange. What did they think of us, the denizens of the most trans-friendly joint in town? Now I knew: no better than anyone else in town. The most enlightened factions of the City's queer sex culture hated us for what we represented, our kind of unabashed femininity which had no room for the daddy-worshipping culture up on the streets. For all the dicks that got sucked at the Power Exchange, and for as many of them as were sucked by Soma on a given night, there was still a willful rejection of masculine dominance. Masculinity was the *sine qua non* in the San Francisco queer world to such an extent that a dyke friend had recently told me that when she used to work at Good Vibrations, there was peer pressure to shoot testosterone to prove she was butch. Oh, we do have fun! There were countless gates being kept and fiery hoops to jump through for trans women to get safe access to estrogen, and many of us were still battling the conventional wisdom that we were just gay men who were going too far. Meanwhile, testosterone was so plentiful that cis dykes were taking it on a dare, which goes to show that male privilege kicks in real early. (For more about the unfortunate dominance of masculinity in mid–2000s San Francisco, see my essay "In the Shadow of the Valley" in Jennifer Clare Burke's 2009 anthology *Visible: A Femmethology, Volume Two*. Like the Criterion Collection's 2020 Blu-ray of *Crash*, please do not judge *Visible* by its hideous cover.)

I left the Barracks before Soma, but she knew I was there and told me later that if anyone had said anything unkind to or about me, she would have responded with ***if you say one more bad thing about my girlfriend, i'll rip the skin off your balls and choke you with it***. It never came to that, but it would have been hot to hear. We returned to the Indus River Valley and slept until 11:00 a.m.—dogs love sleeping, it's a fact—before heading back into the world for food, still in last night's clubwear. Granted, I went for *last night's clubwear* as my daily look when possible even if I hadn't been to a club the night before, which was something else I'd picked up from c0g in 1999. As Soma and I leaned against a railing at 5th and Market waiting for the bus in 2006, my back against the railing and Soma up against me, a fellow with a camera asked if he could take our picture. We declined, and he informed everybody within earshot that we broke his heart. Then a little man with a thick moustache, a thicker Southern accent, and what Soma called Dick-Sucking Lips stopped in front of us and said: ***damn, that's the sexiest thing i seen all day! can i have a kiss?*** He puckered up his DSL in anticipation. Soma said no, so he looked at me and said: ***what about that one?*** This one shook her head. As the little Southern man stomped away, he shouted: ***you fucked up my whole day!*** A couple of heartbreaking day-ruiners, that was Soma and me.

Some Semen Is Saltier Than Others

We were a couple of heartbreaking day-ruiners with a taste for ephemera, which was why Soma joined me at the Artists Television Access for the release party for Rick Prelinger's new book, *The Field Guide to Sponsored Films*. Prelinger was an archivist who collected and preserved old industrial and educational reels, for which he had coined the term **ephemeral films**. I was a fan of his work from way back: the first laserdiscs I rented from San Francisco's best video store Le Video in 1994 were Prelinger's compilations *To New Horizons* and *You Can't Get There from Here*, and I also owned the CD-ROM editions of those titles. (My friend Lilah had once called me **the queen of arcane media**, which I took as high praise.) More recently, I had downloaded the short films *Three Little Kittens* and *The Private Life of a Cat* from the Prelinger Archives and incorporated them into *kittyprOn* Episode #5 ("An Instructional Sound Film") and Episode #9 ("Complicated Interior Lives"), respectively. I had met Prelinger once before, and I think he found me overwhelming—many do, because I can be a lot!—so I did not fangirl all over him at the ATA.

Soma and I hung out at Checkpoint Charlie later that night, and Artwhore mused that while he used to be ready to fuck at the drop of any hat, working at the Power Exchange had desensitized him so much that he never wanted to have sex while on the job or even when he was there off the clock. Soma concurred, saying that while she loved sucking dick and was addicted to spooge, she was desensitized to sex otherwise. Pulling me close, she added that her level of pleasure depended on how she felt about the person she was with. I hugged her a little tighter, and she kissed my cheek. By virtue of being in the best place to see people coming and going, Checkpoint Charlie was also the best place to be seen—especially if you *wanted* to be seen, as Soma and I did. We were tactile exhibitionists, our hands often wandering to the other, and before long we were making out on Artwhore's stool. A few Towelboys sat on the couch watching us, par for this course. They were replaced by two cis women, and Soma and I put on an extra-special show, hoping to lure them over. No such luck.

I did some time on the cross with Al while Soma went off on her own, and when she returned, she reported that she had sucked three out of four nearby dicks. (The fate of the fourth dick remained shrouded in mystery.) Soma took my hand and led me into the Blue Room, where we lay down on the bed and started making out. Men lined the low wall and stood in the doorway, and Soma asked me, **lover, do you want to show them what a good little dicksucker you're becoming?** I glanced at the audience and asked Soma if she was comfortable outing herself. Some men would feel a bulge if Soma let their hand travel far enough on nights when she didn't tuck, but word that she was not cis hadn't made it onto the grapevine, and Soma was good enough at her job that those who did know she was trans could convince themselves otherwise if they needed to.

Soma shrugged and said, **i'm ambivalent, but it would be worth it.**

If it was okay by Soma, it was okay by me. I pulled down her skirt and her underwear, and as I untucked her, there was a murmur in the crowd at the big reveal of *le petit soma*. (For more about the sexuality and objectification of trans women *vis-à-vis* genitalia expectations, see my essay "The Big Reveal" in Kate Bornstein and S. Bear Bergman's 2010 anthology *Gender Outlaws: The Next Generation*. Like "The Slimming Effect" in *It's So You*, "The Big Reveal" did not get me into any trouble at the time, and it is full of words and ideas which have all aged well!) Perhaps because we had an audience, Soma was being rougher than usual. I gagged a few times, the Sophie to her Johnny as Soma's firm hand gripped my pigtailed hair and pushed me in close, me pulling away so I could breathe, her pushing me back in as I gasped for oxygen during this most anaerobic of exercises. I had a lot to learn, and she was happy to teach me. When I was able to look up, I saw a glee in her eyes which made me want to follow Soma to the ends of the Earth and which translated into words as ***this is so hot, sherilyn!***

I was aware that a few Tourists had moved inside the room—which, again, was a room in name only, and people were also watching us from across the way inside the Cage—and one of the Tourists reached new levels of banality by commenting, ***hey, she's sucking you off good, isn't she?*** Ever polite in the face of idiocy, Soma agreed that I was sucking her off good. Soma didn't come, but if she did, I knew to close my eyes. I'd learned that one the hard way.

* * *

We were cuddling in bed at the Black Light District when Soma told me that a taxi driver had recently given her a ride home from the Power Exchange. Soma figured the cabbie thought she was a sex worker, since he told her to get in the front seat. He soon started groping her, and by the time they got to the Indus River Valley, he told her to blow him.

I said, *i hope you did, puppy!*

Soma hugged me and said, ***of course, mommy!*** She was proud of blowing the cabbie, considering it a *sleazy achievement* and a ***new, dirty low to sink to,*** but she was also a bit puzzled by how nonchalant the guy had been. Was that typical for cabbies, she wondered, to give rides to whores in exchange for free services? And what if he'd pinned Soma wrong? Since I seldom took cabs and never provided those kinds of services, I couldn't say. Soma ruminated that she had been dressed in *a ho-tastic fashion*, but most of the women in and around the Power Exchange at the time were similarly attired, so that didn't narrow it down. On the plus side, the cabbie picking her up saved her from having to wait for the bus, and—

Soma snapped her fingers. ***oh, that's it! it's because i was standing at*** *the corner, and not sitting in the bus stop shelter. that's why he thought i was a hooker. duh!*

I asked if she had been standing at the tangled corner where Otis, 12th, South Van Ness, and Mission all converge. Soma confirmed that she had been, and I said, *that makes sense, pup. that's where the magic happens.*

*   *   *

We were having lunch at the Third Street Café around the corner from NakedSword when, apropos of nothing, Soma made a gesture representing breasts larger than her own considerable aftermarket pair and said, *i want really big tits, out to here, so the audience can see them get all cut up and crushed on the dashboard.* I had been taking a drink of water at that moment, and it nearly came back out of my nose. Good heavens, Soma just quoted *Crash* at me! Once I was sure I could do so with a relative minimum of splatter, I replied, *seagrave? you couldn't wait for me? you did the jayne mansfield crash without me?*

Soma smiled and said, **cronenberg is a weird guy.**

I took her hand, nodded, and said, *gotta love 'im.*

And if I hadn't known before that moment, and I kinda did know, I knew it for sure now: Soma and I were falling in love.

*   *   *

Feeling bored after her *World of Warcraft* subscription expired, Soma organized a bukkake scene via Craigslist. I thought it had a nice symmetry with Pamela Holm's *The Toaster Broke, So We're Getting Married*—one small thing can lead to the biggest thing of all!—and Soma invited me to be there to watch. The timing didn't work out, so I settled for knowing the address and room number of the motel so I'd have a last known location if she went missing, and I asked her to keep me posted in general.

While Soma was doing her thing at the Rodeway Inn at Eddie and Franklin, I ended up at the Power Exchange, the same night a group of Traditionalists from the Citadel made their monthly visit. In my experience from being around them on a few occasions at the Citadel, which was considered the respectable sex club for respectable sex people, the Trads considered the Power Exchange to be a blight. Also in my experience from being around them on a few occasions at the Citadel, the Trads were no damn fun. Sex and kink were serious business to them, with no place for smiling and laughing. This resulted in me and Al smiling and laughing and making silly jokes in loud voices, just to get dirty looks from the Trads. Tourists being loud and raucous at the Power Exchange were dealt with swiftly by the staff, and there was zero tolerance for disrespect, but Locals like us were given more leeway, and it may have helped that we were trolling known meanies. As though Al and I weren't making enough noise, my cell phone rang from inside my boot; it was Soma, informing me that Buk-kakeCon 2006 was not the success she'd hoped for. Though she got many responses to her Craigslist ad, most of the guys couldn't get past the front desk blockade, a large gay man who was unhappy about the depravity happening under his roof. (Maybe because it was a woman doing the dicksucking?) As a result, Soma only sucked about 10 dicks, a couple dozen short of her goal. Still, it was good to have goals, and I was proud of her for pursuing them.

A few nights later we were bundled up in her bed at the Indus River Valley, Soma playing *Elite Beat Agents* on her Nintendo DS while I wrote in my notebook. I told Soma how after I'd gotten off the phone with her the night of BukkakeCon 2006, I had spent a few hours with a cis woman named Zuki in the Undersea Room. As Zuki and I made out we were surrounded by men who were constantly groping us, which respected the room's oceanic premise by feeling like tentacles, as though Zuki and I were in a *hentai* porn. Soma appreciated that imagery, and she told me about one of her recent fellatio marathons—not BukkakeCon 2006, but a regular night at the Power Exchange. As the next man in line put his dick in her face, Soma saw his shirt and almost laughed. But she had a job to do, so Soma went right to work, though she didn't have to work hard because *he pretty much came up to me and blew a massive load in my face. just massive.* It was only after the massive load had been blown in Soma's face that she told him she loved his flux capacitor shirt, and the man replied, *this is what makes time travel possible.* Soma was finally able to laugh, and I joined her.

* * *

I helped Soma get an intake appointment at the Waddell Clinic, the city-run department through which I had managed to maintain an estrogen-and-spironolactone prescription during my own less-employed years. I also helped Soma get a barista job at a coffeehouse near the Indus River Valley, and I spent some days writing there while she was working her shift. She liked my writing, and she said that when people asked her about me, she led off with *sherilyn is a writer!* One day while I was writing at Soma's coffeehouse, I ruminated on how glad I was that we were each responsible for our own lives and that we both had a work ethic, and while we both just wanted to have fun, we always waited until the working day was … oh, for fuck's sake. Not *that* song again. But at least now I was on its good side.

When we arrived at the Power Exchange that evening, Soma went off to do her own thing and I went off to do mine, which in this case was hanging out with Artwhore upstairs and watching a member of the cleaning crew do their thing. Artwhore told me the entire staff was fastidious, including himself, because the Health Inspector dropped in every few weeks. Throughout the three large floors which received regular usage, the Inspector had never found more than a dozen errant condoms out of the hundreds which were used. I'd seen the floors getting mopped and surfaces sprayed down on a nightly basis, which went against the gospel preached by many of the club's most ardent critics. I also knew those critics could accompany the Inspector and see all the past bills of health, but they would still insist that the Power Exchange was a squalid pit where blood-transmitted pathogens evolved into airborne parasites which spread a combination of aphrodisiac and venereal disease. And with teeth, probably.

Soma was getting throatfucked in the Blue Room around 3:00 a.m., and when she was finished, she waved me over. Her glasses were off, and in the blue light I could see her makeup had smudged and run, cut by multiple streams. We cuddled and made out, the bed a swamp of wet spots of lube and spooge and sweat and other fluids which only Martin Landau's forensics team from the already-canceled *The Evidence* could identify. In the hushed, conspiratorial tone she did so well, Soma asked: **isn't this hot, mommy?** I groomed her face and paws, licked them clean, and Soma said **you're a dirty kitty**. I kissed her, hugged her tight, and thought to myself, *pee cat gets the belt.*

At any given time at least two men would be watching over the low wall, and a third would be in the room with us, sitting on the chair next to the bed. Soma always told them she was spent, she simply couldn't suck any more dicks tonight. I noticed that her dick estimate kept getting higher: she told the first guy that she'd already sucked 11 dicks tonight, the next guy that she'd sucked 12, then 13, 14, and capping out around 18. I decided that it should be a prime number, and furthermore, that prime number should be 47. This led into a debate about whether 47 *was* a prime number. We were pretty sure it was, but on this fluid-drenched bed at half past three in the morning, our math-brains weren't up for the task. We asked every man who entered the Blue Room if 47 was a prime number, and they all ignored the question, instead trying to talk Soma into sucking their dick. Soma had put her glasses back on, so I kept mine on as a show of solidarity, and if we were wearing braces you could have put us on the platform in the Green Door Show and the O'Farrell would have a line around the block during Fleet Week while North Beach would be a ghost town.

Some of the songs from the mix CD I gave Robin had made it into the Power Exchange's rotation. Robin herself had fallen in love with Bigod 20's "The Bog," and I now felt an extra charge of giddiness when Madonna's "Hung Up (SDP Extended Dub)" started playing as I cuddled with

Soma. The song still took me back to descending the Maritime Hall stairs down to Shrine of Lilith, and I now wished I could pull a *Prince of Darkness* and use 1999 Sherilyn's brain's electrical system as a receiver for a broadcast of this moment of tenderness and personal connection in the year two zero zero six—not for the purpose of causality violation, but to give the poor raccoon-eyed schmuck a glimmer of hope, so she would know as her self-esteem was getting flayed that it would grow back stronger than ever and she would discover happiness she hadn't thought possible. But the transmitter in my consumer-grade, FM-radio-equipped flip phone was not strong enough to reach her as a dream, let alone her conscious state of awareness, so 1999 Sherilyn would have to stumble through the darkness on her own. She would have to go for it and crash and burn and get back up and go for it again and crash and burn again and get back up again, however long it took. When an angry biped started stepping on her tail at the end of the year, she would have to live through that, too.

The men watching 2006 Sherilyn and Soma in the Blue Room ignored me. They knew Soma was the virtuoso dicksucker and I was not, and I was pretty sure that would always be the case, though there was a rather tasty piece of well-dressed Eurotrash who kept going on about how cute we were and how he wanted us as a package deal. He was pleasant enough that I was tempted to volunteer, to make him the first cis male dick I sucked—but to do so would have meant detaching myself from Soma, and I wasn't ready to do that. Cuddling with the puppy felt like my purpose, to be the ***mommy slash lover*** who gave her unconditional warmth and support and pride after whatever sleazy thing she had just done, making sure she never felt abandoned or disregarded or like she was a bad person who did a bad thing just by being herself. Maybe that was what it meant to be her Catherine.

Prophecy Is Ragged and Dirty

But the problem with me being Soma's Catherine had always been right there in those final lines:

i think i'm all right.
maybe the next one, darling. maybe the next one.

Deborah Kara Unger got a lot of static for her opaque performance as Catherine Ballard, but the opacity was appropriate because she's the most alienated character in the film. It pays off with that single tear at the end, and I take back what I said before about how the scene would be just as powerful even if the film's costume designer Denise Cronenberg hadn't put Unger into that certain long-sleeved, bruise-violet-colored cut velvet blouse, for the blouse makes it look like Catherine's skin has been flayed, representing her newfound vulnerability. She is the first character in *Crash* to cry, to be in touch with her emotions—the only time anyone else comes close is Helen's existential frustration when the crash test video freezes right before impact because the tape player's fucked, it always does that— and what Catherine is at long last feeling is the pain of the insurmountable gulf between her and James.

You don't get to choose your crash. And mine had long since happened.

*   *   *

Soma had been joining me at the Dark Room, and everyone there liked her, as well they should have. On the last Sunday of January 2007, a *San Francisco Chronicle* writer interviewed me and Jim about Bad Movie Night for the Sound Scene column on *SFGate*. I wasn't on mic that evening, but I had started producing the show that month, and I was happy that the slideshow which ran with the article included a few photos of me and Soma in the audience. The only one which is still viewable online at the time of this writing is my favorite: our backs to the camera during the final moments of *The Matrix Reloaded,* Soma's red mop next to my blonde mop, my arm up in the air as I'm demanding that the movie just end already.

What the Sound Scene photo didn't show was the wall my ego had hit in recent weeks, how I had been feeling like deadweight compared to Soma, like I was the bulky Kit Kat Girl to Soma's sexy Kit Kat Girl, the Comingore to her Novak, the Beta Twin to her Alpha Twin, the Love to her Auf der Maur (or, in my darkest moments, the Erlandson to her Auf der Maur). None of that was Soma's fault, but she could tell I was starting to withdraw, and she did her best to pull me back from the brink. What Soma could not do was not be herself any more than I could not be myself, and while the one boundary I had put in place was to ask her to not cruise at the Dark Room, she wanted to pursue Anomaly. I got it, I did: Anomaly was hot and charismatic and a proud whore on the level to which Soma herself aspired. Certain other cracks were also starting to show in our interpersonal dynamic, the ways Soma and I differed—or how we could complement each other if I gave us the chance, and Soma was open and honest enough that I knew she and I could make it work.

All I had to do was not let myself be held back by fear … my own fear, or anyone else's.

*   *   *

My former bestie had been banned from the Dark Room for being a source of the bad kind of drama, usually involving whatever straight cis man she was involved with. The Dark Room folks made it clear they did not hold me responsible for her behavior, but I was still mortified that they were having to deal with her now because of my bad decisions in the past, because I had internalized the way my mother dehumanized me for being queer I had then consented to both being made to feel inferior and to getting my tail stepped on. Some of my former bestie's newest drama was tangentially related to her getting involved with Anomaly's ex-boyfriend, and I was further horrified by the thought of new waves being caused by introducing Soma into the mix. That was not fair to Soma, who was more mature and self-assured at 23 than my former bestie had been at 33, but I was too busy panicking about the angry biped to be fair to my puppy.

While Soma and I were chatting one Friday night in mid–February, I asked her to please not pursue Anomaly. Soma replied that she could not acquiesce to limits about who she could or could not socialize with, and then added. *isn't that what cally did to you?*

Oh, fuck. Fuck fuck fuck fuck fuck fuck *fuuuck.*

I ended the chat. Which was a very Cally move.

A Universe Gone Quickly

Dancing. I was pretty sure Soma and I had just broken up, not that she knew it yet, and I needed to go dancing. All I knew for sure was that I was angry and frustrated with a self-righteous *soupçon* of betrayal thrown in for good measure and that I needed to dance it away. I made myself up and put on my most reliable uniform of shiny black PVC pants and a black chemise top and my Formula X jacket all while fighting the temptation to stay home where it was warm and safe and uncomplicated. Sooner rather than later, I found myself at Divas. I first walked upstairs to the fourth-floor lounge, which was decorated more like a traditional bar, complete with a pool table with one of those faux-stained-glass lamps hanging overhead. There was karaoke on Sunday nights, but on this Friday night there were about half a dozen cis men and no women of any stripe. This was a common ratio downstairs on slow weekdays, but it felt creepy on a busy weekend night. I considered channeling Soma: perch on a barstool and be flirty and coquettish, have a man buy me a drink, and maybe I would get a little drunk and loosen up and…

I went downstairs to our Revolution Ballroom, *glory glory hallelujah om namah shivaya*, and I was relaxing between tours of dancing duty when a familiar-looking blonde walked by and into the restroom. Was it Lilah? Naaah. But it was a face I knew, and I was intrigued. I stood and edged a little closer to the restroom. Someone else went in, and I peeked through as the door was closing. Well, no wonder, she looked just like ... but, no, it couldn't be. To the best of my knowledge she wasn't alive, and if she was alive, it was unlikely she was currently getting made up in the third-floor restroom at Divas. But still...

When the mystery blonde came back out, I asked: *excuse me, are you kelly michaels?* The rumors of her death had been exaggerated, for it was indeed Kelly Michaels, and I geeked out all over her: *oh my god, i'm a huge fan from way back and i am just so super-thrilled to meet you, this means so much, can i buy you a drink?* Despite my babbling like an adrenalized Mouseketeer, Kelly understood me. She ordered a white wine, and as I got the money out of my wallet, I realized my hands were shaking. I said: *i'm sorry, i'm having a total fangirl moment.*

Kelly laughed and said: **that's okay, i don't mind at all. say, me and some friends are going to the endup in a little while. you wanna come with us?**

The EndUp at 6th and Harrison was one of the few clubs in town which stayed open after 2:00 a.m., hence it was where people tended to end up. I had chilled in the outdoor courtyard on a few Sunday mornings myself, and it was a great place to enjoy a daytime Ecstasy buzz. Presently, I wanted to go *squee!!!* the way you do when your hero invites you to join their entourage after knowing you exist for all of ninety seconds. Instead, I reined myself in and said: *sure, that sounds like fun.*

Kelly took a drink of wine, then said: **great! but first, wanna dance?**

Madonna's "Vogue" soon started playing because the DJ knew what was up as 33-year-old Sherilyn did what 17-year-old Sherilyn watching *Sally Jessy Raphael* would have considered an impossible dream, more impossible than pointing at the television and saying, *that's me! that's me, mom! that's me!* As we danced, I turned back into a mirror-gazer so I could burn this moment into my retinal memory, because there they were across the dimly-lit room, dancing in time with us: the beautiful ghosts of Kelly Michaels and Sherilyn Connelly.

When we went back downstairs, I discovered Kelly had been around all along and I was just never at Divas at the right time, and she had a maternal relationship with the Motherlode Girls. She checked in with each one and made sure they were doing all right, and I could tell most of them looked up to her. I didn't get a clear look at Kelly until we were outside under the streetlights, and for someone who'd had as rough a life as hers, she was holding up quite well. Her eyes had a translucent blueness which the standard-definition video I'd always seen her on hinted at but couldn't do justice to, and they were sparkly tonight because she was tweaking. Kelly said as much herself, then asked, **do you get high?** I replied *yes*, which was not a lie. Bouncing, Kelly asked, **meth?** I said, *um, no. not that. but just* *about anything else.* Which was a lie, since I would never do bug powder or crack, having seen the effects of both in person. But what was I going to tell Kelly? That I'd worked at NakedSword for almost two years and was starting to get curious about cocaine and had gone to gay porn industry parties where people were doing rails, but nobody invited me to join them, and I was starting to take it personally? It was all true, but I didn't want to expose how much of a dilettante I was, that I was forever the undergraduate film student in the graduate-level writing group.

Kelly said the EndUp expedition would happen when she tracked down her roommate Violet. I got out my notebook and showed Kelly the Ursula sketch, and because San Francisco is a closed system where lines always converge, Kelly confirmed that it was by the Violet in question. She appeared a few minutes later, though the EndUp expedition did not happen upon her arrival as predicted. I had no idea where the evening would go, only that however we got there, I would not be driving. My Neon was parked a few blocks to the west, which by Tenderloin standards was safer than a few blocks to the east, and since it wasn't at risk of being ticketed or towed until Monday, I decided not to mention I was vehicular, lest I have to find parking far deeper into San Francisco's clubland.

A few doors down at the corner of Polk and Post was a sketchy liquor store with a perpetual contingent of dealers out front. I always felt nervous walking past it on my way to Divas, but I felt safe with Kelly and Violet. The dealers outside and the employees inside knew them, as I reckoned they knew all the Motherlode Girls, much like the owner of the market across from the O'Farrell knew the dancers. The dealers held no ill will toward me; they were capitalists first and foremost, and it wouldn't do to alienate a potential customer. All the same, I knew I would never go back in the store by myself. (Some programming is hardwired.)

Instead of going to the EndUp, which I was sure was going to happen sooner rather than later, we walked the Circuit as Kelly turned the occasional trick, in and out of the car in about ten minutes. As usual for around closing time, the streets were packed with slow-driving men checking out the Motherlode Girls (*and me! i'm here, too! don't forget kelly's needy little sister!*) while seeking that nightcap blowjob. Some of the hardier tricks were on foot, and Violet was on the clock and vigilant, saying **wanna date?** to every passing car or pedestrian even if they were too far away to hear her. (Some programming is hardwired.) She was a bit more reactive when we rounded the corner onto Sutter and saw one of her colleagues getting harassed. Violet handed me her purse and rushed off to help the other woman, and being nobody's hero, I kept a safe distance until the situation was resolved.

Kelly was a bit further up, talking to a well-dressed, pleasant-looking gay man across from the R Bar. He offered to take us to his place in North Beach to do … something. That part of the plan was vague, but I got the impression drugs would be involved. Sure! I was down for bearing sober witness to a groovy North Beach drug party. He soon drifted away, and before long Kelly disappeared back among the wraiths and strays of San Francisco whence she came. By a quarter to three, it was just me and Violet. Well, phooey. I liked Violet well enough, but Kelly and I were supposed to be hanging out, and we were going to have adventures, and … well, I didn't know what would have happened if we'd gone to the EndUp or to the groovy North Beath drug party, but the unexpectedness was the point. And now, nothing. The Bombers had long since left Torchie's, and the streets were empty and *sans feu.*

Things only happen once, and most things don't happen at all.

I was pouting to myself about impermanence when a man walked up to me and said ***tell her not to!*** Violet exposited that she was trying to get a lift to the Power Exchange, but this man was not having it, insisting that it was a dangerous and unsafe place. I'd heard a lot of people talk a lot of shit about it over the years, moreso in recent months since I'd become a regular, but this was the best yet: dude was telling a sex worker that the Power Exchange was more dangerous than getting into a stranger's car in the middle of the night. Several Motherlode Girls had been found murdered in recent years, and it was sometimes followed by candlelight vigils and speeches by respectable queers, which was the only time the wider community pretended to care. Those respectable queers made a far bigger, more media-friendly fuss about Gwen Araujo's murder because she was young and photogenic and blameless, but because the Motherlode Girls tended to be immigrant women of color plying a disreputable trade, their murders were forgotten by the time the candles went out. My friend Gwendolyn Smith's Transgender Day of Remembrance had been doing good work to raise awareness about the fact that our people got murdered on a regular basis and our murderers often got away with it, but in San Francisco at its most progressive in the mid–2000s, nobody in the power structure gave a damn about a dead immigrant hooker with a dick.

I offered Violet a lift to the Power Exchange, and by the time I brought my Neon around her would-be savior was gone, no doubt off to warn someone about fluoridation. Violet remained on the job as we drove off, saying ***wanna date? wanna date? wanna date?*** to everyone she saw out the window, not letting the window being rolled up slow her own roll. As we passed the corner of Van Ness and Eddy, Violet said: ***i need a bump. ooh, there's sammy! pull over!*** Forgetting that I had every right to draw the line at picking up a stranger at three in the morning, I pulled over. Violet opened the door and Sammy climbed in the back. My heart pounding,

I drove off and tried to keep my cool about the goddamn *drug dealer* in my car. Hey, I'd hoped the evening would go in unexpected directions, right? I was getting my wish in a big way. The sketchy liquor store at Polk and Post was one thing but this was quite another, and I kept an eye on my jacket and purse which I'd tossed onto the backseat a few minutes earlier, and since I was born white and middle-class in Fresno, scenarios worse than losing my stuff went through my head, like Sammy pointing a gun and telling me to get out or to drive somewhere in particular or just pulling the trigger—

None of that happened. Maybe the blue sparkles still embedded in the backseat brought me good fortune, but more likely is that Sammy didn't want to be in my car any longer than I wanted him to be. He wanted to conduct the transaction and get out to conduct other transactions. I was merely assisting in his job. Besides, I was a trans woman, which was the safest thing I could be in this instance; for all he knew I was a fledgling Motherlode Girl, and being with Violet counted for something. Sammy and Violet did their business, I dropped Sammy off, and that was that. I parked outside the Power Exchange, Violet had her bump, and I declined her generous offer to share. When we went inside, Violet continued on her own timeline while I stopped at Checkpoint Charlie. Artwhore asked if I'd seen Soma tonight, and I said I hadn't, not mentioning that I was pretty sure I had broken up with her earlier in the evening. I also neglected to mention that detail later to Robin when she asked about Soma. It wasn't something I felt like announcing, since I hadn't *officially* broken up with her, not in so many words. All Soma knew was that I was miffed at her. Was I miffed at *her*, though? Yes. No. Sorta. It was hitting me from all directions, as it so often did. I knew Soma would never ask me to be exclusive, but us having feelings for each other was scary, too. I was also terrified that Soma was right, that I was trying to do to her what an angry biped had once done to me. That whatever else domestic abuse may be, it is also a cycle.

Everything ended, and sometimes it was for the best if it ended sooner rather than later.

Epilogue

Under the Zodiacal Light

Eighteen months later, on the last Friday of July 2008, I went to the Center for Sex and Culture at 1519 Mission to see Beth Lisick and Tara Jepsen's new show Getting In on the Ground Floor and Staying There, which they described as *a ten year retrospective of our comedic "career" together*. I'd last been at the Center in June for the launch party for Carol Queen's anthology *More Five Minute Erotica: 35 Tantalizing Tales of Sex and Seduction,* which included my story "Outlet." It was my fourth piece to be published in a book; the third had been "The Slimming Effect" in Michelle Tea's 2007 anthology *It's So You,* and the second had been in *Good Advice for Trendy Young People of All Ages.* Like "Two-Sixteen-Ought-Four" in *I Do / I Don't* before it, the *Good Advice* piece was a stylistic experiment which didn't quite work, and its name was changed by the editors from my original "HQ77" to the garish "Sherilyn's Skool for Girlz" to align it with Lynn Breedlove's "Lynnee's Skool for Boyz" during the brief epoch when our careers were entangled.

It's So You's "The Slimming Effect" was significant because it was my first attempt to reckon with the madness of my 1999 in print and because I nailed the long-form essay format after *I Do / I Don't* and *Good Advice.* (I still loved those first two awkward, misshapen efforts; after all, I was a failed experiment myself.) But I was most proud of *More Five Minute Erotica*'s "Outlet," both because it was the kind of smut which Tom Lehrer might have enjoyed and because it was the fictionalized fruit of my once-forbidden Exhibit A about public sex in a Gilroy store. Seeing the story in print gave me a wonderful feeling of *getting away with it,* of embracing my sinful vanity in full *Velvet Goldmine* mode. I also posted the story about the night Lenore and I attended Fetish Diva Midori's piercing class in my goddamn blog, the night I kept on the down-low yet still got punished because I broke the Eleventh Commandment. If three years wasn't enough time to tell my story, when would it ever be? And who had the right to make that decision? The *More Five Minute Erotica* book launch was only my second-most-recent gig; the most recent was at the Legbutt in June for Meliza Bañales' 2008 National Queer Arts Festival show, Coming Out … Again. I read an essay called "Garden Party" which looked back on the ways I'd gotten in trouble for being a memoirist, including my bestie's early anger at me about my online diary and the later *Rent Girl* furor.

Flyer for Coming Out … Again at the LGBT Center, June 2008. Meliza wasn't wrong, because coming out once … is never enough.

There were many old friends in the audience for Beth and Tara's show in July, including Horehound and Lynnee, but there were more unfriendly faces, so I made an Irish exit when the lights came up. As I approached Phoebe, my recently-acquired secondhand Saturn I named after the darkest of the Saturnian satellites, I heard my own name; it was Lynnee, inviting me to join him and Tara at Burger Joint on Valencia. Awww! It felt good to hang out with people who had been a significant part of my world six years ago when I first dove into the queer lit scene, a scene which I was growing away from. Because San Francisco is a closed system where lines always converge, when KrOB walked by Burger Joint and saw me through the window, he came in and joined us.

After the Burger Joint nosh I returned to the Black Light District and woke up to a crisp, gorgeous Saturday. I topped off Perdita's food and water in case I didn't return that night, as I always did when I left the house, then headed to the Dark Room. Now more than ever it was my home away from home, a place where I was welcome any time of the day or night, the third most important key on my ring after the Black Light District and Phoebe. I made myself comfortable at the front desk in the lobby and spent the morning working on the schedule for Working for the Weakened, my upcoming four-night variety show. The theme was employment horror stories, and it was a continuation of the show of the same name I'd curated for SF in Exile at the Jon Sims Center for the 2006 National Queer Arts Festival. (That was the thing about doing the work: it led to more work.) I subtitled the 2008 Dark Room iteration of Working for the Weakened *a wicked messenger production* as a shout-out to my old series with Frankie, whom I hadn't heard from in years. Though I was hosting all four nights, I knew I was box office poison, so I only called attention to my name on the flyer by partially covering it with clip-art of a blood splatter.

December 31, 2007, was the last day of my acquaintance with Anais. Things were never the same between us after Ryder, and I had been superseded in Anais' heart by a third party long before I met Soma Red. Anais was also never comfortable with how the stories I wrote about us made it seem like I was a gravedigging cat who wants a pony princess to be her friend, nor did she care for the way I would follow her around in real life like a needy little sister when she wanted to have adventures without me. We stayed together for a year longer than we should have because I was still no good at ending things, and sometimes those twelve months felt like that painful moment in Orson Welles' 1965 *Chimes at Midnight* when Henry is telling Falstaff to fuck off and Falstaff is just crumpled there, in too much pain to move. Shortly after Anais and I broke up things fell apart with another cis woman I was seeing, Proxima. She wanted me to be exclusive, and I again got the trapped and panicky feeling, 'twas ever thus. Much

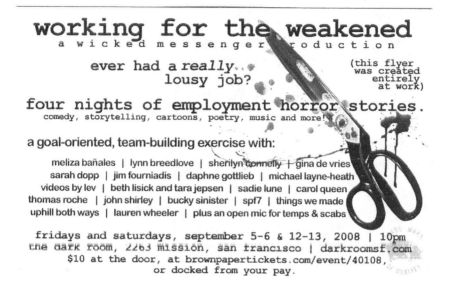

working for the weakened
a wicked messenger production

**ever had a *really*
lousy job?**

(this flyer
was created
entirely
at work)

four nights of employment horror stories.
comedy, storytelling, cartoons, poetry, music and more!

a goal-oriented, team-building exercise with:

meliza bañales | lynn breedlove | sherilyn connelly | gina de vries
sarah dopp | jim fourniadis | daphne gottlieb | michael layne-heath
videos by lev | beth lisick and tara jepsen | sadie lune | carol queen
thomas roche | john shirley | bucky sinister | spf7 | things we made
uphill both ways | lauren wheeler | plus an open mic for temps & scabs

fridays and saturdays, september 5-6 & 12-13, 2008 | 10pm
the dark room, 2263 mission, san francisco | darkroomsf.com
$10 at the door, at brownpapertickets.com/event/40108,
or docked from your pay.

Flyer for Working for the Weakened at the Dark Room, September 2008. You can always tell which flyers I designed because they're wall-to-wall lowercase text. I know what puts asses in seats!

like Soma, my relationship with Proxima was a brief light rather than a sustained one, and it burned all the hotter because Anais didn't approve of me dating Proxima, so we had to keep on the dark end of the street. Turns out my consensual, closed-mouth stage kiss in an acting class ten years earlier did prove I was capable of all manner of immoral malfeasance, but it was worth it for the way Proxima and I clicked on that first bareback night, both of our tendencies toward ferality finding a kindred soul and a kindred flesh in the other with her sharp bits in my soft parts and vice versa, the way her appearance chameleoned under the black light when she tied her hair back, sometimes looking like the rank stranger with large, tired eyes she had been a week before and sometimes eerily familiar, the raised skin, scratching and biting and leaving mini-nebulae and galactic clusters, flecks of inked skin and blood under our nails, her deep sharp gasps when touched or bitten or twisted just so, the sheer amount of sweat we generated and shared and mixed, the way she smelled and tasted and that wonderful sound she made when she orgasmed, and around half past midnight, brief sleep: Proxima cuddling my leg, murmuring with little tremors passing through her body as she dozed off, a mid-coital *pieta* during which I napped as well until we both jolted awake a little after 1:00 a.m., and for the next few hours we were aware that we both had to work the next day and that she needed to go home but we kept at each other all the same, energy levels dipping and then spiking again, the green and purple fog beginning to glow, the tenacity that comes with the thrill of discovery, and most of all that Meredith Monk was right about impermanence, that this is it, right now, this moment, this last minute, and as much as I wanted to will the night to last forever every moment comes to an end *and now the longing begins*. Another big plus was that the blood-and-raven-haired Proxima was my height, and nothing was hotter than being at eye level with a cis woman.

After I broke up with Soma and then Proxima I felt all the guilt that I got punished for for *not* exhibiting when I broke up with my bestie, but still nothing compared to the guilt I would never stop feeling about hurting Ivy. Sometimes you're Falstaff being told by Henry to fuck off and sometimes you're Henry telling Falstaff to fuck off: both are exquisitely painful, and both are necessary experiences. That's what I told myself after experiencing both, and it continued to confirm that Tira was right, that I did these things in the worst way possible. For sure, I knew I would never forgive myself for not becoming friends with Kelly Michaels. We had dinner a few weeks after we met, and it didn't work. Our worlds were too different, and it was like meeting the sister who had disappeared into my brother Jim's closet and discovering that we had nothing in common, nothing to offer each other. I did book Kelly to perform when my unearned confidence resulted in me producing the Trans Stage at the official 2007 Pride Sunday Celebration, and I was super-frazzled on that day because of the sheer scale of the production and all the fires I had to put out, but that was no excuse for how curt I was with Kelly when she arrived late. It was a failure of compassion on my part, and though I never saw her again (*dingdingdingding!*) I knew the look in her blue eyes on that late June day would always haunt me. My heart was not big enough, and if you should never meet your heroes then I taught Kelly that you should never meet your fans, because fans are the worst. *I* was the worst. I was a bad person, which was why I drove people away.

Positivity accentuation via sinful vanity: with all the heartbreak there was plenty of adventure, and I maintained my decadent spiral in the eighteen months after breaking up with Soma. It never reached *Valencia* levels of Lambda Literary Award-winning hedonism because I was not and never would be Michelle Tea, and Lou Reed's week would always beat my year, but by Sherilyn Connelly standards it was a damn good ride. The euphemism *meeting perdita* was coined when a cis woman named Hayley and I were on our first date at Divas, me on my second drink and Hayley on her third. We were talking about cats, and when I told Hayley about Perdita, Hayley said wistfully: *i want to meet her. i want to meet perdita*. So, we went to the Black Light District so Hayley could meet Perdita, and so Hayley and I could have fantastic sex. It was during this era of feral fecundity,

The author at the end of a long night in 2007, a night that may still be happening, the night she became Mehitabel (author photograph).

this era of impressions rather than ideas and of situations rather than subjects, that I discovered that casual sex with women I was not emotionally attached to could approach the hallucinatory levels Annie Sprinkle had written about, that it could become a swirling descent into pure aesthetic attractions and chemical reactions where the only emotion is an insatiable hunger for those aesthetics and chemicals, creating the most delicious feedback loop, the most virtuous of circles.

I hooked up with not just once-and-future-porn stars, but also strippers and rent girls. Not because any of them had been those things, but by virtue of where and when I was, most everyone I dated was either a former, current, or future sex worker. I wanted to have sex with Hayley because she was tall and had a Sharon Kane quality about her, but knowing she had also been a dancer at the Lusty Lady made it feel all the more like we were living inside *Exile on Main St.*'s kickoff "Rocks Off," which had been my favorite Rolling Stones song since long before I realized it was the greatest song ever recorded about achieving sleazy apotheosis through fucking. The hint is right there in the title, but 14-year-old Sherilyn did not know what the phrase **rocks off** meant, let alone that most rock and roll songs are about sex. She only knew "Rocks Off" was high-energy ear candy about being bored by sunshine and preferring to chase shadowy mysteries by moonlight and getting to a place where she can't even feel the pain anymore, and it was so addictive that years passed before she listened to the rest of *Exile on Main St.* and discovered her second-favorite Stones song, "I Just Want to See His Face." Thirty-four-year-old Sherilyn still loved "Rocks Off" for all the potential it represented and came to learn that any night on the dirty road which ended with honey and glitter splattered on her skin and clothes was by definition a good night. Sometimes it was red marks from candle wax, and those were good nights, too.

Jim Fourniadis emerged from his bedroom in the early afternoon of that Saturday in July 2008, and after smoking me out, he picked up his guitar and sang me his newest song, "The Tale of Job." It was for the Dark Room's upcoming stage musical based on Robin Hardy's 1973 film *The Wicker Man*, the story of a repressed Christian policeman named Howie who investigates the disappearance of a young girl on the pagan island of Summerisle. Jim's adaptation began with Howie singing "The Tale of Job" as he preaches at his church, and the lines which stuck with me were God talking to Job during the middle eight break. After pointing out that it was none of Job's business why God made the world the way He did, God exposits that Job had best slow his roll: ***yours is not understanding / yours is utterly this: / you must worship in sadness as you worship in bliss.*** The song was sung by Flynn DeMarco on the Dark Room's stage and in the studio recording which I would listen to for comfort hundreds of times over the years to come, and Howie's point in "The Tale of Job" is that no matter what happens, you must supplicate before the Christian God. That's fine if finding God in the church of your choice or perhaps Woody Guthrie in Brooklyn State Hospital is what gets you through the night, but I took the concept of worshipping equally in sadness or bliss as an argument for persistence. You keep going no matter how dark things get, if everyone is telling you you're bad and wrong and you ruined everything for everyone and if an angry biped is stepping on your tail and punishing you for the sins of strangers thousands of miles away and telling you to stop writing down your feelings because their feelings are more important than yours will ever be, and you keep going when you're the shiny new object and people want to listen to your words and you also keep going when your luster fades and people don't want to listen to your words as much because they've come to realize you're not a good person, and you don't take it personally either way 'cuz it ain't up to you.

I got gussied up later that evening, and Jim and I took a cab to the Center for Sex and Culture for a last-minute show I was reading in called Transtastic. It was happening the same night as the Human Rights Campaign's big 2008 fundraising dinner, and Transtastic was counterprogramming to protest that the HRC was the only major queer organization to not insist transgender people be included in the Employment Non-Discrimination Act. The show was hosted by Theresa Sparks, a trans woman who had been elected president of the San Francisco Police Commission in 2007, and she had been the Grand Marshal of the 2008 Pride Parade. In addition to the HRC dinner elsewhere, Perverts Put Out! and the second night of Beth and Tara's show were also happening at the CSC, so Transtastic's turnout was wickedmessengerfoür-level minimal but enthusiastic. It was also the first time I heard Macy Gray's "Sexual Revolution," and Ms. Gray was right: a certain authority figure had lied to me all this time, and I would never again keep my freak to myself.

Jim returned to the Dark Room after Transtastic, but since it was pushing midnight and I was already dressed for excess, I went to the Power Exchange. Artwhore filled me in on recent events, including rumors of an impending closure in November. I'd heard those rumors from a few different directions, which only confirmed that the rumor was spreading. Artwhore assured me that the issues had been cleared up, and the Power Exchange on Otis would not be shuttering in November 2008 or at any point in the foreseeable future.

The Dungeon seemed slow for a Saturday night, at least as I remembered them; it had been so long since I'd been there on a regular basis, I felt like I'd lost track of the patterns. Robin and Al were happy to see me as always, and Al showed off his latest toys. I picked up a classic Hitachi Magic Wand and turned it on, and a cis woman who had been watching us asked if I would use it on her, promising that she would only take a few minutes. I assured her she could take her time as she made herself comfortable on the red couch, pulled down her underwear, spread her legs—and as predicted, she came in about three minutes. A German cis couple had also been watching, and the Teutonic woman asked if she could go next. Sure, why not? I was holding the vibrator steady while they went to town, and I could do that all night. I headed back to the Dark Room around 3:00 a.m., and the traffic was sparse enough that I was able to walk down the middle of Mission. This allowed me to keep an eye on my surroundings in an unsafe area, but I also did it because the only thing better than a Walk of Shame—and I facilitated the orgasms of a nonzero number of strangers tonight, so this damn well qualified—was a Walk of Shame down the middle of a city street at three in the morning. If I had been photographed by Diane Arbus or Weegee, it would have been iconic.

I slept on the couch in the Dark Room's green room, and as we often did when I spent the night, the next morning Jim and I enjoyed a big, delicious breakfast of plantains and pupusas at the Salvadoran restaurant across the street. Afterward, I leveled up my day-old makeup and met up with

Helena, whom I was starting to hang out with again. We should have been close friends ever since Shrine of Lilith, but then my tail got stepped on. (Stupid kitty, letting a thing like that happen.) Helena and I went to Phred's apartment for Dore Alley, which was a precursor to the Folsom Street Fair. Dore Alley was smaller and raunchier and more intense than Folsom in most appreciable ways, and Phred lived in a second-floor apartment in the middle of it all.

Newspaper advertisement template for *Shinbone Alley,* from the original 1971 press kit and campaign manual. It's no *this story is about beauty,* but the tagline *it's sophisticated enough for kids, simple enough for adults!* is still pretty great.

Watching Dore Alley got me to thinking about an animated film I'd recently stumbled across at Mission Bay: John David Wilson's 1971 *Shinbone Alley*, based on an unsuccessful yet oft-revived 1957 Broadway musical which was itself based on the poems of Don Marquis from the 1910s. Though the movie predated Ralph Bakshi's *Fritz the Cat* by a year, *Shinbone Alley* already had the eyesore visual palette and wobbly, poorly-dubbed animation style associated with Bakshi. The ostensible protagonist is a man named Archy (voiced by Eddie Bracken) who is reincarnated as a cockroach after committing suicide, and he falls for an aging alley cat named Mehitabel (voiced by Carol Channing). Mehitabel's philosophy since long before Archy showed up on her doorstep was *toujours gai,* meaning to always be cheerful and open to new experiences, but newcomer Archy disapproves, telling Mehitabel early on **sometimes i think you're too toujours gai**. When Mehitabel later does her own Walk of Shame back to Shinbone after getting fucked and then discarded by the tomcat Big Bill, she looks at her bleary, sagging reflection in the mirror and admits to herself that yeah, she's over the hill, but what the hell—she's still in the ring, and that's what matters. She then launches into her theme song of hope and positivity and belief in herself, about how it's all good because she's going to live her life to the fullest. Archy barges into Mehitabel's home after she finishes the song, and at first, Archy is all sheepish and aw-shucks shy about how much he missed her. But when Mehitabel declares that she's a little raggeder but also a little wiser and still ready for anything, and she then reprises her theme song, Archy throws a sudden but inevitable tantrum. He's a cartoon cockroach so the only object he can throw is his adorable little hat, and Archy does indeed throw his adorable little hat onto the ground in anger before screaming at Mehitabel to stop singing. When Mehitabel's song of hope and positivity and (heaven forbid!) belief in herself screeches to halt, Archy slut-shames her: **aren't you the least bit ashamed? aren't you chastened?** She refuses to consent to Archy making her feel inferior, and Carol Channing makes a meal out of Mehitabel's awesome reply: *not since big bill chastened me—he chastened me over every back alley in new york!* Angrier than ever at Mehitabel for not prioritizing Archy's feelings, Archy shouts at Mehitabel that **your morals are the lowest, the loosest, the limpest!**

    Shinbone Alley doesn't work as a movie, but that scene made me think of the maxim which Roger Ebert attributed to Howard Hawks, that a good movie needs **three good scenes and no bad scenes**. It's probably a bastardization of Hawks himself recalling the advice he gave to John Wayne during the filming of *Red River*: **you do three good scenes and don't annoy the audience the rest of the time and you'll be a star**. (That's fine for the John Waynes of the world, but the *Velvet Goldmine* path to stardom sounds a lot more fun.) There are many bad scenes in *Shinbone Alley*, and it's a stretch to say there are as many as three good scenes, but it has that one scene which rings emotionally true. Speaking of films with a dearth of good scenes, I also checked out the DVD of *Flashdance* from Mission Bay and was pleasantly surprised that director Adrian Lyne acknowledged in the bonus features that Marine Jahan did much of Jennifer Beals' dancing. Lyne did not mention that he had chosen to leave Jahan uncredited at the time, and he pretended to be bemused that the press found out or that anybody cared. I then revisited *Flashbeagle* and picked up on something that went over my 10-going-on-11-year-old head in 1984: after his night at the disco, we see a bleary-eyed Snoopy doing a Walk of Shame against a vanilla sky at the break of dawn. He's dead to the world that day until someone starts playing music, at which point Snoopy comes back to life and starts busting out his Jahan moves because he can't *not* dance. *Flashbeagle* is far from good, but as a child's first celebration of pleasure for its own sake, that getting *fuuucked up* tonight is worth feeling like you got hit by a truck tomorrow, it's kinda great.

I parted company with Phred and Helena after Dore Alley and returned to the Dark Room for Bad Movie Night. I wasn't on the mic for that evening's feature, Hyung-rae Shim's *Dragon Wars*, though I sat next to Jim in the front row because I could. *Dragon Wars* was the finale of Urban Monsters Month, following Matt Reeves' *Cloverfield*, Rob Bowman's *Reign of Fire*, and Roland Emmerich's *Godzilla*. Doing themes made the scheduling easier and more fun; August 2008 was going to be Legendary Flops Month, consisting of Michael Lehmann's *Hudson Hawk*, Kevin Reynolds' *Waterworld*, Paul Weiland's *Leonard Part 6*, John McTiernan's *Last Action Hero*, and Willard Huyck's *Howard the Duck*. Bad Porn Night ended after a few months, and Bad Movie Night itself no longer did porn—though I was proud that Anomaly and I heckled Mel Gibson's *The Passion of the Christ*, which isn't *not* a porn movie—and I was already scheming to have my revenge on *Pulp Fiction* during Blasphemy Month in 2009. My last official birthday reading had been Wicked Words at Modern Times in 2004, so my friend Rhiannon and I held our first annual Rhiannon and Sherilyn's Birthday Sleepover at Bad Movie Night in 2008, a tradition we maintained until Bad Movie Night wrapped and the Dark Room closed for good.

I cleaned up the theater after *Dragon Wars* let out. I had creative control over Bad Movie Night, and though I also got half of the door (usually no more than a sawbuck on a good night) I felt that I earned that creative control by doing as much of the physical labor as possible, setting up the chairs and the microphones and the free popcorn beforehand, then stacking the chairs and sweeping up the spilled popcorn afterward, and a million other things in between. As Jim often said when faced with an unglamorous chore: *what, and quit showbiz?* While I was sweeping up, I got to thinking about how one of the pictures in the Sound Scene slideshow had been of Soma sweeping the floor that night after *The Matrix Reloaded* and how there was no good reason that the puppy and I weren't still seeing each other, not to mention that for as much self-righteous pride as I took in avoiding chemical dependency I was jonesing so goddamn much for the delicious feedback loop known as Fucking Proxima that I had to keep telling myself that engaging in the time-honored tradition known as the **booty call** would be a bad idea. So, I would not do that. Definitely, for sure, I would not get back into touch with Proxima to get sexually junksick with her, no matter how strong the longing. Besides, what if she turned me down?

As I was trying to put those thoughts out of my head, my old acquaintance Becky entered the theater. I'd never seen her at the Dark Room before, and she asked if I had time to get a drink. I was already planning to go to karaoke at Divas, so after I finished restoring the theater to factory settings, Becky accompanied me into the Tenderloin. As we sat at the bar on the first floor of Divas, she told me about the problems she was having with her partner. Things had not been going well for a while now, and Becky had been having an affair. She wasn't asking for advice; she just needed to talk to someone who would hear her and who would be sympathetic and not judge her. This had been happening a lot lately, and it was always people who had witnessed Operation Archangel. An unexpected consequence of that late heavy PR bombardment was that I had become someone people felt safe confiding in about infidelities and peccadilloes both real and desired as well as other unspeakable thoughts and deeds. If they asked for advice, I told them to follow their heart, even if it meant blowing up their life. It was super-basic advice, real Self-Help 101 stuff, but I gave them the encouragement that I felt like I'd lacked for so long, and nobody ever told me to not write any of it in my goddamn blog.

When Becky left, I went up to the fourth floor and signed up for a song I've known all my life, one which aged and changed along with me. I was also thinking about something my seldom-mentioned father said while we were having lunch in Fresno back in March. He was always interested in my latest adventures in trying to get words into print, and I was telling him about how since I couldn't focus on my writing at home, I would bounce from coffeehouse to coffeehouse as they closed for the night, often riding that wave to the 24-hour Starbucks in Laurel Heights. My father said my newfound work ethic didn't surprise him. I had been **scattered** when I was younger, as he put it, but I now seemed much more focused, much more clear-headed. It summed up my father's feelings about me being trans: he didn't fully get it, but it did him no harm, and he couldn't argue with the results.

As I waited at Divas for my song, I thought about how my ten-year estrogen-and-spironolactone anniversary was approaching, and I felt like I had indeed gained a sort of clarity over the emotionally brutal past decade. I was still a deeply flawed human being and always would be, there was a good chance that every bad thing which had ever been said about me was true, and the people who cut me out of their lives probably made the right call. I would make many more mistakes going forward, and I would continue to get punished for things which were not mistakes—like breaking up with Tira and coming out as trans, which I now knew were not very bad and wrong things but were instead two of the three most necessary and positive things I had ever done. I would always try to be a better person today than I was yesterday, but I was starting to suspect that the ability to forgive myself sooner rather than later was, if not the beginning of wisdom, then at least the only way to avoid further mistreatment, to never let my tail get stepped on again. And that included forgiving myself for my own lack of compassion, which was by far the greatest of my sins.

When my song came on, I didn't need to look at the screen because I knew it as well as I've ever known anything. Instead, I closed my eyes and announced to the world that at long last, my mind was clearer now.

The Beautiful Ghosts Mixtape

Some of the songs mentioned in *Beautiful Ghosts*. If you are reading this book in the 2020s, there is a good chance the mixtape can be accessed online at https://www.youtube.com/user/lndgnwtr/playlists.

"Waving Goodbye," Sia, *The Neon Demon*
"The Golden Section," Coil, *Horse Rotorvator*
"Couples Must Fight," Jonathan Richman, *Her Mystery Not of High Heels and Eye Shadow*
"Garden Party," Rick Nelson, *Garden Party*
"Cities in Dust," Siouxsie and the Banshees, *Tinderbox*
"Joining You," Alanis Morissette, *Supposed Former Infatuation Junkie*
"Smut," Tom Lehrer, *That Was the Year That Was*
"Christianity Is Stupid," Negativland, *Escape from Noise*
"Stage Fright," The Band, *Stage Fright*
"Macho Shithead," Rats of Unusual Size, *Id, Ego, Superego and Burns Ltd.*
"Superstar," The Carpenters, *Carpenters*
"Sunset Strip (Demo)," Courtney Love (non-album track)
"Let's Get Fucked Up," The Cramps, *Flamejob*
"Hung Up (SDP Extended Dub)," Madonna (non-album track)
"Nowhere Fast," Fire Inc., *Streets of Fire*
"Celebrity Skin," Hole, *Celebrity Skin*
"Cleanin' Out My Closet," Eminem, *The Eminem Show*
"Rocks Off," The Rolling Stones, *Exile on Main St.*
"Toujours Gai," Carol Channing, *Shinbone Alley*
"Beautiful Ghosts (Victoria's Song)," Francesca Hayward, *Cats*

Index